Drescher / Kahrmann   The Contemporary English Novel

THE
CONTEMPORARY ENGLISH NOVEL

An Annotated Bibliography of
Secondary Sources

by

Horst W. Drescher
and Bernd Kahrmann

Athenäum-Verlag

Alle Rechte vorbehalten
© 1973 by Athenäum-Verlag, Frankfurt am Main
Printed in Germany
Gesamtherstellung : Schwetzinger Verlagsdruckerei GmbH
ISBN-3-7610-1809-6

PREFACE

The purpose of this bibliography is to mirror international
discussion and research on the contemporary English novel. In
listing as many as possible of the critical publications on the
contemporary English novel the bibliography attempts to show
what has already been achieved and, indirectly, what remains
to be done. And we hope it will help to avoid superfluous
work in areas already explored and on findings adequately
established.

First of all, a word about the novelists we have selected
for inclusion. A bibliography cannot define the ambiguous term
'contemporary English novelist'. For this reason we employed
formal and external criteria in deciding which novelists to
include and which to omit. That means that those novelists
have been covered who have been considered to be 'contemporary'
and 'English' by the majority of literary scholars and critics
over the past twenty years.

On the whole the works covered in this bibliography do not
date back beyond 1954, which can be seen as the beginning of
a new era of the English novel.[1] It was in 1954 that the first
novels of great promise such as *Lucky Jim*, *Under the Net* and
Lord of the Flies were published. The preceding years are
frequently considered a period of transition and of new be-
ginnings by literary critics who were aware of changes in form
and subject of the English novel much earlier than the university critics.[2] As a general principle therefore, the compilers
of this bibliography included only novelists who began publish-
ing in this period, and none who were already prominent before
World War II. Anthony Powell and C.P. Snow and their ambitious
sequence novels which appeared over a longer period of time
are exceptions.

It is easier to decide which novels are 'contemporary' than
to decide which are 'English'. Emigration-immigration patterns
complicate the question of national identity. How, for example,
should Brian Moore, who emigrated to Canada and is viewed by
Canadians as a Canadian author, be classified? And how should
West Indian writers who have made their home in the UK be
classified? Are Samuel Selvon or V.S. Naipaul 'English'

authors? Here again a bibliography can only reflect the pre-
vailing state of affairs; in our case a state of confusion and
uncertainty. It cannot decide questions some of which have not
even been raised by scholars or critics.

And now a word about the secondary literature we have selected for inclusion. Publications relevant to Parts I-III which
appeared in book form and which were printed in either England
or America are listed in their entirety - as far as they were
known to us. As a rule we have included those articles published in scholarly periodicals, in intellectual reviews and
newspapers which are indexed in the *MLA International
Bibliography*, the *Abstracts of English Studies*, the "Current
Bibliography" in *Twentieth Century Literature*, the *Annual
Bibliography of English Language and Literature*, the *Year's
Work in English Studies*, or the former "Newsletter and Roll
Call" in *Modern Fiction Studies*.[3] In addition, this bibliography includes an extensive selection of foreign language
publications, particularly from European countries. Further-
more, a greater number of articles from non-academic journals
have been included than is usual in bibliographies of this
kind. In deciding what to select the compilers considered it
neither necessary nor useful to distinguish between scholarly
journals and literary reviews. But we confined the choice of
newspaper and review articles to those which are important for
the appreciation of the authors discussed or which give
information about authors on whom few other critical analyses
have been published.

There is no commonly accepted uniform system for numbering
and paginating periodicals and reviews.[4] In fact a single
journal may use various systems at various times (*Twentieth
Century* is an extreme example). We have consistently used the
following system:
1) If the individual issues are combined in a single volume,
and if the whole volume rather than the individual issue is
paginated our reference reads either *CQ*, VII (1965), 87-92 or
Renascence, X (1957/58), 214-221. The latter form is used when
the first issue was published in one year and the following
issues in the next year.

2) If the individual issues are combined in a volume but each issue is paginated individually the reference includes the month or quarter in which the issue was published as well as the number of the volume; for example, *Shenandoah*, XVIII (Summer 1967), 55-68.

3) If the issues are numbered individually and not combined in a volume the reference gives the number of the issue in Arabic numerals and the month or quarter in which the issue was published; for example, *Caliban*, 4 (mars 1967), 10-23.

4) If the issues appear weekly we have omitted any reference to volume or issue and have given only the exact date of the individual issue; for example, *TLS*, 18 January 1963, 17.

Part III is probably the most important and complete section of this bibliography. It lists first of all under each author's name all his novels which appeared before 1972 and their dates of publication in chronological order. Only the titles of the editions published in England are given. The list of novels is followed by a compilation of bibliographies and/or checklists (if available), of anonymously published secondary literature and finally of publications about the author in alphabetical order. The author's own comments on his works are listed as secondary literature. If there are several publications by the same writer on a novelist these are entered chronologically according to the date of publication.

To help the researcher the entries are annotated to identify subject matter and point of view. Annotations have been omitted where the subject of the article or the point of view is evident from the title. Serial publications on a common principle (such as CEMW, WTW and TEAS) have not been annotated individually.

We have quoted the latest edition or reprint of a book. Glaring printing errors have been unobtrusively corrected. Whenever possible all entries have been verified by the compilers. When the inaccessability of material made this impossible, various bibliographical aids were used to countercheck available information in order to eliminate errors as far as possible.

The completion of this bibliography has taken more time
than was originally foreseen. Without the kind assistance and
encouragement of many individuals and institutions it would
still not be ready for publication. The staffs of the depart-
mental libraries of the Englische Seminar of the University
of Münster and of the Fachbereich Angewandte Sprachwissen-
schaft of the University of Mainz in Germersheim, of the University Library of Münster and of the British Museum Library
have generously given their help. A grant from the Deutsche
Forschungsgemeinschaft made a longer period of work in the
British Museum Library possible. Thanks are due to all these
for their help and also to Dr. Cordula Kahrmann and Judith
Schluchter (Münster) and to J.K. Bunjes, E. Heene, G. Heinrichs
and H.J. Stellbrink (Germersheim) who at various stages assist-
ed the compilers of this bibliography.

Mainz-Germersheim   H.W.D.
Münster   B.K.

December 1972

[1] We have included none of the novelists Mark Longaker and
Edwin C. Bolles cover in their book *Contemporary English
Literature* (New York, 1953).

[2] Marghanita Laski writes as early as 1951: "Indeed, there
would seem to be definite indications that the novel of personal relationships has had its day, at least for a time,
and that we are moving into a period whose main literary
theme will be man's moral relationship with society."
(*Spectator*, 19 January 1951, 90).

[3] For a more complete list see Marjorie Stephenson, "Twentieth-Century Literature in English: Sources of Criticism."
CE, XXVI (1964/65), 151-153.

[4] Paul Witherington has made some critical remarks on this
chaotic situation in his "Winter and Discontent." *CE*, XXXI
(1969/70), 238.

VIII

CONTENTS

MASTER LIST AND TABLE OF ABBREVIATIONS

ALitASH	Acta Litteraria Academiae Scientiarum Hungaricae
ALM	Archives des Lettres Modernes
Alphabet	
Alta	
America	
Approach	
AQ	American Quarterly
AR	Antioch Review
ArQ	Arizona Quarterly
ASch	American Scholar
Aspect	
Atlantic	Atlantic Monthly
AWR	Anglo-Welsh Review
BA	Books Abroad
B&B	Books and Bookmen
BB	Bulletin of Bibliography
BBN	British Book News
BC	Book Collector
BDEC	Bulletin of the Department of English (Calcutta)
BI	Books at Iowa
BJA	British Journal of Aesthetics
BJES	British Journal of Educational Studies
BlakeS	Blake Studies
BLM	Bonniers Litterära Magasin
Brotéria	
BSTCF	Ball State Teachers College Forum
BSUF	Ball State University Forum
BuR	Bucknell Review
Caliban	
CamR	Cambridge Review
CanL	Canadian Literature
Carnegie Magazine	
CathW	Catholic World
CE	College English
CEA	CEA Critic
CEMW	Columbia Essays on Modern Writers

NYHTBR	New York Herald Tribune Book Review
NYRB	New York Review of Books
NYTBR	New York Times Book Review
Observe	
Observer Colour Supplement	
Overland	
P&P	Plays and Players
Paris Match	
Paris Rev	Paris Review
PBSA	Papers of the Bibliographical Society of America
Person	Personalist
Perspective	
PLL	Papers on Language and Literature
PMASAL	Papers of the Michigan Academy of Science, Arts, and Letters
PMLA	Publications of the Modern Language Association of America
Poetica	
Poetry	
Ponte	
PP	Philologica Pragensia
PR	Partisan Review
Praxis	Praxis des neusprachlichen Unterrichts
Preuves	
PrS	Prairie Schooner
Punch	
QQ	Queen's Quarterly
QR	Quarterly Review
Ramparts	
RdP	Revue de Paris
Réalités	
REL	Review of English Literature
Renascence	
Reporter	
RevN	Revue Nouvelle
RGB	Revue Générale Belge
RLMC	Rivista di Letterature Moderne e Comparate
RLV	Revue des Langues Vivantes

Samtiden	
SAQ	South Atlantic Quarterly
SatR	Saturday Review
SGG	Studia Germanica Gandensia
Shenandoah	
SHR	Southern Humanities Review
SIN	Studies in the Novel
SLitI	Studies in the Literary Imagination
SoR	Southern Review
SoRA	Southern Review (Australia)
SovL	Soviet Literature
Sowjetliteratur	
Spectator	
SR	Sewanee Review
SRAZ	Studia Romanica et Anglica Zagrabiensia
SSF	Studies in Short Fiction
STC	Studies in the Twentieth Century
STCM	Sunday Times Colour Magazine
Studies	
Sunday Times	
SWR	Southwest Review
SZ	Stimmen der Zeit
TamR	Tamarack Review
TC	Twentieth Century
TCL	Twentieth Century Literature
TEAS	Twayne's English Authors Series
Thought	
ThQ	Theatre Quarterly
Time and Tide	
Times	
Tirade	
TLS	Times Literary Supplement
TM	Temps Modernes
Topic	
TQ	Texas Quarterly
TR	Table Ronde
TSLL	Texas Studies in Literature and Language
TWA	Transactions of the Wisconsin Academy of Sciences, Arts, and Letters

I BIBLIOGRAPHIES AND REFERENCE WORKS

ANON. *A selection of contemporary British fiction 1950-1970.*
British Council: London, n.d. (1971). Pp. 27.

Selected by Ian Scott-Kilvert. Only works published between 1950 and 1970 are included. Lists also British
publishers of contemporary fiction.

BENNETT, J.R. "Style in twentieth-century British and American fiction: A bibliography." *WCR*, II (Winter 1968), 43-51.

Partially annotated; based upon *PMLA* annual bibliography
(1946-1965) and the *Annual Bibliography of English Language and Literature* (1925-1956).

BUFKIN, E.C. *The twentieth-century novel in English. A
checklist.* Georgia UP: Athens, 1967. Pp. VI + 144.

"The object of this book is to provide a full listing of
the novels of all the major and many of the minor writers
in English, regardless of nationality, who have published
the entirety or the greater part of their work in the
twentieth century."

*Contemporary authors. The international bio-bibliographical
guide to current authors and their works.* Vol. I ff. Gale:
Detroit, 1962 ff.

International in scope, but concerned mainly with English-
speaking writers. Published quarterly, with cumulative
indexes.

CROOK, ARTHUR. *British and Commonwealth fiction since 1950.*
National Book League: London, 1966. Pp. 30.

"The titles in this list ... should be looked at as a
personal choice."

CULPAN, NORMAN & W.J. MESSER. *Contemporary adult fiction
1945-1965 for school and college libraries. A list of
books, with a short list of critical works on the modern
novel, chosen and annotated for the use of sixth-form and
other students.* School Library Association: London, 1967.
Pp. XIV + 66.

DAICHES, DAVID, ed. *The Penguin companion to literature.
Britain and the Commonwealth.* Lane & Penguin Press: London, 1971. Pp. 576.

FLEISCHMANN, WOLFGANG BERNARD, ed. *Encyclopedia of world literature in the 20th century. An enlarged and updated edition of the Herder "Lexikon der Weltliteratur im 20. Jahrhundert".* 3 vols. Ungar: New York, 1967-1971. I: A-F (publ. 1967); II: G-N (publ. 1969); III: O-Z (publ. 1971).

FRAMPTON, MARALEE. "Religion and the modern novel: A selected bibliography." *The shapeless God. Essays on modern fiction*, eds. Harry J. Mooney, Jr. & Thomas F. Staley. Pittsburgh UP: Pittsburgh, 1968. Pp. 207-217.

GOETSCH, PAUL & HEINZ KOSOK. "Literatur zum modernen englischen Roman: Eine ausgewählte Bibliographie." *Der moderne englische Roman. Interpretationen*, ed. Horst Oppel. Schmidt: Berlin, 1971 (rev. ed.). Pp. 419-432.

JONES, BRYNMOR. *A bibliography of Anglo-Welsh literature, 1900-1965.* Published by The Wales and Monmouthshire Branch of the Library Association, 1970. Pp. VIII + 139.
An "enumerative bibliography" of 20th century "writers of Welsh birth or extraction who write imaginative literature in English, locating their narratives against a Welsh background and portraying Welsh characters and idiom. ... In assigning 'localities' to prose fiction, only named or recognisable places have been noted and fictional or conjectured places are shown as such." Section B lists bibliographical and critical works on Anglo-Welsh literature in general and on individual authors.

KINDLERS LITERATUR LEXIKON. 7 vols. Kindler: Zürich, 1965-1972. I: A-Cn, pp. XXXII, 2710 columns (publ. 1965); II: Co-Fk, pp. XXVIII, 2974 columns (publ. 1966); III: Fl-Jh, pp. XXVIII, 2898 columns (publ. 1967); IV: Ji-Mt, pp. XXXI, 2994 columns (publ. 1968); V: Mu-Ra, pp. XXXI, 3092 columns (publ. 1969); VI: Rb-Tz, pp. XXXI, 3246 columns (publ. 1971); VII: U-Z, Essays, Register, pp. XXXV + 1098, 1526 columns (publ. 1972).

KLEINES LITERARISCHES LEXIKON, eds. Horst Rüdiger & Erwin Koppen. II: *Autoren II. 20. Jahrhundert. Erster Teil: A-K.* Francke: Bern, 1972 (rev. ed.). Pp. 449.

LENNARTZ, FRANZ. *Ausländische Dichter und Schriftsteller unserer Zeit. Einzeldarstellungen zur schönen Literatur in fremden Sprachen.* Kröner: Stuttgart, 1971. Pp. VII + 861.

Contains bio-bibliographical articles on Amis, Durrell, Golding, Murdoch, Powell, Sillitoe, Snow, Spark, Storey, and Angus Wilson.

MAY, DERWENT. *British and Commonwealth novels of the sixties.* National Book League: London, 1970. Pp. 27.

An annotated list.

OLLES, HELMUT, ed. *Literaturlexikon 20. Jahrhundert.* Rowohlt: Reinbek bei Hamburg, 1971. Pp. 850.

Contains bio-bibliographical articles on various contemporary English novelists.

SCHÜTZE, SYLVIA. *Englische Literatur der Gegenwart. Prosa, Drama, Lyrik, Schauspiel, Hörspiel. Ein Auswahlverzeichnis.* Völker im Spiegel der Literatur, ed. Fritz Hüser. Folge 13. Stadtbücherei Dortmund: Dortmund, 1969. Pp. VIII + 125.

Bio-bibliographical entries, German translations of titels; introduced by a short article by A. Norman Jeffares on "Die moderne englische Literatur" (III-VII).

TEMPLE, RUTH Z. & MARTIN TUCKER, eds. *A library of literary criticism. Modern British literature.* 3 vols. Ungar: New York, 1966. I: A-G, pp. XXXII + 441; II: H-P, pp. XXXII + 510; III: Q-Z, pp. XXXII + 482.

Informs about authors and criticism. Over 400 twentieth-century British authors are included, novelists ranging from the classics (Conrad, Joyce, Woolf, etc.) to present-day authors (Amis, Braine, Brigid Brophy, Sillitoe, etc.). Each vol. contains author bibliographies. Studies on the authors are listed at the end of each entry.

TEMPLE, RUTH Z. & MARTIN TUCKER, eds. *Twentieth century British literature. A reference guide and bibliography.* Ungar: New York, 1968. Pp. X + 261.

Part One contains a special section on the novel (90-102); Part Two is based on the bibliographies in *A library of literary criticism. Modern British literature.* The listings have been brought up to date.

WARD, A.C. *Longman companion to twentieth century literature.* Longman: London, 1970. Pp. 593.

Arranged alphabetically throughout and fully cross-referenced. Bio-bibliographical entries on writers in English, including writers in foreign languages whose works have appeared in English editions.

WEINSTOCK, DONALD J. "The Boer War in the novel in English, 1884-1966: A descriptive and critical bibliography." *DA,* XXIX (1968), 1910A (U.C.L.A.).

WILPERT, GERO VON, ed. *Lexikon der Weltliteratur. Vol. I. Biographisch-bibliographisches Handwörterbuch nach Autoren und anonymen Werken. Unter Mitarbeit zahlreicher Fachgelehrter.* Kröner: Stuttgart, 1963. Pp. 1471.

WILPERT, GERO VON, ed. *Lexikon der Weltliteratur. Vol. II. Hauptwerke der Weltliteratur in Charakteristiken und Kurzinterpretationen. Unter Mitarbeit zahlreicher Fachgelehrter.* Kröner: Stuttgart, 1968. Pp. 1254.

WRIGHT, ANDREW. *A reader's guide to English and American literature.* Scott, Foresman: Glenview, Ill., 1970. Pp. XIX + 166.
Chap. on "The Recent Past (1920-1960)" (98-107) lists editions, biography and criticism. The "present compilation claims the virtue of selectivity."

YATES, J.V., ed. *The author's and writer's who's who.* Burke's Peerage: London, 1971 (6th ed.). Pp. XXI + 887.
Biographical entries with full or selected lists of works.

4

ANON. "Experience of a lifetime." *TLS*, 20 June 1958, 345.

There is no English term equivalent to *roman fleuve*, but there are works that it might describe: Snow's *Strangers and Brothers*, Powell's *The Music of Time*, Durrell's *The Alexandria Quartet*.

ANON. "Two views of fiction." *TLS*, 7 November 1958, 641.

Contrasts the traditional postwar English novel and the French *nouveau roman*.

ANON. "The British imagination: The workaday world that the novelist never enters." *TLS*, 9 September 1960, VII.

"Work is something of which our novelists are ignorant, or which they do not choose to write about ... The things our novelists know about are the grades and subtleties and shifts of society." Refers to Snow, Powell, Golding, Angus Wilson, and others.

ALDISS, BRIAN W. "'One that could control the moon': Science fiction plain and coloured." *ILA*, III (1961), 176-189.

With bibliography of primary sources.

ALDISS, BRIAN W. "SF serious, popular and S-and-S." *London Mag*, n.s. X (April 1970), 74-78.

A short history of science fiction and its different forms.

ALDISS, BRIAN W. *The shape of further things. Speculations on change*. Faber & Faber: London, 1970. Pp. 185.

Contains chaps on the history and development of SF, "the subliterature of change".

ALDRIGE, JOHN W. *Time to murder and create. The contemporary novel in crisis*. McKay: New York, 1966. Pp. XVIII + 264.

Assails the contemporary novel for a sense of boredom and for a failure of creative imagination. "... we crave something original and exciting. We crave even more intensely something true, something that represents a vital engagement of experience as it is and that wrenches us out of our old habits of perception..." English novelists are briefly dealt with in "The Brief, Stale Anger of the English" (230-244): Colin Wilson and Sillitoe.

ALLEN, WALTER. *The novel to-day*. Longmans, Green: London, 1960 (rev. ed.). Pp. 44.

General survey of the situation of the novel. Quite extensive on Powell, Snow, Angus Wilson, and the 'university wits'.

ALLEN, WALTER. *Reading a novel*. Phoenix House: London, 1963 (rev. ed.). Pp. 64.

Chap. 3 is on "The Classic and Contemporary Fiction". See chap. 8 for a discussion of Snow's *The Masters,* Amis's *Lucky Jim* and Murdoch's *The Bell.*

ALLEN, WALTER. *Tradition and dream. A critical survey of British and American fiction from the 1920s to the present day.* Penguin Books: Harmondsworth, 1964. Pp. 365.

Comprehensive critical survey from Joyce to Murdoch. Sees modern English novelists as part of the English literary tradition, though he admits that social changes are undermining the validity of this statement (Sillitoe, Storey, Waterhouse). Refers to numerous writers, also lesser ones. Sequel to *The English novel* by the same author.

ALLEN, WALTER. "Recent trends in the English novel." *English,* XVIII (1969), 2-5.

Mentions Snow, Golding, Angus Wilson, and others.

ALLSOP, KENNETH. *The angry decade. A survey of the cultural revolt of the nineteen-fifties.* Owen: London, 1958. Pp. 212.

Analyses the novels of the Angry Young Men as well as their personal background which is related to the aftermath of the Second World War.

AMIS, KINGSLEY. "Laughter's to be taken seriously." *NYTBR,* 7 July 1957, 1, 13.

The Angry Young Men.

AMIS, KINGSLEY. *New maps of hell. A survey of science fiction.* Harcourt, Brace: New York, 1960. Pp. 161.

Regards science fiction as a serious form of literature.

ANDERSON, DAVID. *The tragic protest. A Christian study of some modern literature.* SCM Press: London, 1969. Pp. 208.

Amis, Braine, Brigid Brophy, Dennis, Golding, Murdoch, Wain, Angus Wilson, and others.

ANDRAE, IRMGARD. "Der englische Roman der Gegenwart." *Leserzeitschrift,* VII: 3 (1966), 1-13.

Angus Wilson, Spark, Murdoch, Snow, Powell, the Angry Young Men, Golding, Durrell, and others. Bibliography.

BAILHACHE, JEAN. "Angry Young Men." *LanM,* LII (1958), 143-158.

Amis, Wain, Braine, Colin Wilson, and Osborne are the leading figures among the Angry Young Men. Short analysis

of the works of the authors concerned. They have created
a new, revolutionary, "anti-snob" hero, who has become the
ideal of the young generation, even if society silenced
the angry voices by enriching their authors.

BALAKIAN, NONA. "The flight from innocence: England's newest
literary generation." *BA*, XXXIII (1959), 261-270.

Mentions Amis, Wain, Murdoch, Braine.

BARZUN, JACQUES. "Meditations on the literature of spying."
ASch, XXXIV (1964/65), 167-178.

Mentions le Carré, Ambler and Fleming. Thinks that spy
books have little merit.

BEAR, ANDREW. "Popular reading: The new 'sensation novel'."
The twentieth century, ed. Bernard Bergonzi. History of
Literature in the English Language, 7. Barrie & Jenkins:
London, 1970. Pp. 336-361.

Discusses a number of "overall bestsellers" which have
dominated the market in the period since World War II
(Monsarrat's *The Cruel Sea*, Robbins and Fleming). Bibliography.

BENNEMANN, HEINRICH. "Der II. Weltkrieg im englischen Roman."
WZUL, XII (1963), 533-537.

Preview of a dissertation in progress which analyses from
a Marxist viewpoint sixty-four "war-novels" by fourty-four
English speaking authors.

BENNEMANN, HEINRICH. *Der zweite Weltkrieg im englischen Roman*. Diss. Leipzig, 1963. Pp. 319.

English novels about World War II are analysed from a
Marxist viewpoint. Bibliography.

BENTLEY, PHYLLIS. "Yorkshire and the novelist." *EDH*, XXXIII
(1965), 145-157.

Novels written by Yorkshire novelists and set in Yorkshire: Braine, Storey, Barstow, Waterhouse, Bradbury.

BERGONZI, BERNARD. "The novel no longer novel." *Listener*,
19 September 1963, 415-416.

Discussion of the "generic novel". Argues that there is
not much originality in today's fiction. As exceptions,
Spark and Amis are mentioned; Golding's *Lord of the Flies*
considered excellent, though traditional.

BERGONZI, BERNARD. *The situation of the novel*. Macmillan:
London, 1970. Pp. 226.

Discussion of the present condition of the novel in England
and America. Examination of the crisis of the novel form,

which is mainly a "crisis of identity", and the way the novel reflects the surrounding culture. Study of the work of Powell, Snow, Angus Wilson, and Amis. Argues that English fiction is still mainly traditional, centred on character and concerned with liberal values.

BIRD, STEPHEN B. "Natural science and the modern novel." *ER*, XVI (February 1966), 2-6.

Correspondences between literary works and scientific experiments; refers among others to Durrell's *The Alexandria Quartet* and Golding's *Lord of the Flies*.

BODE, CARL. "The Redbrick Cinderellas." *CE*, XX (1958/59), 331-337.

The Angry Young Men - Amis, Wain, Osborne.

BOILEAU, PIERRE & THOMAS NARCEJAC. *Le roman policier*. Payot: Paris, 1964. Pp. 235.

Historical and synchronic study of the detective novel. Special chap. on the spy novel. Quite detailed on Christie, Highsmith and Fleming.

BOWEN, JOHN. "One man's meat: The idea of individual responsibility." *TLS*, 7 August 1959, XII-XIII.

On "Angus Wilson's stoical humanism, William Golding's semi-Manichean religious vision, Iris Murdoch's common sense, Lawrence Durrell's mystique of love."

BOWEN, JOHN. "The virtues of science fiction." *Listener*, 31 December 1964, 1063.

BRADBURY, MALCOLM. "Myths and manners." *TLS*, 19 October 1967, 983-984.

On the international standing of the English novel. The view that the English novel is too traditionalist is rejected. The importance of the "social" nature of the English novel is often exaggerated.

BRADBURY, MALCOLM. *What is a novel?* Arnold's General Studies. Arnold: London, 1969. Pp. 72.

Refers to a great number of contemporary novelists.

BRADBURY, MALCOLM. "Our writers today: Who they are - how they live (I, II)." *Encounter*, XXXVI (February 1971), 16-23; XXXVI (March 1971), 15-26.

BRADBURY, MALCOLM & DUDLEY ANDREW. "The sugar-beet generation: A note in English intellectual history." *TQ*, III (Winter 1959), 38-47.

On the Colin Wilson group and English novels which depict this world and movement.

BRADY, CHARLES A. "The British novel today." *Thought*, XXXIV (1959/60), 518-546.

The Angry Young Men, Powell, Snow, and the "new romancers" (Charles Williams, C.S. Lewis, Tolkien, T.H. White) are discussed.

BRISSENDEN, R.F. "The phenomenon of science fiction." *Meanjin*, XIII (1954), 203-213.

BROCKWAY, JAMES. *Waar zijn de Angry Young Men gebleven? En andere stukken*. Contact: Amsterdam, 1965. Pp. 151.

BROICH, ULRICH. "Tradition und Rebellion: Zur Renaissance des pikaresken Romans in der englischen Literatur der Gegenwart." *Poetica*, I (1967), 214-229.

Wain's *Hurry on Down*, Amis's *Lucky Jim* and Murdoch's *Under the Net* are considered the most significant examples of the revival of the picaresque novel in England in the 50s.

BRONZWAER, W.J.M. "De smalle basis van de Engelse roman." *Vormen van imitatie. Opstellen over Engelse en Amerikaanse literatuur*. Athenaeum - Polak & Van Gennep: Amsterdam, 1969. Pp. 13-34.

Durrell, Snow, Murdoch, Golding, Dennis, Angus Wilson, Amis, Wain, Cooper, Hinde, Storey, Braine, Sillitoe, and others.

BROOKE-ROSE, CHRISTINE. "Le roman expérimental en Angleterre." *LanM*, LXIII (1969), 158-168.

Discusses Spark, Golding, Burgess, Heppenstall, and others.

BRYDEN, RONALD. "British fiction, 1959-1960." *ILA*, III (1961), 40-53.

Golding, Murdoch and Angus Wilson are considered the "only three contenders for major status"; mentions various other writers: Snow, Powell, Braine, Sillitoe, MacInnes, and Pamela Hansford Johnson.

BURGESS, ANTHONY. *The novel today*. Longmans, Green: London, 1963. Pp. 56.

Short survey of the situation of the novel in the 60s. Select bibliography of primary sources.

BURGESS, ANTHONY. "What now in the novel?" *Spectator*, 26 March 1965, 400. Repr. in *Urgent copy. Literary studies*. Cape: London, 1968. Pp. 153-156.

Sees a swing "to a new interest in form rather than content".

BURGESS, ANTHONY. "The Manicheans." *TLS*, 3 March 1966, 153-154.

"... there is something in the novelist's vocation which predisposes him to a kind of Manicheeism. What the religious novelist often seems to be saying is that evil is a kind of good, since it is an aspect of Ultimate Reality." Mentions Greene, Waugh, Golding.

BURGESS, ANTHONY. *The novel now. A student's guide to contemporary fiction*. Faber & Faber: London, 1971 (rev. ed.). Pp. 229.

On British and American fiction, on novelists in Europe, Asia, and Africa. Most of the important novelists of the postwar period are included, but the main interest is in contemporary British fiction. Bibliographical summaries at the end of each chap. and indexes of authors and titles complete the book.

CAPEY, ARTHUR. "The post-war English novel." *Literature and environment. Essays in reading and social studies*, ed. Fred Inglis. Chatto & Windus: London, 1971. Pp. 15-40.

CHAMBERS, JOHN. "The cult of science-fiction." *DR*, XL (1960/61), 78-86.

On the *raison d'être* of science-fiction, its origins and traditions and on the vast range of science-fiction plot material in the 50s.

COHN, RUBY. "The contemporary English novel." *Perspective*, X (1958/59), 103-105.

Introduces a special number on contemporary British novelists (Newby, Golding, Amis, Wain, and Powell).

COLEMAN, JOHN. "The facts of fiction." *Spectator*, 23 October 1959, 559-560.

Contemporary novels have made sex boring.

COLLINS, A.S. *English literature of the twentieth century. With a postscript on the nineteen-fifties by Frank Whitehead*. University Tutorial Press: London, 1960. Pp. VII + 410.

A postscript deals with the Angry Young Men, Cary, Murdoch, Angus Wilson, Cooper, and the later works of Huxley and Greene.

CONQUEST, ROBERT. "Science fiction and literature." *CritQ*, V (1963), 355-367.

Defence of science fiction as a form of literature which
is read only for enjoyment. Amis's *New Maps of Hell* is
quoted in support.

COUGHLAN, ROBERT. "Why Britain's 'Angry Young Men' boil
over." *Life*, 26 May 1958, 138-150.

COX, C.B. "The modern novel." *The free spirit. A study of
liberal humanism in the novels of George Eliot, Henry
James, E.M. Forster, Virginia Woolf, Angus Wilson*. Oxford
UP: London, 1963. Pp. 154-184.

Discussion of novels by Amis, Wain, Raymond Williams,
Angus Wilson. Golding as "the one new major novelist".

CRAIG, DAVID. "The British working-class novel today." *ЗАА*,
XI (1963), 29-41.

Argues that because it lacks "whole-hearted socialism",
the British working-class novel has not been successful
as yet. This explains the failure of Raymond Williams's
Border Country, Allen's *All in a Lifetime* and Heinemann's
The Adventurers. Praises the "deeply proletarian qualities"
of Sillitoe.

DAICHES, DAVID. "The background of recent English literature." *Folio*, XXII (Winter 1956/57), 52-64.

On the "consolidated" 50s.

DAICHES, DAVID. *The present age, after 1920*. Introductions
to English Literature, 5. Cresset Press: London, 1958.
Pp. X + 376.

Short survey of the English literary scene ("Fiction",
85-118); bibliography of primary and secondary sources
including contemporary English novelists such as
Angus Wilson, Toynbee and Newby.

DAVIS, ROBERT MURRAY. "Market depressed and unstable: Surveys of the recent English novel." *PLL*, VI (1970),
211-223.

On recent critics of the postwar English novel: James Hall,
Rabinovitz, Allsop, Gindin, Karl, O'Connor, Scholes.

DERLETH, AUGUST. "Contemporary science fiction." *CE*, XIII
(1951/52), 187-194.

Closes with a bibliography of representative science
fiction since 1940.

DIAKONOVA, NINA. "Notes on the evaluation of the *Bildungsroman* in England." *ЗАА*, XVI (1968), 341-351.

Mentions novels by Huxley, Greene, Amis, Braine, Murdoch,
Angus Wilson, MacInnes, Barstow, Durrell, and Cary.

DOOLEY, D.J. "Some uses and mutations of the picaresque." *DR*, XXXVII (1957/58), 363-377.

The last part of this article deals with the "good possibilities" of the picaresque to describe the postwar period: Amis's *Lucky Jim* and *This Uncertain Feeling,* Braine's *Room at the Top,* Wain's *Hurry on Down.*

DRESCHER, HORST W. "Einleitung." *Englische Literatur der Gegenwart in Einzeldarstellungen*, ed. Horst W. Drescher. Kröner: Stuttgart, 1970. Pp. 3-22.

Short but comprehensive survey of contemporary British literature. Traces the main trends in poetry, drama and the novel since 1945.

EADE, D.C. *Contemporary Yorkshire novelists. A study of some themes in the work of Stan Barstow, John Braine, David Storey and Keith Waterhouse.* M.Phil. Leeds, 1968/69.

EARNSHAW, H.G. *Modern writers. A guide to twentieth-century literature in the English language.* Chambers: Edinburgh, 1968. Pp. VI + 266.

Contains short chaps on Huxley, Waugh, Graves, Priestley, Greene, Orwell, Golding, and Durrell.

ENGELBORGHS, MAURITS. "Britse 'Lady novelists'." *DWB*, CXIV (1969), 286-292.

Spark and Edna O'Brien.

EVANS, ROBERT O. "A perspective for American novelists." *Topic*, VI (Fall 1966), 58-66.

English models "provide the American writers with the shot in the arm they need": for example, Spark's *The Mandelbaum Gate* and Amis's *The Anti-Death League.*

FELDMAN, GENE & MAX GARTENBERG, eds. *The Beat Generation and the Angry Young Men.* Citadel Press: New York, 1958. Pp. 384.

FIELD, J.C. "The literary scene: 1968-1970." *RLV*, XXXVI (1970), 652-662; XXXVII (1971), 91-100, 332-347, 621-631, 766-773.

Contains discussions of Amis's *I Want It Now*, Spark's *The Public Image*, Powell's *The Military Philosophers,* Snow's *The Sleep of Reason*, Moore's *I Am Mary Dunne*, Durrell's *Tunc*, Amis's *The Green Man*, Drabble's *The Waterfall*, Brophy's *In Transit*, Murdoch's *The Nice and the Good* and *Bruno's Dream.*

FRASER, G.S. *The modern writer and his world*. Pelican Books: Harmondsworth, 1970 (rev. ed.). Pp. 464.

The book gives an analysis of the major English writers in the twentieth century. An introductory survey relates the overall literary and cultural scene. See particularly Part Two "The Novel" (73-190). Epilogue written in 1970.

FRICKER, ROBERT. *Der moderne englische Roman*. Vandenhoeck & Ruprecht: Göttingen, 1966 (rev. ed.). Pp. 263.

See chap. on "Der englische Roman unserer Zeit" (174-252): Greene, Waugh, Powell, Snow, Angus Wilson, Newby, Compton Burnett, Hartley, Green, Durrell, Golding.

FRICKER, ROBERT. "Das Kathedralenmotiv in der modernen englischen Dichtung." *Festschrift Rudolf Stamm*, eds. Eduard Kolb & Jörg Hasler. Francke: Bern, 1969. Pp. 225-238.

The symbol of the cathedral in modern English literature. There is a religious revival in modern English literature (Greene, Waugh, Murdoch, and Golding in the field of the novel). Discussion of Golding's religious symbolism.

FRIES, UDO. "Zum historischen Präsens im modernen englischen Roman." *GRM*, n.s. XX (1970), 321-338.

Quotations from Dennis (*Cards of Identity*), Murdoch (*The Time of the Angels*) and others.

FURBANK, P.N. "The twentieth-century best-seller." *The Pelican guide to English literature*, ed. Boris Ford. Vol. VII, *The modern age*. Penguin Books: Harmondsworth, 1961. Pp. 429-441.

Tries to answer the question to what best-sellers owe their popularity. Traces their history.

FYTTON, FRANCIS. "The car as a character." *London Mag*, n.s. VI (May 1966), 36-50.

Cars in modern fiction "have earned themselves a place on the same footing - or should it be wheeling? - as human characters." Mentions Huxley's *Those Barren Leaves*, Cronin's *The Citadel*, Braine's *Room at the Top*, Amis's *Take a Girl Like You*, and other novels.

GASKIN, D. BRUCE, ed. *From Lord Jim to Billy Liar. An introduction to the English novel in the twentieth century*. Heritage of Literature Series, 12. Longmans: London, 1969. Pp. 302.

Contains extracts from novels by Cary, Huxley, Hartley, Hughes, Orwell, Waugh, Lehmann, Greene, Snow, Golding, Angus Wilson, Murdoch, Amis, Braine, Sillitoe, Waterhouse. Each extract is preceded by a brief note on the novelist

and information about the novel. Introduction to elements
of a novel and supplementary list for further reading.

GERARD, ALBERT. "Les jeunes hommes furieux." *RGB*, XCVI
(février 1960), 21-30.

The Angry Young Men as a transitory movement.

GEREVINI, SILVANO. *Voci di letteratura inglese contemporanea*.
Cortina: Pavia, 1957. Pp. 68.

Brief biographical sketches of writers, including a bibliography of their works.

GIBBINS, JOHN. "Some thoughts on the state of the novel." *QR*,
CCCI (1963), 48-56.

Discussions of the current novel.

GINDIN, JAMES. "The reassertation of the personal." *TQ*, I
(Winter 1958), 126-134.

Aspects of the comic in contemporary English novels by
Amis, Wain, Angus Wilson.

GINDIN, JAMES. "Comedy in contemporary British fiction."
PMASAL, XLIV (1959), 389-397.

Amis, Murdoch, Angus Wilson, Wain.

GINDIN, JAMES. *Postwar British fiction. New accents and attitudes*. Cambridge UP: London, 1962. Pp. XII + 246.

Deals extensively with Sillitoe, Amis, Lessing, Wain, Angus Wilson, Murdoch, Golding. Regards Sillitoe, Murdoch
and Angus Wilson as outstanding. Argues that Snow, Durrell
and Colin Wilson are overrated. Bio-bibliographical notes
on the authors.

GINDIN, JAMES. "The fable begins to break down." *WSCL*, VIII
(1967), 1-18.

On contemporary British novel-writing: Durrell, Golding,
Murdoch, Angus Wilson, and others.

GINDIN, JAMES. "Well beyond laughter: Directions from fifties' comic fiction." *SIN*, III (1971), 357-364.

Since the fifties Amis, Sillitoe, Murdoch, Angus Wilson,
and Wain have altered their themes and attitudes in different directions.

GINDIN, JAMES. "Compassion in contemporary fiction." *Harvest
of a quiet eye. The novel of compassion*. Indiana UP:
Bloomington, 1971. Pp. 337-359.

Golding, Murdoch, Sillitoe, Fowles, and others.

GLICKSBERG, CHARLES I. "The literature of the Angry Young Men." *ColQ*, VIII (1959/60), 293-303.

GOLDBERG, GERALD JAY. "The search for the artist in some recent British fiction." *SAQ*, LXII (1963), 387-401.

Durrell's *The Alexandria Quartet*, Golding's *Free Fall*, Murdoch's *Under the Net*.

GRAAF, VERA. *Homo futurus. Eine Analyse der modernen Science-fiction*. Claassen: Hamburg, 1971. Pp. 238.

Examples are taken mainly from American science fiction; extensive bibliography of primary and secondary sources.

GRANSDEN, K.W. "Rebels and timeservers." *TC*, CLXI (1957), 220-226.

Differences observeable, in their writing, between the post- and prewar intellectual. Orwell (*The Road to Wigan Pier*), Amis, Snow (*The Masters, Homecomings*), Osborne (*Look Back in Anger*).

GRANSDEN, K.W. "Thoughts on contemporary fiction." *REL*, I (April 1960), 7-17.

Extended references to Snow, Powell and Amis. "We could ... classify the novel under three headings: (1) the novel of sensibility, exploring character and relationships in the great Austen-Forster-James tradition; (2) the novel of articulation, the 'novel as gesture', mud in the face of other people, the universe, etc.: e.g. the first novels of John Braine, John Wain, Amis; some of Joyce; (3) the novel as chronicle."

GREACEN, ROBERT. "Social class in post-war English fiction." *SoR*, n.s. IV (1968), 142-151.

Postwar English novelists do not write thesis novels. Authors mentioned are Compton-Burnett, Greene, Waugh, Snow, Powell, Priestley, Amis, Wain, Sillitoe, Braine, Lessing, MacInnes, Angus Wilson, and others.

GREEN, MARTIN. "Room at the middle." *Commonweal*, 8 April 1960, 38-39.

The novel of the Angry Young Men. Short survey mentioning Amis, Braine, Sillitoe, Waterhouse. Sees connection between the modern British novel and Salinger and Nabokov.

GREENBERG, ALVIN. "The death of the psyche: A way to the self in the contemporary novel." *Criticism*, VIII (1966), 1-18.

Quotes from Beckett's *Watt* and Bellow's *Henderson the Rain King*. Mentions Golding's *Pincher Martin*.

GRÖGER, ERIKA. *Die Widerspiegelung der Atomproblematik im*
englisch-amerikanischen Roman (1946-1962). Diss. Leipzig,
1963. Pp. 279.

Based on an analysis of seventy novels - mainly published
between 1946 and 1962 in Britain and America - which deal
with the challenge of nuclear weapons.

GRÖGER, ERIKA. "Der bürgerliche Atomwissenschaftler im
englisch-amerikanischen Roman von 1945 bis zur Gegenwart."
ZAA, XVI (1968), 25-48.

HAGOPIAN, JOHN V. & MARTIN DOLCH, eds. *Insight II. Analyses*
of modern British literature. Hirschgraben: Frankfurt/M.,
1965 (rev. ed.). Pp. 371.

Includes critical analyses of Durrell's *Clea* (94-103),
Greene's *The Power and the Glory* (152-164), Huxley's *Brave*
New World (175-185), Snow's *The Masters* (330-336) and of
short stories by Amis, Bates, Elizabeth Bowen, Cary, Lessing, Orwell, Sansom, Wain, and Angus Wilson. Selected
bibliography of full-length discussions of the authors.

HALIO, JAY L. "A sense of the present." *SoR*, n.s. II (1966),
952-966.

Rev. art. Novelists discussed are Murdoch, Elizabeth Bowen,
Angus Wilson, Powell, Bates, Hartley, Burgess, Compton-
Burnett, Tuohy, Fowles, Wain, Sillitoe.

HALL, JAMES. *The tragic comedians. Seven modern British*
novelists. Indiana UP: Bloomington, 1966 (3rd printing).
Pp. VIII + 176.

Contains individual chaps on Forster, Huxley, Waugh, Green,
Cary, Hartley, and Powell. Refers also to Wain, Amis and
Braine. Selected bibliography.

HALL, JAMES. *The lunatic giant in the drawing room. The*
British and American novel since 1930. Indiana UP: Bloomington, 1968. Pp. 242.

Discusses writers concerned with the Freudian conflict between the *id* - the "lunatic giant" - and the *super-ego* -
the "drawing room" of established social restraints -.
Deals extensively with novels by Elizabeth Bowen, Greene
and Murdoch (chaps on each writer). Mentions Golding, Snow,
Waugh, and others. Selected bibliography of recent criticism.

HARKNESS, BRUCE. "The lucky crowd: Contemporary British
fiction." *EJ*, XLVII (1958), 387-397.

Wain's *Hurry on Down* and Amis's *Lucky Jim* as examples of
the "new voice" in British fiction.

HART, FRANCIS R. "Region, character, and identity in recent
Scottish fiction." *VQR*, XLIII (1967), 597-613.

Deals with seven recent Scottish novels by Gunn, Jenkins,
Duncan, Spark, McLean, Linklater, and Sharp.

HARVEY, W.J. "Have you anything to declare? Or Angry Young
Men: Facts and fictions." *ILA*, I (1958), 47-59.

Discusses the myth of the Angry Young Men. Amis, Wain,
Colin Wilson, Braine, and Osborne are mentioned as typi-
cal examples.

HARVEY, W.J. "The reviewing of contemporary fiction." *EIC*,
VIII (1958), 182-187.

Rev. art. on Golding, *Pincher Martin;* Hinde, *Happy as
Larry;* Murdoch, *The Sandcastle;* Fuller, *Image of a
Society.*

HARVEY, W.J. *Character and the novel.* Cornell UP: Ithaca,
1965. Pp. X + 222.

Refers to various contemporary English novels.

HARRIS, WENDELL V. "Molly's 'Yes': The transvaluation of sex
in modern fiction." *TSLL*, X (1968/69), 107-118.

Discussion of various novelists from Joyce to Durrell.

HASSAN, IHAB H. "The anti-hero in modern British and American fiction." *Comparative literature. Proceedings of the
second congress of the international comparative literature association,* ed. Werner P. Friederich. North Carolina
UP: Chapel Hill, 1959. Vol. I, pp. 309-323.

HAYMAN, RONALD. "Le roman anglais d'après-guerre." *La situation de la littérature anglaise d'après-guerre.* Les Cahiers
des Lettres Modernes. Lettres Modernes: Paris, 1955.
Pp. 81-112.

Refers to West, Koestler, Greene, Waugh, Orwell, Huxley,
Hartley, Sansom, and Green. General description of the
postwar novel scene.

HAYWARD, JOHN. "Nya namn." *BLM*, XXIII (1954), 280-283.

The new generation of novelists: Wain, Amis, Murdoch,
Larkin.

HEBBLETHWAITE, PETER. "How Catholic is the Catholic novel?"
TLS, 27 July 1967, 678-679.

Greene, Waugh, Spark, Fielding.

HEJE, JOHAN. "Efterkirgstidens engelske roman." *Fremmede*

digtere i det 20. århundrede. III, ed. Sven M. Kristensen. G.E.C. Gad: Copenhagen, 1968. Pp. 531-549.

HENFREY, NORMAN V. "The Angry Young Men: Les raisons d'une colère." *Culture*, XXVII (1966), 176-194.

HILLEGAS, MARK R. *The future as nightmare. H.G. Wells and the anti-utopians*. Oxford UP: New York, 1967. Pp. XI + 200.
Huxley and Orwell are discussed as anti-utopians. Wells's influence on present-day science fiction and other types of fiction, such as Golding's *The Inheritors*, is shown.

HOBSBAUM, PHILIP. "University life in English fiction." *TC*, CLXXIII (Summer 1964), 139-147.
Contains discussions of novels by Snow, Amis, Bradbury, Larkin, and others.

HOLLOWAY, JOHN. "Tank in the stalls: Notes on the 'School of Anger'." *HudR*, X (1957/58), 424-429. Repr. in *The charted mirror. Literary and critical essays*. Routledge & Kegan Paul: London, 1960. Pp. 137-145.
Amis, Wain, Braine, Hinde, and others.

HOOK, SIDNEY. "The politics of science fiction." *Encounter*, XX (May 1963), 82-88.
Rev. art. on *Fail-Safe* by Eugene Burdick & Harvey Wheeler. Touches on general problems of the "new genre".

HOPE, FRANCIS. "Faces in the novel." *TC*, CLXXIII (Autumn 1964), 56-61.
On the way contemporary British novelists mirror their country.

HORTMANN, WILHELM. *Englische Literatur im 20. Jahrhundert*. Dalp-Taschenbücher, 379. Francke: Bern, 1965. Pp. 204.
Detailed survey of 20th-century literature in Great Britain, which also includes minor and present-day writers.

HOWE, IRVING. "Novels of the post-war world." *NewR*, 10 November 1958, 16-18.
American and English.

HOWE, IRVING. "Mass society and post-modern fiction." *PR*, XXVI (1959), 420-436.
The novels of Amis, Braine, and Wain are characterized by a "quick apprehension and notation of contemporary life which ... has become somewhat rare in serious American fiction."

18

HUNTER, JIM, ed. *The modern novel in English. Studied in extracts.* Faber & Faber: London, 1966. Pp. 224.

Authors included are Greene, Cary, Golding, Angus Wilson, Storey.

HYMAN, STANLEY EDGAR. "Some trends in the novel." *CE*, XX (1958/59), 1-9.

Refers to American, English, German, French, Italian, and Soviet writers; mentions the Angry Young Men.

HYNES, SAM. "The 'poor sod' as hero." *Commonweal*, 13 April 1956, 51-53.

Themes and characterizations in the contemporary English novel (Angry Young Men).

HYNES, SAM. "The beat and the angry." *Commonweal*, 5 September 1958, 559-561.

IVASHEVA, V. "The English novel of the fifties." *InLit*, 1 (January 1958), 211-217.

Mainly on the Angry Young Men.

IVASHEVA, V. "The struggle is not over yet." *InLit*, 5 (May 1959), 180-188.

On the polemics by British critics about the problems of developments in modern art. A certain enlivening of English literature is in many respects due to the success of writers who develop social problems in their works: Wain, Davidson, Stewart.

IVASHEVA, V. "The struggle continues: Some comments on English modernist esthetics." *ZAA*, VIII (1960), 409-421.

On the "considerable strengthening of the realist camp in English literature". Mentions Lessing, Baron, Lindsay, and others.

IVASHEVA, V. *Anglijskij roman poslednego desjatiletija (1950-1960).* Sov. Pisatel: Moskva, 1962. Pp. 413.

IVASHEVA, V. "Sovremennyj anglijskij 'rabočij roman'." *VMU*, XXI: 4 (1966), 31-51.

On the working-class novel in contemporary English literature.

IVASHEVA, V. "Novye tendencii v anglijskoj proze 60-x godov." *VLit*, XI: 3 (1967), 177-194.

New tendencies in the English novel of the sixties.

IVASHEVA, V. *Anglijskaja literatura. XX vek.* Izdatel'stvo "Prosveščenije": Moskva, 1967. Pp. 476.

Contains passages on Aldington, Cronin, Priestley, Huxley, Greene, Waugh, Snow, Fleming, Orwell, Lessing, Murdoch, Golding, Colin Wilson, Angus Wilson, the Angry Young Men, Aldridge, and others.

JACQUE, VALENTINA. "Soviet critics on modern English writing." *SovL*, 4 (1963), 163-167.

Translations of novels by Lindsay and Gwyn Thomas. Soviet interest in the Angry Young Men and the Kitchen Sink Dramatists.

JOHANNSEN, KARIN. *Wiederkehrende Elemente in der Motivik und Form englischer Künstlerromane*. Diss. Kiel, 1965. Pp. II + 232.

Concerned with English novels of the nineteenth and twentieth centuries which present the artist as the central character. Modern English novels discussed are: Kennedy, *The Constant Nymph*; Huxley, *Point Counter Point* and *Time Must Have a Stop*; Orwell, *Keep the Aspidistra Flying*; Cary, *The Horse's Mouth*; Priestley, *Jenny Villiers*; Angus Wilson, *Hemlock and After*; Humphreys, *Hear and Forgive*; Linklater, *The House of Gair*; Hartley, *A Perfect Woman*; Cronin, *Crusader's Tomb*; Waugh, *The Ordeal of Gilbert Pinfold*; Amis, *I Like It Here*; Durrell, *The Alexandria Quartet*.

JOHNSON, PAMELA HANSFORD. "Modern fiction and the English understatement." *TLS*, 7 August 1959, III.

Modern English fiction understates national characteristics. Waugh, Snow, Powell, and Amis are mentioned.

KAHRMANN, BERND. *Die idyllische Szene im zeitgenössischen englischen Roman*. Linguistica et Litteraria, 8. Gehlen: Bad Homburg v.d.H., 1969. Pp. 150. Summary in *EASG*, II (1970), 74-76.

Analyses of three functions that the idyllic scenes may assume for the figure or figures in contemporary novels: escape, release, self-securement. The material is provided by the novels of Orwell and Murdoch. Further writers included are Braine, Wain, Sillitoe, Golding, Penelope Mortimer, Waugh, Storey, and Cary.

KARL, FREDERICK R. *A reader's guide to the contemporary English novel*. Thames & Hudson: London, 1963. Pp. 304.

A short survey of the contemporary English novel is followed by detailed studies of Beckett, Durrell, Snow, Greene, Bowen, Cary, Orwell, Waugh, Green, Compton-Burnett and the 'Angries'. Chaps XIII and XIV deal with Powell, Angus Wilson, Dennis, Golding, Murdoch, Warner, and Newby. Chap. XV includes "several novelists whose work warrants mention although for many reasons they have not been or are not yet in the first rank": Pamela Hansford Johnson, Lehmann, Taylor, Manning, Spark, Lessing,

Sillitoe, King, Glanville, Jones, Sansom, Gerald Hanley, Fuller.

KATONA, ANNA. "The decline of the modern in recent British fiction." *ZAA*, XIII (1965), 35-44.

Only socially engaged novelists like Amis, Wain and Silli- toe give a true picture of reality. Stephen Spender's distinction between modern and contemporary (*The struggle of the modern*) is considered to be very helpful when applied to 20th-century English fiction.

KENNEDY, JAMES G. "More general than fiction: The uses of history in the criticism of modern novels." *CE*, XXVIII (1966/67), 150-163.

Attack on those who read novels for universals. Contains a section on Wyndham Lewis's *Self Condemned*. Mentions Graves, Cary, Snow, Angus Wilson, Amis.

KERMODE, FRANK. "Myth, reality, and fiction." *Listener*, 30 August 1962, 311-313.

The views of Murdoch, Greene, Angus Wilson, Compton-Bur- nett, Snow, Wain, and Spark on the proportion of fanciful to realistic elements in modern fiction.

KERMODE, FRANK. "The house of fiction: Interviews with seven English novelists." *PR* , XXX (1963), 61-82.

Free and unprepared talks with Compton-Burnett, Greene, Murdoch, Snow, Spark, Wain, and Angus Wilson.

KETTLE, A. "Quest for new ways (notes on contemporary English literature)." *InLit*, 8 (August 1961), 182-188.

Braine, Sillitoe, Wallis, Heinemann, Raymond Williams.

KING, ROGER. "Is Bond broken? Or, is Hercule Poirot unbreak- able?" *TC*, CLXXVI (Second/1968), 49-51.

"... at this moment, there is no obvious successor to Bond" (Fleming).

KITCHIN, LAURENCE. "The zombies' lair." *Listener*, 4 November 1965, 701-702, 704.

On the collision in literature between the country-house intelligentsia and the industrial workers: D.H. Lawrence, Cary, Storey, Middleton, Barstow, Braine, Amis, Murdoch (*The Bell*).

KLUTH, KÄTHE. "Audiatur et altera pars (Zum englischen Frauen- roman der Gegenwart)." *WZUG*, X (1961), 253-261.

Written from a Marxist point of view. Refers to Compton Burnett, Elizabeth Bowen, Lehmann, Mitford, Murdoch, Les- sing, Christie, Spark, and Pamela Hansford Johnson.

KLUTH, KÄTHE. "The contemporary English short story." *PP*, V (1962), 84-95.

Most present-day English novelists make also use of the short story.

KOSTELANETZ, RICHARD. "Contemporary literature." *On contemporary literature. An anthology of critical essays on the major movements and writers of contemporary literature,* ed. Richard Kostelanetz. Avon Books: New York, 1964. Pp. XV-XXVII.

Introduces a collection of essays dealing with Burgess, Durrell, Golding, Lessing, Murdoch, Spark, and others.

KVAM, RAGNAR. "Teddy-boys og Nietzsche-boys." *Vinduet,* XII (1958), 179-187.

Critical review of the Angry Young Men: Colin Wilson, *The Outsider*; Amis, *Lucky Jim*; Braine, *Room at the Top*; Murdoch, *The Flight from the Enchanter*.

KVAM, RAGNAR. "Ny engelsk prosa." *Samtiden*, LXIX (1960), 549-557.

Snow's *The Affair*, Colin Wilson's *Ritual in the Dark* and Durrell's *The Alexandria Quartet* reflect the current antithesis between the "socially engaged novel" and the aestheticism of the Bloomsbury school.

LECLAIRE, LUCIEN. *Le roman régionaliste dans les Iles Britanniques (1800-1950)*. Société d'Edition "Les Belles Lettres": Paris, 1954. Pp. 300.

Detailed study of the regional novel in Great Britain. References to Bates, Cronin, James Hanley, Humphreys, Linklater, Llewellyn, O'Connor, O'Faolain, Jameson, Gwyn Thomas, and Williamson.

LEHMANN, JOHN. "Foreword." *London Mag*, IV (August 1957), 7-9.

"... the characteristic mood and interest of the English novel in our time is social comedy." Mentions Amis, Wain, Braine, Murdoch.

LEHMANN, JOHN. "English letters in the doldrums?: An editor's view." *TC*, IV (Autumn 1961), 56-63.

On the state of English letters since 1945; mentions Greene, Waugh, Sansom, Angus Wilson, Wain, Amis, Braine, Murdoch, Powell, Snow, Durrell, Dennis, Golding.

LEWIS, C.S., KINGSLEY AMIS & BRIAN ALDISS. "Unreal estates: On science fiction." *Encounter*, XXIV (March 1965), 61-65.

A recorded discussion on the topic of science fiction.

LINDSAY, JACK. *After the 'thirties. The novel in Britain, and its future.* Lawrence & Wishart: London, 1956.

Pp. 239.

Only part I is dedicated to the contemporary literary scene, while part II deals with problems of writing. Hardly an overall view of the novel between 1930 and 1956, rather thoughts and ideas of a novelist on the novel and its authors. Many minor works are discussed, while there is no systematic presentation of trends or individual authors. Contains discussions of the following novels: *The Diplomat* (Aldridge), *Secret Valleys* (Coussins), *All Things Betray Thee* (Gwyn Thomas), *Soldier at the Door* (Pargeter), *The Caravan Passes* (Tabori), *Hunger* (Lessing), and *The New Men* (Snow).

LOCKWOOD, BERNARD. "Four contemporary British working-class novelists: A thematic and critical approach to the fiction of Raymond Williams, John Braine, David Storey and Alan Sillitoe." *DA*, XXVIII (1967), 1081A (Wis.).

Examines mainly *Border Country* and *Second Generation; Room at the Top; This Sporting Life* and *Flight into Camden; Saturday Night and Sunday Morning* and *The Loneliness of the Long-Distance Runner*. These novels present a "class-divided, dog-eat-dog society" and "the search for values and a more meaningful life". Their contribution to British fiction: "... they expand its bounderies to include the working classes as a normal and acceptable subject matter for a novelist, and they add a new perspective to the genre - a working-class view of the world."

LODGE, DAVID. "Le roman contemporain en Angleterre." *TR*, 179 (décembre 1962), 80-92.

Braine, Amis, Wain, Sillitoe, Durrell, Murdoch, Golding, Snow, Angus Wilson, and others.

LODGE, DAVID. "The contemporary novel, and all that jazz." *London Mag*, n.s. II (August 1962), 73-80.

Concerned with the jazz-content of recent fiction. Novels discussed are MacInnes's *Absolute Beginners*, Amis's *Take a Girl Like You*, Wain's *Strike the Father Dead*, and others.

LODGE, DAVID. "The novelist at the crossroads." *CritQ*, XI (1969), 105-132. Repr. in *The novelist at the crossroads and other essays on fiction and criticism*. Routledge & Kegan Paul: London, 1971. Pp. 3-34.

Whither the novel? Distinguishes between different kinds of novels. Refers to a great number of contemporary English novelists.

MCCORMICK, JOHN. *Catastrophe and imagination. An interpretation of the recent English and American novel.* Longmans, Green: London, 1957. Pp. XI + 327.

Extended references to Elizabeth Bowen, Cary, Hartley, Huxley, Lehmann, Newby, Powell, Pritchett, Warner, and Waugh. Mentions briefly Amis, Baron, Brigid Brophy, Compton-Burnett, Cooper, Green, Greene, Koestler, Lowry, Manning, Monsarrat, Orwell, Sansom, Snow, and Angus Wilson.

MCDOWELL, FREDERICK P.W. "'The devious involutions of human character and emotions': Reflections on some recent British novels." *WSCL*, IV (1963), 339-366.

Murdoch, Lessing, Powell, and others.

MCDOWELL, FREDERICK P.W. "Recent British fiction: Some established writers." *ConL*, XI (1970), 401-431.

Rev. art. on recent novels by Amis, Braine, Sillitoe, Waterhouse, Hinde, Glanville, Snow, Spark, Durrell, Powell, Newby, Burgess, Murdoch, Lessing, Fowles, and others.

MCDOWELL, FREDERICK P.W. "Recent British fiction: New or lesser-known writers." *ConL*, XI (1970), 540-578.

Rev. art. on recent novels by Middleton, Hyams, Barstow, Raven, Charteris, Gordon M. Williams, Robert Shaw, Drabble, Bragg, Frayn, Mosley, Julian Mitchell, P.-P. Read, and others.

MACKWORTH, CECILY. "Le roman anglais d'aujourd'hui." *Critique*, XIV (1958), 32-41.

Discusses the novels of the Angry Young Men: Braine, Amis and Wain.

MERTNER, EDGAR. "Der Roman der jungen Generation in England." *Sprache und Literatur Englands und Amerikas*, III, ed. Gerhard Müller-Schwefe. Niemeyer: Tübingen, 1959. Pp. 101-123.

Mainly on the novels of the Angry Young Men and their social criticism (Wain, Amis, Braine). Refers to Lessing, Murdoch, Golding.

MERTNER, EDGAR. "Der Roman und andere Prosa seit dem ersten Weltkrieg." Ewald Standop & Edgar Mertner: *Englische Literaturgeschichte*. Quelle & Meyer: Heidelberg, 1971 (rev. ed.). Pp. 629-664.

Concludes (651-664) with discussions of Powell, Snow, Wain, Amis, Braine, Sillitoe, Storey, Durrell, Angus Wilson, Golding, Murdoch, Lessing, and Spark.

MILLER, KARL, ed. *Writing in England today. The last fifteen years*. Penguin Books: Harmondsworth, 1968. Pp. 362.

24

Contains an introduction by the editor, extracts from
novels by Waugh, Amis, MacInnes, Bedford, Sillitoe,
Storey, Golding, Spark, Moore, Lessing, Burgess, Brigid
Brophy, Drabble, Fleming, Mackay, McGahern, Edna O'Brien,
and Higgins. Biographical notes on the authors.

MILLGATE, MICHAEL. "Contemporary English fiction: Some observations." *Venture,* II (1961), 214-220.

Contemporary English fiction is represented by Snow and
the anti-experimental novel. Golding and Durrell are exceptions. The older generation (Huxley, Waugh and others)
have had their day.

MITCHELL, STEPHEN O. "Alien vision: The techniques of science
fiction." *MFS,* IV (1958/59), 346-356.

MONOD, SYLVERE. *Histoire de la littérature anglaise. De Vic-
toria à Elisabeth II.* Librairie Armand Colin: Paris, 1970.
Pp. 392.

Contains separate chaps on Frank O'Connor, Sansom, Eliza-
beth Bowen, Powell, Orwell, Waugh, Cary, Greene, Green, C.
S. Lewis, Colin Wilson, Larkin, Amis, Angus Wilson, Snow,
Hartley, Wain, Braine, Sillitoe, Durrell, Lowry, Compton-
Burnett, Murdoch, Spark, Heppenstall, Brooke-Rose, and
Golding. Selected bibliography.

MONTEIRO-GRILLO, J. "Tradição e crise no romance inglês con-
temporâneo." *Brotéria,* LXVII (1963), 144-164.

MOODY, PHILIPPA. "In the lavatory of the Athenaeum: Post-war
English novels." *MCR,* VI (1963), 83-92.

Golding, Murdoch, Snow, and Sillitoe. These popular though
lesser novelists draw a picture of contemporary society.

MOORE, HARRY T. "Preface." *Contemporary British novelists,*
ed. Charles Shapiro. Southern Illinois UP: Carbondale,
Edwardsville, 1965. Pp. V-XIV.

Comments on the individual essays by the editor of the
Crosscurrents Series.

MORGAN, EDWIN. "Scottish writing today, II: The novel and the
drama." *English,* XVI (1966/67), 227-229.

Discusses Archie Hind's *The Dear Green Place,* and mentions
Alan Sharp, Hugh Rae, Alexander Trocchi, Alex Neish, and
Spark.

MORGAN, W. JOHN. "Authentic voices." *TC,* CLXI (1957), 138-144.

The "younger generation" of writers and their "spokesmen":
Amis *(Lucky Jim),* Cooper *(Scenes from Provincial Life; The
Struggles of Albert Woods),* Colin Wilson *(The Outsider).*

MURCH, A.E. *The development of the detective novel*. Owen: London, 1968 (rev. ed.). Pp. 272.

General survey of detective fiction writers of all times and countries.

NEW, WILLIAM H. "The island and the madman: Recurrent imagery in the major novelists of the fifties." *ArQ*, XXII (1966), 328-337.

"The adolescent ceases to be the focus of major novels." English novelists discussed are Huxley *(Island)*, Greene *(Our Man in Havana)*, Spark *(Robinson)*.

NEWBY, P.H. *The novel 1945-1950*. Longmans, Green: London, 1951. Pp. 48.

Includes a consideration of the effects of the war upon the writing of fiction. Chaps dealing with tradition and experiment, with satire, and with character and situation. Select bibliography.

O'CONNOR, WILLIAM VAN. "Two types of 'heroes' in post-war British fiction." *PMLA*, LXXVII (1962), 168-174. Repr. in *The new university wits and the end of modernism*. With a preface by Harry T. Moore. Southern Illinois UP: Carbondale, 1963. Pp. 133-149, 162-163.

The younger generation of British novelists has developed a distinct literary response to the social changes taking place in our time. As a result writers like Braine, Murdoch, Wain, and Waterhouse have produced a new type of protagonist.

O'CONNOR, WILLIAM VAN. *The new university wits and the end of modernism*. With a preface by Harry T. Moore. Southern Illinois UP: Carbondale, 1963. Pp. XVI + 168.

"The title, University Wits, of course refers back to the Oxford and Cambridge men ... who became prominent in London literary and theatrical circles during the reign of the earlier Elizabeth." Writers like Amis and Braine should not be labelled Angry Young Men, but rather New University Wits. Studies on Amis, Wain and Murdoch. Extended references to Waterhouse and Sillitoe. Includes a discussion of contemporary English poetry.

OPPEL, HORST. "Einführung." *Der moderne englische Roman. Interpretationen,* ed. Horst Oppel. Schmidt: Berlin, 1971 (rev. ed.). Pp. 7-14.

Introduces a collection of essays on modern English novels, among them Golding's *Lord of the Flies,* Murdoch's *Under the Net,* Angus Wilson's *The Middle Age of Mrs. Eliot,* and Durrell's *The Alexandria Quartet*.

OTTERVIK, ERIC V. "The multiple-novel in contemporary British fiction." *DA*, XXVII (1967), 3877A (Pittsburgh).
Durrell, Snow, Powell, Cary, and others.

PAUL, LESLIE. "The Angry Young Men revisited." *KR*, XXVII (1965), 344-352.
Criticizes "Amis and company" (Wain, Braine, Colin Wilson) as parochial.

PENDRY, E.D. *The new feminism of English fiction. A study in contemporary women novelists.* Kenkyusha: Tokyo, 1956.
Pp. 198.
Compton-Burnett, Elizabeth Bowen, Lehmann, Manning.

PEREZ MINIK, DOMINGO. *Introducción a la novela inglesa actual.* Guadarrama: Madrid, 1968. Pp. 332.

PESCHMANN, HERMANN. "The nonconformists: Angry Young Men, 'Lucky Jims', and 'Outsiders'." *English*, XIII (1960/61), 12-16.
Contains discussions of novels by Wain and Amis.

PHELPS, GILBERT. "The novel today." *The Pelican guide to English literature,* ed. Boris Ford. Vol. VII, *The modern age.* Penguin Books: Harmondsworth, 1961. Pp. 475-495.
Powell, Snow, Amis, Wain, Braine, Sillitoe, Colin Wilson, Angus Wilson, Durrell, Murdoch.

PLANK, ROBERT. "Lighter than air, but heavy as hate: An essay on space travel." *PR*, XXIV (1957), 106-116.
Typology of science fiction.

PRICE, MARTIN. "The novel: Artifice and experience." *YR*, LI (1961/62), 152-158.
Surveys the major novels of the last fifty years. Mentions Snow, Angus Wilson, Murdoch, and Amis.

PRIESTLEY, J.B. "Thoughts in the wilderness: The newest novels." *New Statesman,* 26 June 1954, 824, 826.
Does not mention names: "The New English Novel is now emerging."

PRITCHETT, V.S. "These writers couldn't care less." *NYTBR*, 28 April 1957, 1, 38-39.
The Angry Young Men.

PRITCHETT, V.S. "Saints and rogues." *Listener,* 6 December 1962, 957-959.

Picaresque elements in recent English novels.

PRITCHETT, V.S. *The living novel & later appreciations.*
Random House: New York, 1964. Pp. VIII + 467.

Revised and expanded edition of *The living novel*, originally published in 1947. Twenty-seven new essays have been
added which were first published in the *New Statesman*. Three
of them deal with contemporary English novelists: Powell
("The Bored Barbarians", 294-303), Durrell ("Alexandrian
Hothouse", 303-309), Golding ("Pain and William Golding",
309-315). These essays are also published in *The working
novelist*. Chatto & Windus: London, 1965. Pp. 30-35, 56-61,
172-180.

PROCTOR, MORTIMER R. *The English university novel*. University of California Publications, English Studies, 15. California UP: Berkeley, 1957. Pp. IX + 228.

Brief references to Snow (*The Light and the Dark; The
Masters*) and Amis (*Lucky Jim*).

QUINTON, ANTHONY. "The post-Freudian hero." *London Mag*, IV
(July 1957), 56-61.

Rev. art. on King's *The Widow*, Braine's *Room at the Top*,
Longrigg's *Switchboard*, and Glyn's *The Ram in the Thicket*.
Tries to describe the characteristic novelist's young man
of the 50s.

QUINTON, ANTHONY. "Masculine, feminine and neuter: Or three
kinds of the contemporary novel." *London Mag*, VII (April
1960), 63-67.

Representatives of the first type are Cozzens, Snow and
Balchin, of the second Elizabeth Bowen and Lehmann, of
the third Camp and Sinclair.

QUINTON, ANTHONY, LETTICE COOPER, FRANK KERMODE & MAURICE
CRANSTON. "The new novelists: An enquiry." *London Mag*, V
(November 1958), 13-31; V (December 1958), 57-58.

Full scale discussion of postwar English novelists.

RABAN, JONATHAN. *The technique of modern fiction. Essays in
practical criticism*. Arnold: London, 1968. Pp. 203.

Modern fiction has responded directly to social processes
of our time, and its technique is influenced by new media
and by changes in social structure. Under the headings
"Narrative", "Character" and "Style and Language" fifteen
basic aspects of fictional technique are dealt with. Chaps
contain extracts from representative writers followed each
by a close analysis of the text: Drabble, *Jerusalem the
Golden*; Mortimer, *The Pumpkin Eater*; Orwell, *1984*;
Storey, *Flight into Camden*; Waterhouse, *Billy Liar*; Angus

Wilson, *Anglo-Saxon Attitudes.* Amis, Barstow, John Bowen, Bradbury, Fuller, Golding, Huxley, le Carré, MacInnes, Powell, Sillitoe, Spark, and Waugh are mentioned. A selected descriptive bibliography and a list of recent English and American novelists and their work conclude this sourcebook.

RABINOVITZ, RUBIN. *The reaction against experiment in the English novel, 1950-1960.* Columbia UP: New York, 1967. Pp. XII + 243.

General survey of the 1950s: Barstow, Braine, Cary, Cooper, Dennis, Durrell, Golding, Hartley, Humphreys, Pamela Hansford Johnson, Larkin, Murdoch, Powell, Sillitoe, Spark, Storey, Wain, Waterhouse, Waugh, Colin Wilson. Next follows a detailed study of Amis, Snow and Angus Wilson as leading figures in the traditionalist revival. A comprehensive bibliography lists books, essays, articles, and reviews written by these mid-twentieth-century novelists. Selective bibliography of works concerning each of them, as well as a selected bibliography of more general books and articles on contemporary fiction.

RATCLIFFE, MICHAEL. *The novel today.* Longmans, Green: London, 1968. Pp. 48.

Very brief but detailed study of the situation of the novel, its main representatives (also minor novelists are mentioned) and their work.

RIPPIER, JOSEPH S. *Some postwar English novelists. Angus Wilson, William Golding, Iris Murdoch, Lawrence Durrell, Kingsley Amis, John Wain, John Braine, Alan Sillitoe.* Studien zur Sprache und Literatur Englands, 1. Diesterweg: Frankfurt, 1965. Pp. 208.

Short study of each of the novels written by the authors mentioned in the title. Select bibliography for each author.

ROBSON, W.W. *Modern English literature.* Oxford UP: London, 1970. Pp. xv + 172.

Mentions among others Huxley, Greene, Waugh, Cary, Angus Wilson, Orwell, and contains an epilogue on "Literature since 1950".

ROSENTHAL, T.G. "The death of fiction." *New Statesman,* 22 March 1968, 389.

Being unfashionable is not synonymous with being dead, and fiction continues to survive and even to grow. Mentions Golding, Powell, Spark, and Greene.

SALE, RICHARD B. "An interview in New York with Walter Allen." *SIN,* III (1971), 405-429.

Main subjects: the comic novel in twentieth-century British
literature and the concept of the anti-hero. Mentions
Powell, Murdoch, Spark, Amis, and others.

SAMUELSON, DAVID N. "Studies in the contemporary American and
British science fiction novel." *DA*, XXX (1969), 1181A (So.
Calif.).

SARBU, ALADAR. *Szocialista realista törekvések a modern angol
regényben*. Akadémiai Kiadó: Budapest, 1967. Pp. 133.
With bibliography.

SCHIRMER, WALTER F. "Aldous Huxley, Graham Greene und die
Jüngeren." *Geschichte der englischen und amerikanischen
Literatur. Von den Anfängen bis zur Gegenwart*. Fünfte unter Mitwirkung von Arno Esch neubearbeitete Auflage. Niemeyer: Tübingen, 1968. Pp. 778-786.
Refers in its concluding chap. to Snow, Newby, Angus Wilson, the "Angries", Murdoch, Golding, and Durrell.

SCHLEUSSNER, BRUNO. *Der neopikareske Roman. Pikareske Elemen-
te in der Struktur moderner englischer Romane 1950-1960*.
Abhandlungen zur Kunst-, Musik- und Literaturwissenschaft,
61. Bouvier: Bonn, 1969. Pp. 201. Summary in *EASG*, I
(1969), 76-78.
Elements of the Spanish picaresque novel are traced - in
modified or reverse form - in Wain's *Hurry on Down*, Amis's
Lucky Jim, Waterhouse's *Billy Liar*, Murdoch's *Under the
Net*, Braine's *Room at the Top*, and Sillitoe's *Saturday
Night and Sunday Morning*.

SCHOLES, ROBERT. *The fabulators*. Oxford UP: New York, 1967.
Pp. X + 180.
Contemporary non-realistic fiction. Contains chap. on
Durrell's *Alexandria Quartet* (17-28) and a close exegesis
of Murdoch's *The Unicorn* (106-132).

SCHREY, HELMUT. *Didaktik des zeitgenössischen englischen Romans. Versuch auf der Grenze von Literaturkritik und Fachdidaktik*. Beiträge zur Fachdidaktik, 10. Henn: Wuppertal,
1970. Pp. 158.
Contains chaps on the novels of the Angry Young Men, Angus
Wilson, Golding, Snow, Murdoch, Durrell, and others.

SCHWARTZ, SHEILA. "The world of science fiction." *ER*, XXI
(February 1971), 27-40.
With bibliography.

SCOTT, J.D. "Britain's Angry Young Men." *SatR*, 27 July 1957,
8-11.
Amis, Braine, Wain, Osborne.

SCOTT, NATHAN A., JR. "The 'conscience' of the new literature." *The shaken realist. Essays in modern literature in
honor of Frederick J. Hoffman*, eds. Melvin J. Friedman &
John B. Vickery. Louisiana State UP: Baton Rouge, 1970.
Pp. 251-283.
General study of recent literature in its "post-modern
form", which contrasts strongly to the "grand style".

SCOTT-JAMES, R.A. *Fifty years of English literature, 1900-
1950. With a postscript 1951 to 1955*. Longmans, Green:
London, 1956 (2nd ed.). Pp. XI + 282.
See chaps XIV ("Novelists - Recent and Contemporary",
163-187) and XVII ("Postscript - 1951 to 1955", 240-263)
for a survey of Balchin, Bates, Elizabeth Bowen,
Cary, Charteris, Comfort, Compton-Burnett, Garnett,
Gerhardi, Golding, Green, Greene, James Hanley, Hartley,
Hughes, Huxley, King, Lehmann, Macaulay, Manning, Newby,
Orwell, Priestley, Waugh, and Rebecca West.

SCOTT-KILVERT, IAN. "English fiction 1958-60, I." *BBN*, 247
(March 1961), 163-168.

SCOTT-KILVERT, IAN. "English fiction 1958-60, II." *BBN*, 248
(April 1961), 237-244.

SCOTT-KILVERT, IAN. "English fiction 1961." *BBN*, 261
(May 1962), 309-314.

SCOTT-KILVERT, IAN. "English fiction 1963." *BBN*, 282
(February 1964), 85-91.

SCOTT-KILVERT, IAN. "English fiction 1964." *BBN*, 298
(June 1965), 383-388.

SCOTT-KILVERT, IAN. "English fiction 1965." *BBN*, 310
(June 1966), 397-402.

SCOTT-KILVERT, IAN. "English fiction 1966." *BBN*, 322
(June 1967), 409-414.

SCOTT-KILVERT, IAN. "English fiction 1967." *BBN*, 331
(March 1968), 165-169.

SEEBER, HANS ULRICH. *Wandlungen der Form in der literarischen
Utopie. Studien zur Entfaltung des utopischen Romans in*

England. Göppinger Akademische Beiträge, 13. Kümmerle: Göppingen, 1970. Pp. VIII + 296.

Utopian novels discussed at some length are Huxley's *Brave New World* and Orwell's *1984*. Novels mentioned are: Golding, *Lord of the Flies*; Hartley, *Facial Justice*; Frayn, *A Very Private Life*; Graves, *Seven Days in New Crete*; C.S. Lewis, *Out of the Silent Planet*; Mackenzie, *The Lunatic Republic*.

SEEHASE, GEORG. "Kapitalistische Entfremdung und humanistische Integration: Bemerkungen zum englischen proletarischen Gegenwartsroman." *ZAA*, XV (1967), 383-400.

Three types of writers are distinguished: Those defending capitalism and the present system of alienation (Waugh, Murdoch, Golding, Durrell), those trying to overcome alienation by "humanist integration" (Aldridge, Greene, Snow), and the proletarian authors (Lindsay, Sillitoe, Heinemann). Discussion of the methods used by the proletarian authors to mirror their attitudes in their works (socialist realism).

SEEHASE, GEORG. "Abbild des Klassenkampfes: Aspekte der Wertung demokratischer und sozialistischer Literatur in Großbritannien." *ZAA*, XVII (1969), 392-405.

Mentions Lindsay, Lambert, Smith, Ash, Sillitoe, Aldridge, Allen, Raymond Williams, Heinemann, Willis, and others.

SERVOTTE, HERMAN. *Literatuur als levenskunst. Essays over hedendaagse Engelse literatuur*. Nederlandsche Boekhandel: Antwerpen, 1966. Pp. 136.

Contains essays on Greene, Durrell, Waugh, and Golding.

SEWARD, WILLIAM WARD. *Contrasts in modern writers. Some aspects of British and American fiction since mid-century*. Fell: New York, 1963. Pp. 185.

SHAPIRO, STEPHEN A. "The ambivalent animal: Man in the contemporary British and American novel." *DA*, XXVI (1965), 2760-2761 (Seattle).

Powell, Lessing, and others.

SHAPIRO, STEPHEN A. "The ambivalent animal: Man in the contemporary British and American novel." *CentR*, XII (1968), 1-22.

Angus Wilson, Wain, Lessing, Powell, Durrell, Amis, Braine, Sillitoe, Spark, Storey, and others.

SNOW, C.P. "Science, politics, and the novelist: Or the fish and the net." *KR*, XXIII (1961), 1-17.

Waugh, Powell, Cooper, and the Angry Young Men.

SPANN, EKKEHARD. *"Problemkinder" in der englischen Erzähl-
kunst der Gegenwart (Greene - A. Wilson - Wain - Amis -
Murdoch - Golding - Braine - Sillitoe).* Diss. Tübingen,
1970. Pp. 177. Summary in *EASG*, III (1971), 101-103.

SPENDER, STEPHEN. "Anglo-Saxon attitudes." *PR*, XXV (1958),
110-116.
The Angry Young Men.

SPENDER, STEPHEN. "When the angry (young) men grow older."
NYTBR, 20 July 1958, 1, 12.

SPENDER, STEPHEN. *The struggle of the modern.* University
Paperbacks, 141. Methuen: London, 1965. Pp. XIII + 266.
"Here I am chiefly concerned with writers and artists who
show in their work a consciousness of modern art as an
aim, whether they accept or resist it." Differentiates
between "modern" and "contemporary".

SPOLTON, L. "The secondary school in post-war fiction."
BJES, XI (1962/63), 125-141.

STANFORD, DEREK. "Beatniks and Angry Young Men." *Meanjin*,
XVII (1958), 413-419.

STEVENSON, LIONEL. *The English novel. A panorama.* Constable:
London, 1961. Pp. 539.
Chap. 17: "Exploring the Psyche (Since 1915)." Brief mention of various contemporary novelists. Bibliography and
chronological summary.

STEVENSON, LIONEL. *Yesterday and after.* The History of the
English Novel, 11. Barnes & Noble: New York, 1967.
Pp. 431.
See chaps VII ("Traditionalists between the Wars") and
VIII ("Moods of Scorn and Protest") for discussions of
Snow, Golding, Powell, Durrell, Angus Wilson, Murdoch,
Amis, Braine, and Wain. Select reading and reference list.

STEVICK, PHILIP. "The limits of anti-utopia." *Criticism*, VI
(1964), 233-245.
Orwell's *1984*, Huxley's *Brave New World*, Golding's *Lord
of the Flies*.

STOKES, FRASER. "Current British fiction." *ER*, XVI (February 1966), 7-12.
Spy stories, romance and satire dominate the scene.

STRAUMANN, HEINRICH. "Zum Problem der Interpretation und Wertung zeitgenössischer Romanliteratur." *Sprache und Litera-*

tur Englands und Amerikas, III, ed. Gerhard Müller-Schwefe. Niemeyer: Tübingen, 1959. Pp. 79-99.

On the difficulty of evaluating current novels.

SUDRANN, JEAN. "The necessary illusion: A letter from London." *AR*, XVIII (1958/59), 236-244.

On current English literature: Angus Wilson, Taylor, Amis, Dennis, Hartley, Sansom.

SÜHNEL, RUDOLF. "Eine Betrachtung über die englischen Klassiker der Moderne." *Englische Dichter der Moderne. Ihr Leben und Werk. Unter Mitarbeit zahlreicher Fachgelehrter,* eds. Rudolf Sühnel & Dieter Riesner. Schmidt: Berlin, 1971. Pp. 1-15.

Introduces a collection of essays on twentieth-century British writers. Contemporary English novelists dealt with are Angus Wilson and Golding.

SYMONS, JULIAN. "Crime novels and detective stories." *London Mag*, n.s. I (May 1961), 76-81.

Illustrates the differences between the old form and the new one by various examples.

SYMONS, JULIAN. *The detective story in Britain.* WTW, 145. Longmans, Green: London, 1962. Pp. 48.

SYMONS, JULIAN. "An end to spying: Or, from pipe dream to farce." *TLS*, 12 December 1968, 1411-1412.

On spy stories in the past fifteen years. Stresses the importance and quality of Fleming's James Bond books, but is gloomy about the spy story's immediate future.

SYMONS, JULIAN & EDMUND CRISPIN. "Is the detective story dead?: A recorded dialogue." *TLS*, 23 June 1961, IV-V.

TODD, OLIVIER. "Jeunes gens en colère?" *TM*, XIV (1958/59), 895-910.

The Angry Young Men.

TOYNBEE, PHILIP. "Experiment and the future of the novel." *London Mag*, III (May 1956), 48-56. Repr. in *The craft of letters in England. A symposium*, ed. John Lehmann. Cresset Press: London, 1956. Pp. 60-73.

"... the modern English novelist who is deeply concerned about his fellows and his society will also be concerned with new methods, new ideas, new sensitivities and new material." Mentions Elizabeth Bowen, Green, Amis, and Chapman Mortimer.

TUCKER, MARTIN. *Africa in modern literature. A survey of contemporary writing in English.* Ungar: New York, 1967. Pp. XII + 316.

Contains discussions of novels by Burgess, Cary, Greene, Lessing, Monsarrat, Plomer, Waugh, and others. Selected reading list.

VALENCIA, WILLA F. "The picaresque tradition in the contemporary English and American novel." *DA*, XXIX (1968), 618A (Ill.).

VAN DER VEEN, ADRIAAN. "Boze jongelieden in een zich vernieuwend Engeland." *VlG*, XLIII (1959), 232-236.

Amis, Wain and Braine are disillusioned by the Welfare State. Their essays in *Declaration* reveal their ideas more clearly than their novels.

VANCURA, Z. *Dvadcat' let anglijskogo romana (1945-1964 gg.).* Vysšaja škola: Moskva, 1968. Pp. 115.

VANSITTART, PETER. "Men-gods: A note on the political hero in historical fiction." *London Mag*, n.s. X (September 1970), 85-91.

Mentions Renault, Treece, Golding, Graves, Warner, Mervyn Jones, and others.

VOGT, JOCHEN, ed. *Der Kriminalroman. Zur Theorie und Geschichte einer Gattung.* 2 vols. Fink: München, 1971. Pp. 595.

Collection of essays by various authors on the history and characteristics of the crime novel.

WAGNER, JEAN. "Richard Sorge ou l'anti-James Bond." *TM*, XXI (1965/66), 1317-1326.

On images of the spy in modern crime novels (Fleming).

WAIN, JOHN. "The conflict of forms in contemporary English literature." *CritQ*, IV (1962), 7-30, 101-119. Repr. in *Essays on literature and ideas.* Macmillan: London, 1963. Pp. 1-55.

General survey of new literary forms. Today the novel has lost much of its confidence, but there is no reason to be pessimistic about its future.

WALCUTT, CHARLES CHILD. *Man's changing mask. Modes and methods of characterization in fiction.* Minnesota UP: Minneapolis, 1966. Pp. VIII + 368.

See Part V: "Modern Consequences." A few remarks on
Durrell's *Alexandria Quartet* and passages on Powell's
Music of Time (336-339).

WALKER, BRENDA MARY, ed. *The Angry Young Men. Aspects of
contemporary literature*. Library Association: London, 1957.
Pp. 17.

WALL, STEPHEN. "Aspects of the novel 1930-1960." *The twentieth century,* ed. Bernard Bergonzi. History of Literature
in the English Language, 7. Barrie & Jenkins: London,
1970. Pp. 222-276.
Individual chaps on Powell, Angus Wilson, Golding, Durrell,
Murdoch, and others. Bibliography.

WARD, A.C. *Twentieth-century English literature 1901-1960.*
Methuen: London, 1964. Pp. VIII + 239.
Chap. II "Novelists" (25-89) includes some discussion of
the works of Amis, Elizabeth Bowen, Braine, Compton-Bur-
nett, Cary, Christie, Durrell, Golding, Greene, Huxley,
Innes, Murdoch, Orwell, Powell, Snow, Wain, Waugh, Angus
Wilson, Wodehouse, and John Wyndham.

WATSON, COLIN. *Snobbery with violence. Crime stories and
their audience*. Eyre & Spottiswoode: London, 1971.
Pp. 256.
General survey. Chap. XVIII deals with Fleming's James
Bond novels (233-251).

WEAVER, ROBERT LEIGH. "England's 'Angry Young Men': Mystics,
provincials and radicals." *QQ*, LXV (1958), 183-194.
"An unusually noisy and pretentious group of minor writers."

WEBSTER, HARVEY CURTIS. *After the trauma. Representative
British novelists since 1920*. Kentucky UP: Lexington, 1970.
Pp. XII + 203.
Contains individual chaps on Macaulay, Huxley, Compton-
Burnett, Waugh, Greene, Cary, Hartley, and Snow. Refers to
Allen, Amis, Bradbury, Durrell, Golding, Pamela Hansford
Johnson, Murdoch, Newby, Sillitoe, Spark, Toynbee, and
Angus Wilson in a final chap.

WEIMANN, ROBERT. "Die Literatur der 'Angry Young Men': Ein
Beitrag zur Deutung englischer Gegenwartsliteratur." *ZAA,*
VII (1959), 117-189.
Starting out from developments in English society after
the war, Amis's *Lucky Jim, That Uncertain Feeling, I Like
It Here* and Braine's *Room at the Top* are analysed. Closes
with a survey of the works of the Angry Young Men.

WEST, PAUL. *The modern novel*. Hutchinson University Library:
London, 1963. 2 vols. Pp. XIII + 450.

Concise but comprehensive survey. Vol. I, which covers
England and France, deals with Amis, Balchin, Elizabeth
Bowen, John Bowen, Bradbury, Braine, Brooks, Brigid Brophy,
Burgess, Cary, Compton-Burnett, Cooper, Dennis, Donleavy,
Durrell, Edelman, Fielding, FitzGibbon, Fuller, Garnett,
Gerhardi, Glanville, Godden, Golding, Green, Greene, James
Hanley, Hartley, Heppenstall, Hinde, Hughes, Humphreys,
Huxley, Pamela Hansford Johnson, King, Lehmann, Lessing,
Linklater, Longrigg, Lowry, MacInnes, Mackenzie, Manning,
Mitford, Murdoch, Newby, O'Connor, O'Faolain, Orwell,
Powell, Priestley, Sansom, J.D. Scott, Paul Scott, Robert
Shaw, Shute, Sillitoe, Sinclair, Snow, Spark, Storey, Toyn-
bee, Tracy, Wain, Warner, Waterhouse, Waugh, Williamson,
Angus Wilson, Colin Wilson.

WEST, ROBERT H. "Science fiction and its ideas." *GaR*, XV
(1961), 276-286.

WIGHT, MARJORIE. "An analysis of selected British novelists
between 1945 and 1966, and their critics." *DA*, XXVIII
(1968), 4651A-4652A (So. Calif.).

Cary, Durrell, Powell, Greene, Golding, Angus Wilson, and
Murdoch.

WILLIAMS, RAYMOND. "Realism and the contemporary novel." *PR*,
XXVI (1959), 200-213. Repr. in *The long revolution*.
Chatto & Windus: London, 1961. Pp. 274-289.

Attempts to redefine "realism" with regard to the methods
and substance of contemporary fiction (Huxley, Orwell,
Golding, Greene, Cary, Amis, Wain, Angus Wilson, John
Bowen, and others).

WILSON, ANGUS. "A plea against fashion in writing." *MSpr*,
LV (1961), 345-350.

Snow, Leavis, Durrell, and the climate of literary opinion
in England.

WILSON, ANGUS. "Evil in the English novel. Pt. III: Evil and
the novelist today." *Listener*, 17 January 1963, 115-117.

Golding (*Lord of the Flies*), Angus Wilson (*Hemlock and
After*); mentions Sillitoe.

WÖLCKEN, FRITZ. *Der literarische Mord. Eine Untersuchung
über die englische und amerikanische Detektivliteratur.*
Nest: Nürnberg, 1953. Pp. 348.

WOLFE, BERNARD. "Angry at what?" *Nation*, 1 November 1958, 316-322.

The target of the anger is woman and not 'this unbearable society'.

WYNDHAM, FRANCIS. "Twenty-five years of the novel." *The craft of letters in England. A symposium,* ed. John Lehmann. Cresset Press: London, 1956. Pp. 44-59.

Traces two generations of novelists - those who emerged in 1931 and those whose reputations have been made since 1940. Admits the "absence both of giants and of brilliant newcomers".

YUILL, W.E. "Tradition and nightmare: Some reflections on the postwar novel in England and Germany." *Affinities. Essays in German and English literature. Dedicated to the memory of Oswald Wolff (1897-1968),* ed. R.W. Last. Wolff: London, 1971. Pp. 154-167.

Lists a host of names. Contemporary English novelists depend on the tradition of "plain narration and social observation". Golding prefers symbolic patterns.

ZMEGAC, VIKTOR, ed. *Der wohltemperierte Mord. Zur Theorie und Geschichte des Detektivromans.* Schwerpunkte Germanistik, 4. Athenäum: Frankfurt a.M., 1971. Pp. 278.

Collection of essays on the genre and history of the detective novel.

III INDIVIDUAL AUTHORS

ALDRIDGE, JAMES (1918)
Signed with Their Honour, 1942; *The Sea Eagle,* 1944; *Of Many Men,* 1946; *The Diplomat,* 1949; *The Hunter,* 1950; *Heroes of the Empty View,* 1954; *I Wish He Would Not Die,* 1957; *The Last Exile,* 1961; *A Captive in the Land,* 1962; *The Statesman's Game,* 1966; *My Brother Tom,* 1966.

FINDEISEN, HELMUT. "Eine erste Bibliographie der Werke von James Aldridge." *ZAA,* VI (1958), 428-437.

A list of primary and secondary works. The novels are entered together with various reviews.

ANON. "Scenes of battle." *TLS,* 7 May 1954, 293.

Contains rev. of *Heroes of the Empty View.*

ANON. "The parliamentary novel." *TLS,* 17 August 1956, XVIII.

Mentions, among others, A. *(The Diplomat)* and Edelman as writers of political novels.

ANON. "World weary." *TLS,* 15 November 1957, 685.

Contains rev. of *I Wish He Would Not Die.* Refers also to *Signed with Their Honour* and *The Diplomat.*

ANON. "Inside Egypt." *TLS,* 15 September 1961, 609.

Rev. art. on *The Last Exile.* Refers also to Durrell's *Alexandria Quartet.*

ANON. "East and west." *TLS,* 19 October 1962, 805.

Contains rev. of *A Captive in the Land.* Refers also to *The Last Exile.*

ANIKST, A. "Über die Romane von James Aldridge." *Sowjetliteratur,* 10 (1955), 168-173.

BALASHOV, P. "Freedom of choice and historical necessity." *InLit,* 12 (December 1957), 196-204.
The Diplomat, I Wish He Would Not Die, Heroes of the Empty View.

BALASHOV, P. *Džejms Oldridž. Kritiko-biografičeskij očerk.* Gosizdat: Moskva, 1963. Pp. 245.

A biographical and critical study.

FINDEISEN, HELMUT. "James Aldridge: *I Wish He Would Not Die.*" *ZAA,* VII (1959), 94-97.

Rev. art.

FINDEISEN, HELMUT. *James Aldridge. Schriftsteller und Kämpfer.* Niemeyer: Halle, 1960. Pp. 131.
Contains a section on the novels discussed in chronological order. Bibliography of primary and secondary sources.

ILGNER, BRIGITTE & WOLFGANG WICHT. "James Aldridge und die Sowjetunion: Eine Untersuchung zu Schriftstellerpersönlichkeit und Schaffensmethode." *ZAA*, XVII (1969), 41-59.

LINDSAY, JACK. "Desert values." *Overland*, 2 (Summer 1954/55), 20.
Rev. art. on *Heroes of the Empty View*.

PARTRIDGE, ERIC. "Man of action, words in action: The novels of James Aldridge." *Meanjin*, XX (1961), 256-263.
Life and work with a chronology of his books up to *The Last Exile*.

TURNER, IAN. "The necessity of freedom: A discussion of the novels of James Aldridge." *Overland*, 8 (Spring 1956), 21-24.
The Diplomat, The Hunter, Heroes of the Empty View.

AMIS, KINGSLEY (1922)
Lucky Jim, 1954; *That Uncertain Feeling,* 1955; *I Like It Here,* 1958; *Take a Girl Like You,* 1960; *One Fat Englishman,* 1963; *The Egyptologists,* 1965 (with Robert Conquest); *The Anti-Death League,* 1966; *I Want It Now,* 1968; *Colonel Sun,* 1968 (as Robert Markham); *The Green Man,* 1969; *Girl, 20,* 1971.

VANN, J. DON & JAMES T.F. TANNER. "Kingsley Amis: A checklist of recent criticism." *BB*, XXVI (1969), 105, 111, 115-117.

ANON. "The boy friends." *TLS*, 23 September 1960, 605.
Rev. art. on *Take a Girl Like You*.

ANON. "Iago in America." *TLS*, 14 November 1963, 921. Repr. in *T.L.S. Essays and reviews from The Times Literary Supplement. 1963.* Oxford UP: London, 1964. Pp. 107-109.
Rev. art. on *One Fat Englishman*.

ANON. "Beastly to God." *TLS*, 17 March 1966, 217. Repr. in
*T.L.S. Essays and reviews from The Times Literary Supple-
ment. 1966.* Oxford UP: London, 1967. Pp. 29-31.
Rev. art. on *The Anti-Death League.*

ANON. "Unlucky James." *TLS*, 28 March 1968, 309.
Rev. art. on *Colonel Sun.*

ANON. "In a buyer's market." *TLS*, 10 October 1968, 1145.
Repr. in *T.L.S. Essays and reviews from The Times Literary
Supplement. 1968.* Oxford UP: London, 1969. Pp. 186-188.
Rev. art. on *I Want It Now.*

ANON. "The drunk and the dead." *TLS*, 9 October 1969, 1145.
Repr. in *T.L.S. Essays and reviews from the Times Literary
Supplement. 1969.* Oxford UP: London, 1970. Pp. 214-217.
Rev. art. on *The Green Man.*

ANON. "Having it both ways." *TLS*, 24 September 1971, 1138.
Rev. art. on *Girl, 20.*

AMIS, KINGSLEY. "My kind of comedy." *TC*, CLXX (July 1961),
46-50.
Interview conducted by Pat Williams; mainly concerned
with *Lucky Jim.*

BERGONZI, BERNARD. "Kingsley Amis." *London Mag*, n.s. III
(January 1964), 50-65.
"Amis is getting grimmer as he grows older." Discussion
of the novels up to *One Fat Englishman.*

BERGONZI, BERNARD. "*The Anti-Death League* by Kingsley Amis."
London Mag, n.s. VI (June 1966), 109-112.
Rev. art.

BOYLE, TED E. & TERENCE BROWN. "The serious side of Kingsley
Amis's *Lucky Jim.*" *Crit*, IX: 1 (1966), 100-107.

BRADBURY, MALCOLM. "Delayed orgasm." *New Statesman*, 11 October 1968, 464, 466.
I Want It Now is built on the principle of delayed orgasm.
Sex is delivered but not to the satisfaction of the female.
Lucky Jim's virtues are a particular kind of skeptical
moral realism. A. is trying for a new range of the socio-
logical-moral novel.

BROPHY, BRIGID. "Just Jim." *STCM*, 26 January 1964, 11, 13.
Analyses structure and technique of *Lucky Jim* and other
novels by A.

BURGESS, ANTHONY. "Amis and enemies." *Listener*, 10 October
1968, 475.
Rev. art. on *I Want It Now*: "This novel is funny because
it is serious."

BYATT, A.S. "Mess & mystery." *Encounter*, XXVII (July 1966),
59-62.
Rev. art. on *The Anti-Death League*.

CAPLAN, RALPH. "Kingsley Amis." *Contemporary British novelists,* ed. Charles Shapiro. Southern Illinois UP: Carbondale, Edwardsville, 1965. Pp. 3-15.
Discusses his novels up to *One Fat Englishman*.

CASSON, ALLAN. "Greene's *Comedians* and Amis' *Anti-Death
League*." *MR*, VIII (1967), 392-397.

CHASE, RICHARD. "Middlebrow England: The novels of Kingsley
Amis." *Commentary*, XXII (1956), 263-269.

COLEMAN, JOHN. "King of shaft." *Spectator*, 23 September 1960,
445-446.
Rev. art. on *Take a Girl Like You;* refers to A's previous
novels.

COLVILLE, DEREK. "The sane new world of Kingsley Amis." *BuR*,
IX (1960/61), 46-57.
On his first three novels.

CONQUEST, ROBERT. "Christian symbolism in *Lucky Jim*." *CritQ*,
VII (1965), 87-92.
A piece of so-called 'professional' criticism satirizing
its academic jargon.

COX, C.B. "*Take a Girl Like You* by Kingsley Amis." *CritQ*, II
(1960), 374-375.
Rev. art.

ENGELBORGHS, M. "Nigel Dennis en Kingsley Amis." *DWB*, CII
(1957), 565-571.
Lucky Jim, That Uncertain Feeling, Cards of Identity.

GREEN, MARTIN. "Amis and Salinger: The latitude of private
conscience." *ChiR*, XI (Winter 1957), 20-25.

GREEN, MARTIN. "British decency." *KR*, XXI (1959), 505-532.
Repr. in *A mirror for Anglo-Saxons*. Longmans: London, 1961.
Pp. 95-124.
A's image of the lower middle class (section IV).

GREEN, MARTIN. "British comedy and the British sense of humour: Shaw, Waugh, and Amis." *TQ*, IV (Autumn 1961), 217-227.
Lucky Jim.

GREEN, MARTIN. "Mailer and Amis: The new conservatism." *Nation*, 5 May 1969, 573-574.

GREEN, MARTIN. "Amis and Mailer: The Faustian contract." *Month*, n.s. III (February 1971), 45-48, 52.
Both seen as anti-liberal conservatives.

GROSS, JOHN. "Makes you sober." *New Statesman*, 14 September 1962, 363-364.
A's achievement is not farcical scenes but verbal jabs with amusing understatement.

HAMILTON, KENNETH. "Kingsley Amis, moralist." *DR*, XLIV (1964/65), 339-347.
"Real comic effects are produced by imaginative clear-sightedness brought into focus by moral integrity." On his novels and short stories.

HARTLEY, ANTHONY. "The way we live now." *Encounter*, XV (December 1960), 80-82.
Rev. art. on *Take a Girl Like You.*

HILTY, PETER. "Kingsley Amis and mid-century humor." *Discourse*, III (1960), 26-28, 37-45.
The use of parody devices prevents him from developing serious themes.

HOPKINS, ROBERT H. "The satire of Kingsley Amis's *I Like It Here.*" *Crit*, VIII: 3 (1966), 62-70.

HURRELL, JOHN D. "Class and conscience in John Braine and Kingsley Amis." *Crit*, II: 1 (1958), 39-53.
Lucky Jim, That Uncertain Feeling, I Like It Here, Room at the Top.

JONES, D.A.N. "Amis's English usage." *NYRB*, 16 April 1964, 13-14.
Rev. art. on *One Fat Englishman.*

KNOWLES, A. SIDNEY, JR. "The need for loners: Nine novels of the sixties." *SoR*, n.s. IV (1968), 817-833.
Contains rev. of *The Anti-Death League.*

LEBOWITZ, NAOMI. "Kingsley Amis: The penitent hero." *Perspective*, X (1958/59), 129-136.

At the end of the novels the hero frees himself from his previous artificial roles.

LODGE, DAVID. "The modern, the contemporary, and the importance of being Amis." *CritQ*, V (1963), 335-354. Repr. in *Language of fiction. Essays in criticism and verbal analysis of the English novel*. Routledge & Kegan Paul: London; Columbia UP: New York, 1966. Pp. 243-267, 279.

Differentiates, as Stephen Spender (*The struggle of the modern*) does, between "modern" (Durrell, Golding, Murdoch) and "contemporary" (all the other present-day novelists). The general discussion leads into a closer study of A's novels.

MCGUINNESS, FRANK. "*I Want It Now* by Kingsley Amis." *London Mag*, n.s. VIII (October 1968), 110-113.

Rev. art.

MOBERG, GEORGE. "Structure and theme in Amis's novels." *CEA*, XXV (March 1963), 7, 10.

A mild humorous critique of manners and morals is a unifying factor in his novels.

NOON, WILLIAM T., S.J. "Satire: Poison and the professor." *ER*, XI (Fall 1960), 53-56.

Refers to *Lucky Jim* and Snow's *The Masters*.

O'CONNOR, WILLIAM VAN. "Kingsley Amis: That uncertain feeling." *The new university wits and the end of modernism*. With a preface by Harry T. Moore. Southern Illinois UP: Carbondale, 1963. Pp. 75-102, 160-162.

First four novels.

O'CONNOR, WILLIAM VAN. "Parody as criticism." *CE*, XXV (1963/64), 241-248.

The last part of this article deals with A's good-humoured satire of Eliot's *Murder in the Cathedral* in *That Uncertain Feeling*.

OREL, HAROLD. "Amis in the underworld." *YR*, XLIX (1959/60), 602-604.

Rev. art. on *New Maps of Hell*. Short discussion of A's first three novels.

OREL, HAROLD. "The decline and fall of a comic novelist: Kingsley Amis." *KanQ*, I: 3 (1969), 17-22.

Novel-by-novel discussion. Regards *Lucky Jim* as his only
really good novel.

PARKER, R.B. "Farce and society: The range of Kingsley Amis."
WSCL, II (Fall 1961), 27-38.

On the mixture of farce and social comment.

POWELL, ANTHONY. "Kingsley's heroes." *Spectator*,
29 November 1963, 709-710.

Rev. art. on *One Fat Englishman*. References to *Lucky Jim,
That Uncertain Feeling, I Like It Here,* and *Take a Girl
Like You.*

RAVEN, SIMON. "The Kingsley Amis story." *Spectator*, 17 January 1958, 79.

Rev. art. on *I Like It Here.*

ROSS, T.J. "Lucky Jenny, or affluent times." *NewR*,
27 March 1961, 21-22.

Jenny Bunn in *Take a Girl Like You* is a character in the
tradition of *Lucky Jim.*

ROSS, T.J. "Manners, morals, and pop: On the fiction of Kingsley Amis." *STC*, 4 (Fall 1969), 61-73.

ROTHERMEL, WOLFGANG P. "Kingsley Amis." *Englische Literatur
der Gegenwart in Einzeldarstellungen,* ed. Horst W. Drescher.
Kröner: Stuttgart, 1970. Pp. 150-172.

His main literary importance lies in the fact that he brings
grievances and social injustices into the open by ridicul-
ing them, not by attacking them straightforwardly. Short
biography. Bibliography.

RUTTEN, WILLY. "Nog een geval van Engelse 'Sex': *Take a Girl
Like You* door Kingsley Amis." *VlG*, XLV (1961), 272-273.

SISSMAN, L.E. "Kingsley Amis at halfway house." *NY*,
26 April 1969, 165-170.

Considers *Take a Girl Like You* as his masterpiece.

SMITH, ROBERT BRUCE. "An analysis of the novels of Kingsley
Amis." *DA*, XXVI (1965), 2762 (Washington).

SNOW, C.P. "Italo Svevo: Forerunner of Cooper and Amis." *E&S,*
n.s. XIV (1961), 7-16.

"Part of *Lucky Jim* is owed ... to an intelligent study of
Mr. William Cooper's *Scenes from Provincial Life.*"

WARD, ANTHONY. "Jimsday." *Spectator*, 24 January 1964, 112.

On the 10th anniversary of the publication of *Lucky Jim*. "Has Amis made any progress?"

WILSON, EDMUND. "Is it possible to pat Kingsley Amis?" *The bit between my teeth. A literary chronicle of 1950-1965.* Farrar, Straus & Giroux: New York, 1965. Pp. 274-281.

Lucky Jim and *That Uncertain Feeling* are seen in the comic tradition.

BARKER, A.L. (1918)

Apology for a Hero, 1950; *A Case Examined*, 1965; *The Middling*, 1967; *John Brown's Body*, 1969.

ANON. "The alien hassocks." *TLS*, 27 May 1965, 409.

Rev. art. on *A Case Examined*.

ANON. "Unburdening." *TLS*, 2 November 1967, 1029.

Rev. art. on *The Middling*.

ANON. "Problems of identity." *TLS*, 13 November 1969, 1297.

Rev. art. on *John Brown's Body*.

BARON, ALEXANDER (1917)

From the City, from the Plough, 1948; *There's No Home*, 1950; *Rosie Hogarth*, 1951; *With Hope, Farewell*, 1952; *The Human Kind*, 1953; *The Golden Princess*, 1954; *Queen of the East*, 1956; *Seeing Life*, 1958; *The Lowlife*, 1963; *Strip Jack Naked*, 1966; *King Dido*, 1969; *The In-Between Time*, 1971.

ANON. "Fortunes of war." *TLS*, 10 February 1950, 85.

Contains rev. of *There's No Home*.

ANON. "Sequence of events." *TLS*, 3 April 1953, 217.

Contains rev. of *The Human Kind*.

ANON. "East End polish." *TLS*, 8 March 1963, 165.

Rev. art. on *The Lowlife*.

ANON. "Boy of the thirties." *TLS*, 25 June 1971, 725.

Rev. art. on *The In-Between Time*.

BAKER, WILLIAM "The world of Alexander Baron." *JewQ*, XVII (Winter 1969), 17-20.

"... lower middle class, working class life and war."

GLANVILLE, BRIAN. "The Anglo-Jewish writer." *Encounter*, XIV
   (February 1960), 62-64.
   Mentions Mankowitz, Kersh and B.

BARSTOW, STAN (1928)
A Kind of Loving, 1960; *Ask Me Tomorrow*, 1962; *Joby*, 1964;
The Watchers on the Shore, 1966; *A Raging Calm*, 1968.

ANON. "First fruits." *TLS*, 5 August 1960, 493.
   Contains rev. of *A Kind of Loving*.

ANON. "In search of a plot." *TLS*, 19 October 1962, 805.
   Rev. art. on *Ask Me Tomorrow*.

ANON. "New fiction." *Times*, 13 February 1964, 15.
   Contains rev. of *Joby*.

ANON. "Scholarship boy." *TLS*, 13 February 1964, 132.
   Rev. art. on *Joby*.

ANON. "Old lovers." *TLS*, 12 December 1968, 1401.
   Short rev. art. on *A Raging Calm*.

LERNER, LAURENCE. "New novels." *Listener*, 18 October 1962,
   630.
   Contains rev. of *Ask Me Tomorrow*.

PRICE, R.G.G. "New novels." *Punch*, 24 October 1962, 611-612.
   Contains rev. of *Ask Me Tomorrow*.

BERGER, JOHN (1926)
A Painter of Our Time, 1958; *The Foot of Clive*, 1962;
Corker's Freedom, 1964.

ANON. "The making of an artist." *TLS*, 28 November 1958, 685.
   Contains rev. of *A Painter of Our Time*.

ANON. "Hospitalized." *TLS*, 9 March 1962, 151.
   Rev. art. on *The Foot of Clive*.

ANON. "Corkers all." *TLS*, 19 March 1964, 229. Repr. in *T.L.S.*
   Essays and reviews from The Times Literary Supplement. 1964.
   Oxford UP: London, 1965. Pp. 206-207.
   Rev. art. on *Corker's Freedom*.

ENRIGHT, D.J. "The novel in hospital." *New Statesman*,
16 March 1962, 382-383.
Rev. art. on *The Foot of Clive*.

NICHOLSON, HUBERT. "John Berger as a novelist." *CQ*,
II (1966/67), 194-197.
Corker's Freedom. Puts the work into the context of
A Painter of Our Time and *The Foot of Clive*.

PRITCHETT, V.S. "More from the horse's mouth." *New Statesman*, 15 November 1958, 700-702.
Rev. art. on *A Painter of Our Time*.

WOLLHEIM, RICHARD. "Novel of manners." *Spectator*,
14 November 1958, 656.
Rev. art. on *A Painter of Our Time*.

BOWEN, JOHN (1924)
The Truth Will Not Help Us, 1956; *After the Rain,* 1958; *The
Centre of the Green,* 1959; *Storyboard,* 1960; *The Birdcage,*
1962; *A World Elsewhere,* 1965.

ANON. "John Bowen: *After the Rain*." *TLS*, 31 January 1958, 66.
Rev. art.

ANON. "Family failings." *TLS*, 24 April 1959, 237.
Rev. art. on *The Centre of the Green*.

ANON. "The agency." *TLS*, 4 November 1960, 705.
Rev. art. on *Storyboard*. Refers also to *The Centre of the
Green*.

ANON. "A fairytale." *TLS*, 12 October 1962, 789.
Rev. art. on *The Birdcage*. Refers also to *After the Rain*.

DANIEL, JOHN. "Arts and tarts." *Spectator*, 12 October 1962,
565-566.
Contains rev. of *The Birdcage*.

LERNER, LAURENCE. "New novels." *Listener*, 18 October 1962,
630.
Contains rev. of *The Birdcagè*.

MARCUS, FRANK. "Novel into play." *London Mag*, n.s. VI
(November 1966), 71-73.
On the stage adaption of *After the Rain*.

PRICE, R.G.G. "New novels." *Punch*, 24 October 1962, 611-612.
  Contains rev. of *The Birdcage*.

BRADBURY, MALCOLM (1932)
Eating People Is Wrong, 1959; *Stepping Westward*, 1965.

ANON. "The way we live now." *TLS*, 13 November 1959, 657.
  Contains rev. of *Eating People Is Wrong*.

ANON. "A familiarish destiny." *TLS*, 5 August 1965, 673.
  Rev. art. on *Stepping Westward*.

RAWSON, C.J. "Dr. Johnson in *Eating People Is Wrong.*" *N&Q*,
  n.s. XII (1965), 276-277.

VANSITTART, PETER. "Groves of Academe." *Spectator*,
  6 August 1965, 184-185.
  Contains rev. of *Stepping Westward*.

BRAGG, MELVYN (1939)
For Want of a Nail, 1965; *The Second Inheritance*, 1966;
Without a City Wall, 1968; *The Hired Man*, 1969; *A Place in
England*, 1970; *The Nerve*, 1971.

ANON. "To Oxford and away." *TLS*, 1 July 1965, 553.
  Rev. art. on *For Want of a Nail*.

ANON. "Farmer's boy." *TLS*, 7 July 1966, 589.
  Rev. art. on *The Second Inheritance*.

ANON. "Goodness gracious." *TLS*, 10 October 1968, 1161.
  Rev. art. on *Without a City Wall*.

ANON. "Habits of work." *TLS*, 23 October 1969, 1225. Repr. in
  *T.L.S. Essays and reviews from The Times Literary Supple-
  ment. 1969.* Oxford UP: London, 1970. Pp. 67-69.
  Rev. art. on *The Hired Man*.

ANON. "Between two styles." *TLS*, 13 November 1970, 1317.
  Rev. art. on *A Place in England*. Refers also to *The Hired
  Man*.

ANON. "A mind under attack." *TLS*, 1 October 1971, 1165.
  Rev. art. on *The Nerve*.

MCGUINNESS, FRANK. *"The Second Inheritance* by Melvyn Bragg."
  London Mag, n.s. VI (July 1966), 114-116.
  Rev. art.

WAUGH, AUBERON. "Vanilla slices." *Spectator,*
  14 November 1970, 606-607.
  Rev. art. on *A Place in England.*

BRAINE, JOHN (1922)
Room at the Top, 1957; *The Vodi,* 1959; *Life at the Top,*
1962; *The Jealous God,* 1964; *The Crying Game,* 1968; *Stay
with Me till Morning,* 1970.

ANON. "Combating malevolence." *TLS,* 20 November 1959, 673.
  Rev. art. on *The Vodi.*

ANON. "Near summitry." *TLS,* 5 October 1962, 773.
  Rev. art. on *Life at the Top.*

ANON. "Room for the O.P.?" *TLS,* 26 November 1964, 1053.
  Rev. art. on *The Jealous God.*

ANON. "Rasping at progs." *TLS,* 29 August 1968, 913. Repr. in
  *T.L.S. Essays and reviews from the Times Literary Supple-
  ment. 1968.* Oxford UP: London, 1969. Pp. 73-75.
  Rev. art. on *The Crying Game.*

ANON. "How normal can you get?" *TLS,* 25 June 1970, 679.
  Rev. art. on *Stay with Me till Morning.*

ALVAREZ, A. "Braine at the top." *New Statesman,*
  5 October 1962, 458.
  Room at the Top, Life at the Top, The Vodi.

BARROWS, JOHN. "John Braine." *JOL,* 16 March 1961, 295.
  His outlook is pessimistic.

BERGONZI, BERNARD. "New novels." *NYRB,* 11 March 1965, 19-20.
  Contains rev. of *The Jealous God.*

BRAINE, JOHN. "The penalty of being at the top." *JOL,*
  3 January 1963, 21, 23.

BRAINE, JOHN. "Review of reviewers." *Spectator,*
  6 December 1968, 796.
  B. comments reviews of *The Crying Game.*

BUTCHER, MARYVONNE. "A film in context." *Commonweal*,
3 July 1959, 346-348.
On the film version of *Room at the Top*.

GUTWILLIG, ROBERT. "A talk in London with John Braine." *NYTBR*,
7 October 1962, 5, 20.

HURRELL, JOHN D. "Class and conscience in John Braine and
Kingsley Amis." *Crit*, II: 1 (1958), 39-53.
*Room at the Top, Lucky Jim, That Uncertain Feeling, I Like
It Here.*

JELLY, OLIVER. "Fiction and illness." *REL*, III
(January 1962), 80-89.
Mentions *The Vodi* and Ellis's *The Rack*.

LEE, JAMES W. *John Braine*. TEAS, 62. Twayne: New York, 1968.
Pp. 127.

RICHLER, MORDECAI. "Tougher at the bottom." *Spectator*,
19 October 1962, 602-603.
Rev. art. on *Life at the Top*.

SCHLÜTER, KURT. "Soziale Statussymbole und ihre künstlerische
Verwendung in John Braines Roman *Room at the Top*." *NS*, n.s.
XII (1963), 193-208.

SCHLÜTER, KURT. *Die Kunst des Erzählens in John Braines Roman
"Room at the Top"*. Quelle & Meyer: Heidelberg, 1965. Pp. 126.

SHESTAKOV, DMITRI. "John Braine facing his fourth novel."
SovL, 8 (1964), 178-181.
Room at the Top, The Vodi.

STOLL, KARL-HEINZ. "John Braine." *Englische Literatur der Gegenwart in Einzeldarstellungen*, ed. Horst W. Drescher. Kröner: Stuttgart, 1970. Pp. 173-189.
The main themes of his novels are the dangers of human ex-
tremes - sterile hardness and inefficient softness - and
the difficulties of man's strivings to exist as an unre-
duced, complex human being. Short biography. Bibliography.

SYKES, ADAM. "How I write my novels: John Braine is inter-
viewed by Adam Sykes." *Time and Tide*, 4-11 October 1962,
23-24.

TAYLOR, ARCHER. "John Braine's proverbs." *WF*, XXIII (1964),
42-43.
A collection of proverbs from *Room at the Top* and *The Vodi*.

TODD, OLIVIER. *"Une pièce au soleil,* de John Braine." *TM,* XIV (1958/59), 763-765.
  Rev. art. on the French translation of *Room at the Top.*

WHANNEL, PADDY. *"Room at the Top." ULeftR,* VI (Spring 1959), 21-24.
  On the film version.

BROOKE-ROSE, CHRISTINE (1923)
The Languages of Love, 1957; *The Sycamore Tree,* 1958; *The Dear Deceit,* 1960; *The Middlemen,* 1961; *Out,* 1964; *Such,* 1966; *Between,* 1968.

ANON. "Gallery of rogues." *TLS,* 21 October 1960, 673.
  Contains rev. of *The Dear Deceit.*

ANON. "The go-betweens." *TLS,* 1 September 1961, 577.
  Rev. art. on *The Middlemen.*

ANON. "Colorimetrics." *TLS,* 19 November 1964, 1033.
  Rev. art. on *Out.*

ANON. "In the beginning." *TLS,* 20 October 1966, 953.
  Rev. art. on *Such.*

ANON. "Loded language." *TLS,* 31 October 1968, 1218.
  Rev. art. on *Between.*

BROPHY, BRIGID (1929)
Hackenfeller's Ape, 1953; *The King of a Rainy Country,* 1956; *Flesh,* 1962; *The Finishing Touch,* 1963; *The Snow Ball,* 1964; *In Transit,* 1969.

ANON. "Brigid Brophy: *Flesh." TLS,* 9 November 1962, 861.
  Rev. art.

ANON. "Royal finish." *TLS,* 16 August 1963, 621.
  Rev. art. on *The Finishing Touch.*

ANON. "Some ball." *TLS,* 23 January 1964, 61.
  Rev. art. on *The Snow Ball.*

ANON. "Unscheduled flight." *TLS,* 2 October 1969, 1121.
  Rev. art. on *In Transit.*

AUCHINCLOSS, EVE. "Bad characters." *NYRB*, 24 September 1964,
19-20.
Contains rev. of *The Snow Ball* and *The Finishing Touch*.

MERAS, PHYLLIS. "A talk with Brigid Brophy." *NYTBR*,
21 May 1967, 4-5, 26.

BURGESS, ANTHONY (1917)
The Long Day Wanes (Malayan Trilogy): *Time for a Tiger*, 1956,
The Enemy in the Blanket, 1958, *Beds in the East*, 1959. *The
Right to an Answer*, 1960; *The Doctor Is Sick*, 1960; *Devil of
a State*, 1961; *One Hand Clapping*, 1961 (as Joseph Kell); *The
Worm and the Ring*, 1961; *The Wanting Seed*, 1962; *A Clockwork
Orange*, 1962; *Honey for the Bears*, 1963; *Inside Mr. Enderby*,
1963 (as Joseph Kell); *Nothing Like the Sun*, 1963; *The Eve of
St. Venus*, 1964; *A Vision of Battlements*, 1965; *Tremor of
Intent*, 1966; *Enderby Outside*, 1968; *MF*, 1971.

ANON. "Shading off." *TLS*, 1 May 1959, 262.
Contains rev. of *Beds in the East*.

ANON. "Local boys make good." *TLS*, 3 June 1960, 349.
Contains rev. of *The Right to an Answer*.

ANON. "Portents and symbols." *TLS*, 23 December 1960, 825.
Contains rev. of *The Doctor Is Sick*.

ANON. "Sparing the rod." *TLS*, 7 July 1961, 421.
Contains rev. of *The Worm and the Ring*.

ANON. "Anthony Burgess: *A Clockwork Orange*." *TLS*,
25 May 1962, 377.
Rev. art.

ANON. "The hungry sheep." *TLS*, 5 October 1962, 773.
Rev. art. on *The Wanting Seed*.

ANON. "Going red." *TLS*, 29 March 1963, 213.
Rev. art. on *Honey for the Bears*.

ANON. "Jakes Peer or Jacques Père." *TLS*, 23 April 1964, 329.
Rev. art. on *Nothing Like the Sun*.

ANON. "But hoo!" *TLS*, 10 September 1964, 837.
Rev. art. on *The Eve of St. Venus*.

ANON. "The Ennead." *TLS*, 30 September 1965, 850.
Rev. art. on *A Vision of Battlements*.

ANON. "Spying for laughs." *TLS*, 9 June 1966, 509.
Rev. art. on *Tremor of Intent*.

ANON. "Musings from Morocco." *TLS*, 30 May 1968, 545.
Rev. art. on *Enderby Outside*.

ADAMS, ROBERT M. "Petit Guignol." *NYRB*, 23 January 1964, 7-8.
Rev. art. on *The Wanting Seed* and *Honey for the Bears*.

AGGELER, GEOFFREY. "Mr. Enderby and Mr. Burgess." *MalR*,
10 (April 1969), 104-110.
Inside Mr. Enderby and its sequel *Enderby Outside* as comic
masterpieces.

AGGELER, GEOFFREY. "The comic art of Anthony Burgess." *ArQ*,
XXV (1969), 234-251.
Concerned with his novels as examples of black comedy. Detailed discussion of the Malayan Trilogy, and of *A Clockwork Orange, The Wanting Seed, Nothing Like the Sun, Tremor
of Intent*.

AGGELER, GEOFFREY. "Between God and Notgod: Anthony Burgess'
Tremor of Intent." *MalR*, 17 (January 1971), 90-102.

BERGONZI, BERNARD. "Funny book." *NYRB*, 20 May 1965, 15-16.
Rev. art. on *The Long Day Wanes. A Malayan Trilogy*.

BURGESS, ANTHONY. "Genesis and headache." *Afterwords. Novel-
ists on their novels,* ed. Thomas McCormack. Harper & Row:
New York, 1969. Pp. 29-47.
On the writing of *Nothing Like the Sun*.

CHURCHILL, THOMAS. "An interview with Anthony Burgess." *MalR*,
17 (January 1971), 103-127.
B. discusses his own novels and their reception, Waugh,
Sillitoe, contemporary American novelists, and other subjects.

DAVIS, EARLE. "'Laugh now - Think later!': The genius of
Anthony Burgess." *KM*, (1968), 7-12.

DEMOTT, BENJAMIN. "God's plenty in a flood of proper and
improper nouns." *SatR*, 27 March 1971, 31, 39-41.
Rev. art. on *MF*.

DIX, CAROL M. *Anthony Burgess*. WTW, 222. Longman: London,
1971. Pp. 31.

DONOGHUE, DENIS. "Experiments in folly." *NYRB*, 9 June 1966,
  20-21.
  Contains rev. of *The Doctor Is Sick*.

ENGELBORGHS, MAURITS. "Romans van een woordkunstenaar." *DWB*,
  CXIV (1969), 59-62.
  Inside Mr. Enderby, Enderby Outside.

EVANS, ROBERT O. "Nadsat: The argot and its implications in
  Anthony Burgess' *A Clockwork Orange*." *JML*, I (1970/71),
  406-410.

HOFFMANN, CHARLES G. & A.C. HOFFMANN. "Mr. Kell and Mr.
  Burgess: Inside and outside Mr. Enderby." *The shaken realist. Essays in modern literature in honor of Frederick J.
  Hoffman*, eds. Melvin J. Friedman & John B. Vickery.
  Louisiana State UP: Baton Rouge, 1970. Pp. 300-310.
  "... dark laughter, Burgess's recognition of the absurd
  in life, becomes Enderby's saving grace."

HYMAN, STANLEY EDGAR. "Anthony Burgess." *On contemporary
  literature. An anthology of critical essays on the major
  movements and writers of contemporary literature*, ed.
  Richard Kostelanetz. Avon Books: New York, 1964.
  Pp. 300-305.
  Mainly on *A Clockwork Orange* and *The Wanting Seed*.

ISNARD, MARCEL. "Anthony Burgess." *EA*, XIX (1966), 45-54.
  Language and style.

LECLAIR, THOMAS. "Essential opposition: The novels of
  Anthony Burgess." *Crit*, XII: 3 (1971), 77-94.
  "In novel after novel Burgess plays off culture against
  culture, character against character, value against value
  for both aesthetic and conceptual ends."

MITCHELL, JULIAN. "Anthony Burgess." *London Mag*, n.s. III
  (February 1964), 48-54.
  On the delineation of character in his novels; *The Want-
  ing Seed* as his most successful work.

PAGE, MALCOLM. "Anthony Burgess: The author as performer."
  WCR, IV (January 1970), 21-24.
  Interview.

PRITCHARD, WILLIAM H. "The novels of Anthony Burgess." *MR*,
  VII (1966), 525-539.

General account of his early comic novels and his experimentation in his recent works.

PRITCHARD, WILLIAM H. "The Burgess memorandum." *PR*, XXXIV (1967), 319-323.
Rev. art. on *Tremor of Intent*.

RICKS, CHRISTOPHER. "The epicene." *New Statesman*, 5 April 1963, 496.
Homo- and heterosexuality in B's novels.

SULLIVAN, WALTER. "Death without tears: Anthony Burgess and the dissolution of the West." *HC*, VI (April 1969), 1-11.

VANSITTART, PETER. "Primary colours." *Spectator*, 24 April 1964, 561.
Rev. art. on *Nothing Like the Sun*.

WAIN, JOHN. "Puppeteers." *NYRB*, 22 August 1968, 34-35.
Contains rev. of *Enderby Outside*.

WAUGH, AUBERON. "Seat of pleasure." *Spectator*, 31 May 1968, 745.
Rev. art. on *Enderby Outside*.

CALLOW, PHILIP (1924)
The Hosanna Man, 1956; *Common People*, 1958; *Native Ground*, 1959; *A Pledge for the Earth*, 1960; *Clipped Wings*, 1964; *Going to the Moon*, 1968; *The Bliss Body*, 1969; *Flesh of Morning*, 1971.

ANON. "Scraping a living." *TLS*, 6 April 1956, 205.
Contains rev. of *The Hosanna Man*.

ANON. "Light and shade." *TLS*, 29 August 1958, 481.
Contains rev. of *Common People*.

ANON. "Coining reality." *TLS*, 18 November 1960, 737.
Contains rev. of *A Pledge for the Earth*.

ANON. "The cautious I." *TLS*, 9 July 1964, 585.
Rev. art. on *Clipped Wings*.

ANON. "Sensitive searchings." *TLS*, 1 May 1969, 457.
Rev. art. on *The Bliss Body*, second in the projected sequence of novels about Colin Patten and "his search for self-knowledge and fulfilment".

ANON. "Flashbacks in the provinces." *TLS*, 30 April 1971,
   493.
   Rev. art. on *Flesh of Morning*.

COLEMAN, JOHN. "An apocrypha." *Spectator*, 4 November 1960,
   697-698.
   Contains rev. of *A Pledge for the Earth*.

MCGUINNESS, FRANK. "To be continued." *London Mag*, n.s.
   XI (June-July 1971), 148-151.
   Contains rev. of *Flesh of Morning*.

QUIGLY, ISABEL. "Novels." *Encounter*, XI (November 1958),
   84-86.
   Contains rev. of *Common People*.

CAUTE, DAVID (1936)
At Feverish Pitch, 1959; *Comrade Jacob*, 1961; *The Decline
of the West*, 1966; *The Occupation*, 1971.

ANON. "The diggers." *TLS*, 19 May 1961, 305.
   Rev. art. on *Comrade Jacob*.

ANON. "Public faces, private places." *TLS*, 8 September 1966,
   798.
   Rev. art. on *The Decline of the West*; compared with the
   "contemptible tales" of Harold Robbins.

ANON. "Action and the academic." *TLS*, 3 December 1971, 1496.
   Rev. art. on *The Occupation*. The novel is the third part
   of a trilogy: *The Demonstration* (play), *The Illusion*
   (essay), *The Occupation*.

BERGONZI, BERNARD. "Roundhead utopia." *Spectator*,
   12 May 1961, 689.
   Contains rev. of *Comrade Jacob*.

CAUTE, DAVID. "A writer's prospect - IX." *London Mag*,
   VII (February 1960), 40-46.
   On the supposed contrast between "empirical" and "committed"
   writing. Refers to Green and Snow.

MCGUINNESS, FRANK. "*Decline of the West* by David Caute."
   London Mag, n.s. VI (September 1966), 112-113.
   Rev. art.

CHARTERIS, HUGO (1922)
A Share of the World, 1953; *Marching with April*, 1956;
Picnic at Porokorro, 1958; *The Lifeline*, 1961; *Pictures on
the Wall*, 1963; *The River-Watcher*, 1965; *The Coat*, 1966;
The Indian Summer of Gabriel Murray, 1968.

ANON. "Present problems." *TLS*, 29 June 1956, 389.
  Contains rev. of *Marching with April*.

ANON. "Wider issues." *TLS*, 24 October 1958, 605.
  Contains rev. of *Picnic at Porokorro*.

ANON. "Wha's like us?" *TLS*, 18 August 1961, 545.
  Rev. art. on *The Lifeline*.

ANON. "Humming-bird snare." *TLS*, 22 February 1963, 121.
  Rev. art. on *Pictures on the Wall*.

ANON. "Stream of conscience." *TLS*, 26 August 1965, 729.
  Rev. art. on *The River-Watcher*.

ANON. "Blitz and pieces." *TLS*, 10 November 1966, 1028.
  Rev. art. on *The Coat*.

ANON. "Numinous larks." *TLS*, 13 June 1968, 613.
  Rev. art. on *The Indian Summer of Gabriel Murray*.

CHARTERIS, HUGO. "A novelist on his novels." *London Mag*,
  n.s. VIII (October 1968), 17-35.
  An interview in which Ch. answers questions about his
  methods of writing, the theme of disenchantment in his
  novels, his attitude as a novelist to class, the writers
  who have influenced him, etc.

GALLOWAY, DAVID. "The central image." *Spectator*,
  11 November 1966, 522-523.
  Contains rev. of *The Coat*.

JENNINGS, ELIZABETH. "Five novels." *Encounter*,
  II (April 1954), 74-78.
  Contains rev. of *A Share of the World* (76-78).

MCGUINNESS, FRANK. "*The River-Watcher* by Hugo Charteris."
  London Mag, n.s. V (November 1965), 94-97.
  Rev. art.

MCGUINNESS, FRANK. "Highland fling." *London Mag*, n.s.
  VII (January 1968), 105-108.

A Share of the World to *The Coat* which is Ch's "crowning achievement" so far.

MCGUINNESS, FRANK. "Old soldiers." *London Mag*, n.s.
VIII (June 1968), 107-110.
Contains rev. of *The Indian Summer of Gabriel Murray* (107-109).

ROSS, ALAN. "*Pictures on the Wall* by Hugo Charteris." *London Mag*, n.s. III (May 1963), 85-86.
Rev. art.

VANSITTART, PETER. "Honourable ego." *Spectator*,
14 June 1968, 814, 816.
Rev. art. on *The Indian Summer of Gabriel Murray*.

WYNDHAM, FRANCIS. "*A Share of the World*." *TLS*,
6 August 1954, XLVII-XLVIII.
Rev. art.; regarded as "the most impressive first novel that has appeared since the war."

COOPER, WILLIAM (1910)
Trina, 1934; *Rhéa*, 1935; *Lisa*, 1937; *Three Marriages*, 1946; *Scenes from Provincial Life*, 1950; *The Struggles of Albert Woods*, 1952; *The Ever-Interesting Topic*, 1953; *Disquiet and Peace*, 1956; *Young People*, 1958; *Scenes from Married Life*, 1961; *Memoirs of a New Man*, 1966; *You Want the Right Frame of Reference*, 1971.

ANON. "Success story." *TLS*, 11 July 1952, 449.
Rev. art. on *The Struggles of Albert Woods*.

ANON. "The world of school." *TLS*, 25 December 1953, 829.
Rev. art. on *The Ever-Interesting Topic*.

ANON. "Mariage à la mode." *TLS*, 8 June 1956, 341.
Rev. art. on *Disquiet and Peace*.

ANON. "Youth takes a bow." *TLS*, 28 February 1958, 113.
Rev. art. on *Young People*. Refers also to *The Struggles of Albert Woods* and *Disquiet and Peace*.

ANON. "Work and play." *TLS*, 27 January 1961, 53.
Rev. art. on *Scenes from Married Life* and on the reissue of *Scenes from Provincial Life*.

ANON. "Power game." *TLS*, 12 May 1966, 401.
Rev. art. on *Memoirs of a New Man*.

ANON. "Cultural quandaries." *TLS*, 2 April 1971, 369.

Rev. art. on *You Want the Right Frame of Reference*.

DEAKIN, NICHOLAS. "An appraisal of William Cooper: In search
of banality." *Time and Tide*, 27 January 1961, 140-141.

Rev. art. on *Scenes from Provincial Life* and *Scenes from
Married Life*. Unlike Snow, to whom C. is often compared,
he is a satirist.

ENRIGHT, D.J. "The new pastoral-comical." *Spectator*,
3 February 1961, 154-155.

Rev. art. on *Scenes from Provincial Life* and *Scenes from
Married Life*; compared to Amis's novels.

SCOTT, J.D. "Scenes from Cooper." *New Statesman*,
27 January 1961, 147-148.

Rev. art. on *Scenes from Married Life* and *Scenes from
Provincial Life*.

SNOW, C.P. "Italo Svevo: Forerunner of Cooper and Amis."
E&S, n.s. XIV (1961), 7-16.

"Part of *Lucky Jim* is owed ... to an intelligent study of
Mr. William Cooper's *Scenes from Provincial Life*."

WILSON, ANGUS. "New novels." *Encounter*, VII (August 1956),
83-86.

Contains rev. of *Disquiet and Peace*.

DENNIS, NIGEL (1912)

Boys and Girls Come Out to Play, 1949; *Cards of Identity*,
1955; *A House in Order*, 1966.

ANON. "In the glasshouse." *TLS*, 27 October 1966, 974.

Rev. art. on *A House in Order*. Refers also to his previous
novels.

AUDEN, W.H. "Am I that I am?" *Encounter*, IV (April 1955),
66-72.

Rev. art. on *Cards of Identity*.

BERGONZI, BERNARD. "Updike, Dennis, and others." *NYRB*,
9 February 1967, 28-30.

Contains rev. of *A House in Order*.

BRONZWAER, W.J.M. "Willem Frederik Hermans en Nigel Dennis:
Tweemaal een behouden huis." *Vormen van imitatie. Opstellen
over Engelse en Amerikaanse literatuur*. Athenaeum - Polak

& Van Gennep: Amsterdam, 1969. Pp. 131-144.
Parallels and contrasts between Hermans's *Het behouden huis* and *A House in Order*.

DAVENPORT, JOHN. "New novels." *Observer,* 30 January 1955, 9.
Contains rev. of *Cards of Identity.*

DOOLEY, D.J. "*A House in Order.*" *Crit,* X: 1 (1967), 95-99.

ENGELBORGHS, M. "Nigel Dennis en Kingsley Amis." *DWB,*
CII (1957), 565-571.
Cards of Identity, Lucky Jim, That Uncertain Feeling.

EWART, GAVIN. "Nigel Dennis: Identity man." *London Mag,*
n.s. III (November 1963), 35-46.
Cards of Identity regarded as his masterpiece.

KENNARD, JEAN E. "Towards a novel of the absurd: A study of
the relationship between the concept of the absurd as
defined in the works of Sartre and Camus and ideas and
form in the fiction of John Barth, Samuel Beckett, Nigel
Dennis, Joseph Heller, and James Purdy." *DA,* XXIX (1969),
3144A (Calif., Berkeley).

MCGUINNESS, FRANK. "*A House in Order* by Nigel Dennis."
London Mag, n.s. VI (November 1966), 103-104.
Rev. art.

MACLAREN-ROSS, J. "*Cards of Identity* by Nigel Dennis."
London Mag, II (June 1955), 97-99.
Rev. art.

OLNEY, JAMES. "*Cards of Identity* and the satiric mode." *SIN,*
III (1971), 374-389.

PEAKE, CHARLES. "*Cards of Identity:* An intellectual satire."
LHY, I (July 1960), 49-57.

SCOTT, J.D. "*Cards of Identity* by Nigel Dennis." *Spectator,*
11 February 1955, 164.
Rev. art.

SEYMOUR-SMITH, MARTIN. "Heroic qualities." *Spectator,*
4 November 1966, 592-593.
Contains rev. of *A House in Order.*

WATT, IAN. "'Very funny ... unbelievably tough'." *NewR,*
29 August 1960, 17-19.

D. pleads for the exercise of commonsense and social
responsibility in evaluating the role of both psychiatry
and religion in modern society.

DRABBLE, MARGARET (1939)

A Summer Bird-Cage, 1963; *The Garrick Year,* 1964; *The Millstone,* 1965; *Jerusalem the Golden,* 1967; *The Waterfall,* 1969.

ANON. "Margaret Drabble: *A Summer Bird-Cage*." *TLS,*
12 April 1963, 253.
Short rev.

ANON. "The little woman." *TLS,* 23 July 1964, 645.
Rev. art. on *The Garrick Year*.

ANON. "Ask any girl." *TLS,* 23 September 1965, 820.
Rev. art. on *The Millstone*.

ANON. "Woman's mirror." *TLS,* 13 April 1967, 301. Repr. in
*T.L.S. Essays and reviews from The Times Literary Supple-
ment. 1967.* Oxford UP: London, 1968. Pp. 104-106.
Rev. art. on *Jerusalem the Golden*.

ANON. "Female and male subjects." *TLS,* 22 May 1969, 549.
Repr. in *T.L.S. Essays and reviews from The Times Literary
Supplement. 1969.* Oxford UP: London, 1970. Pp. 209-212.
Contains rev. of *The Waterfall*.

GALLOWAY, DAVID. "Milk and honey." *Spectator,* 14 April 1967,
425-426.
Contains rev. of *Jerusalem the Golden*.

JEBB, JULIAN. "*Jerusalem the Golden* by Margaret Drabble."
London Mag, n.s. VII (May 1967), 85-87.
Rev. art.

TREVOR, WILLIAM. "A life in limbo." *New Statesman,*
23 May 1969, 738.
On the characters of Jane, Rosamund and Clara in *The
Waterfall, The Millstone* and *Jerusalem the Golden*.

DUFFY, MAUREEN (1933)

That's How It Was, 1962; *The Single Eye*, 1964; *The Micro-cosm*, 1966; *The Paradox Players*, 1967; *Wounds*, 1969; *Love Child*, 1971.

ANON. "Photographer's marriage." *TLS*, 16 July 1964, 625.
Rev. art. on *The Single Eye*.

ANON. "In the house of shades." *TLS*, 26 May 1966, 469. Repr. in *T.L.S. Essays and reviews from The Times Literary Supplement. 1966.* Oxford UP: London, 1967. Pp. 176-178.
Rev. art. on *The Microcosm*.

ANON. "Roughing it for art." *TLS*, 28 September 1967, 868.
Rev. art. on *The Paradox Players*.

ANON. "Back to bed." *TLS*, 3 July 1969, 720.
Rev. art. on *Wounds*.

ANON. *Maureen Duffy. A novelist of the 1970's*. Weidenfeld & Nicholson: London, n.d. Pp. 22.
Bio-bibliographical account published by the Publicity Department of W&N.

GRANSDEN, K.W. "Of butches and femmes." *Encounter*, XXVIII (March 1967), 66-68.
Rev. art. on *The Microcosm*. Comments on the "documentary novel".

REES, DAVID. "Woman's world." *Spectator*, 20 May 1966, 640.
Rev. of *The Microcosm*.

DUGGAN, ALFRED (1903-1964)

Knight with Armour, 1950; *Conscience of the King*, 1951; *The Little Emperors*, 1951; *The Lady for Ransom*, 1953; *Leopards and Lilies*, 1954; *God and My Right*, 1955; *Winter Quarters*, 1956; *Three's Company*, 1958; *Founding Fathers*, 1959; *The Cunning of the Dove*, 1960; *Family Favourites*, 1960; *The King of Athelney*, 1961; *The Right Line of Cerdic*, 1961; *Lord Geoffrey's Fancy*, 1962; *Elephants and Castles*, 1963; *Count Bohemond*, 1964.

ANON. "Roman ways." *TLS*, 5 October 1956, 590.
Contains rev. of *Winter Quarters*.

ANON. "Roman trimmer." *TLS*, 11 April 1958, 193.

Rev. art. on *Three's Company*.

ANON. "Into the Duggan country." *TLS*, 22 May 1959, 304.

Rev. art. on *Founding Fathers*. Regards D. as one of the best living historical novelists. Outline of his writing to date.

ANON. "Amiable pietist." *TLS*, 11 March 1960, 157.

Rev. art. on *The Cunning of the Dove*.

ANON. "Crusade without questions." *TLS*, 1 October 1964, 893.

Rev. art. on *Count Bohemond*.

MCLAREN, MORAY. "Alfred Duggan." *JOL*, 25 January 1962, 75-76.

His historical novels guarantee him a permanent place among present-day writers.

NICOLSON, NIGEL. "Leap over the furrow." *New Statesman*, 23 May 1959, 733-734.

Rev. art. on *Founding Fathers*.

VANSITTART, PETER. "The crusaders." *Spectator*, 25 September 1964, 408.

Rev. art. on *Count Bohemond*.

WAUGH, EVELYN. "The art of Mr. Alfred Duggan." *Spectator*, 18 November 1955, 667-668.

Mainly on *Conscience of the King* and *God and My Right*.

WAUGH, EVELYN. "Alfred Duggan: In memoriam." *America*, CXI (1964), 483-485.

WAUGH, EVELYN. "Preface." Alfred Duggan, *Count Bohemond*. Faber & Faber: London, 1964. Pp. 5-7.

DURRELL, LAWRENCE (1912)
Pied Piper of Lovers, 1935; *Panic Spring*, 1937 (as Charles Norden); *The Black Book*, 1938; *Cêfalu*, 1947 (reissued as *The Dark Labyrinth*, 1961); *White Eagles over Serbia*, 1957; *The Alexandria Quartet: Justine*, 1957, *Balthazar*, 1958, *Mountolive*, 1958, *Clea*, 1960. *Tunc*, 1968; *Nunquam*, 1970.

BEEBE, MAURICE. "Criticism of Lawrence Durrell: A selected checklist." *MFS*, XIII (1967/68), 417-421.

KNERR, ANTHONY. "Regarding a checklist of Lawrence Durrell."
PBSA, LV (1961), 142-152.
Mainly primary sources.

LEBAS, GERARD. "Lawrence Durrell's *Alexandria Quartet* and the
critics: A survey of published criticism." *Caliban*,
6 (1969), 91-114.
List of monographs, critical essays from books or periodicals, review articles on *The Alexandria Quartet*, interviews,
and bibliographical surveys. The introduction stresses the
"polemic tendency" of Durrell criticism.

POTTER, ROBERT A. & BROOKE WHITING. *Lawrence Durrell. A checklist.* University of California Library: Los Angeles, 1961.
Pp. 50.

THOMAS, ALAN G. & LAWRENCE CLARK POWELL. "Some uncollected
authors, XXIII: Lawrence Durrell." *BC*, IX (1960, 56-63.

ANON. "Mirrored in Alexandria." *TLS*, 8 February 1957, 77.
Rev. art. on *Justine*.

ANON. "A tale retold." *TLS*, 18 April 1958, 205.
Rev. art. on *Balthazar*.

ANON. "His excellency." *TLS*, 17 October 1958, 589.
Rev. art. on *Mountolive*.

ANON. "Lawrence Durrell answers a few questions." *Two
Cities*, 15 April 1959, 25-28. Repr. in *The world of
Lawrence Durrell,* ed. Harry T. Moore. Southern Illinois
UP: Carbondale, 1962. Pp. 156-160.
Interview, mainly on *Justine*.

ANON. "Ein Abend mit Lawrence Durrell." *Zeit*,
27 November 1959, 9.
Interview, mainly on *The Alexandria Quartet*.

ANON. "Time released." *TLS*, 5 February 1960, 80.
Rev. art. on *Clea*, which is seen in relation to the
other parts of *The Alexandria Quartet*.

ANON. "Profile: Lawrence Durrell." *Observer*,
28 February 1960, 18.
Mainly biographical.

ANON. "The Kneller tape (Hamburg)." *The world of Lawrence
Durrell,* ed. Harry T. Moore. Southern Illinois UP: Carbondale, 1962. Pp. 161-168.

D. answers questions on *The Alexandria Quartet.*

ANON. "The old firm." *TLS*, 25 April 1968, 413. Repr. in
T.L.S. Essays and reviews from The Times Literary Supplement. 1968. Oxford UP: London, 1969. Pp. 63-68.
Rev. art. on *Tunc.*

ANON. "Olives and after." *New Statesman*, 26 July 1968, 143.
D's fiction shows a lazy reliance on the use of place to do the work of thought.

ANON. "The long arm of the firm." *TLS*, 26 March 1970, 328.
Repr. in *T.L.S. Essays and reviews from The Times Literary Supplement. 1970.* Oxford UP: London, 1971. Pp. 33-36.
Rev. art. on *Nunquam.*

ALBERES, R.-M. "Lawrence Durrell ou le roman pentagonal."
RdP, (juin 1965), 102-112.
The Alexandria Quartet.

ALDINGTON, RICHARD. "A note on Lawrence Durrell." *The world of Lawrence Durrell,* ed. Harry T. Moore. Southern Illinois UP: Carbondale, 1962. Pp. 3-12.
Mainly on *The Alexandria Quartet.*

ARBAN, DOMINIQUE. "Lawrence Durrell." *Preuves*, 109 (mars 1960), 86-94.
The Black Book and *The Alexandria Quartet.* His experiments with 'relativity' are not as scientific as it would appear at first glance.

ARTHOS, JOHN. "Lawrence Durrell's gnosticism." *Person,* XLIII (1962), 360-373.
A charge is levelled against his philosophical and artistic positions which are thought to contradict each other. His system of thought is a "pessimistic gnosticism".

BALDANZA, FRANK. "Lawrence Durrell's 'word continuum'."
Crit, IV: 2 (1961), 3-17.
The Alexandria Quartet.

BAUMGART, REINHARD. "Rückblickend von vorn gesehen: Lawrence Durrell." *Merkur*, XVIII (1964), 677-683.
On the implications of his ideology as revealed in *The Alexandria Quartet.*

BECHER, HUBERT, S.J. "Lawrence Durrells Tetralogie und die
literarische Kritik." *SZ*, CLXVIII (1961), 360-369.

BEJA, MORRIS. "Afterword: Contemporaries." *Epiphany in the
modern novel*. Owen: London, 1971. Pp. 211-233.
Contains discussions of *The Alexandria Quartet* (216-220).

BERGONZI, BERNARD. "Stale incense." *NYRB*, 11 July 1968,
37-39.
Contains extensive rev. of *Tunc*.

BLIVEN, NAOMI. "Books: Alexandrine in tetrameter." *NY*,
13 August 1960, 97-103.
Despite its careful structure, *The Alexandria Quartet*
cannot be called a careful work.

BLÖCKER, GÜNTER. "Schlußgalopp in der vierten Dimension."
Bilder und Zeiten. *FAZ*, 22 April 1961, n.p.
Does not regard *Clea* as a satisfying final sequel to *The
Alexandria Quartet*. The master of the multi-dimensional
does not feel at home in one dimension, though *Clea*, if
not seen as the one-dimensional final sequel, is still a
masterpiece.

BODE, CARL. "Durrell's way to Alexandria." *CE*, XXII
(1960/61), 531-538. Repr. as "A guide to Alexandria" in
The world of Lawrence Durrell, ed. Harry T. Moore.
Southern Illinois UP: Carbondale, 1962. Pp. 205-221.
The Alexandria Quartet: central subject, characters,
setting, plot.

BODE, CARL. "Lawrence Durrell." *JOL*, 16 February 1961, 169.
Characters and their meaning in *The Alexandria Quartet*.

BORK, ALFRED M. "Durrell and relativity." *CentR*, VII (1963),
191-203.
Popularized version of Einstein's theory of relativity
in *The Alexandria Quartet*.

BOSQUET, ALAIN. "Lawrence Durrell ou l'azur ironique." *NRF*,
XIV (juin 1966), 1116-1123.
On his indebtedness to Mallarmé and Rimbaud.

BOSTON, RICHARD. "Some notes on *The Alexandria Quartet*." *Delta*,
XXIII (February 1961), 33-38.
Dismisses D's conception of relativity.

BROMBERT, VICTOR. "Lawrence Durrell and his French reputa-
tion." *The world of Lawrence Durrell*, ed. Harry T. Moore.
Southern Illinois UP: Carbondale, 1962. Pp. 169-183.

BROWN, SHARON LEE. "Lawrence Durrell and relativity." *DA*,
XXVI (1966), 7310 (Ore.).

BROWN, SHARON LEE. "*The Black Book:* A search for method."
MFS, XIII (1967/68), 319-328.

BURNS, J. CHRISTOPHER. "Durrell's heraldic universe." *MFS*,
XIII (1967/68), 375-388.

CAMI, BEN. "Lawrence Durrell: Een paar nota's." *VlG*, XLII
(1958), 635-637.
His knowledge of the locale in *The Alexandria Quartet*.

CARRUTH, HAYDEN. "'And I shal clynken yow so mery a belle
that I shal wakyn al this companye'." *Poetry*, XCIII
(1958/59), 323-325.
Explains the "linguistic properties" of *Justine* and compares its composition to that of the symbolic poem.

CATE, CURTIS. "Lawrence Durrell." *Atlantic*, CCVIII
(December 1961), 63-69.
Regards *The Alexandria Quartet* as not particularly original. Its true modernity lies in the exploration of doubt
and uncertainty.

CHAUMEIL, C. "Lawrence Durrell: *Balthazar - Mountolive -
Clea*." *EA*, XV (1962), 298-300.
Rev. art.

COLEMAN, JOHN. "Mr. Durrell's dimensions." *Spectator*,
19 February 1960, 256-257.
Rev. art. on *The Alexandria Quartet*.

COLLIER, PETER. "A talk with Lawrence Durrell." *NYTBR*,
14 April 1968, 14.

CORKE, HILARY. "Mr. Durrell and Brother Criticus."
Encounter, XIV (May 1960), 65-70.
Takes *The Alexandria Quartet* as a test case for re-
viewers.

CORKE, HILARY. "Lawrence Durrell." *LHY*, II (January 1961),
43-49.
The "movement in time" of the conventional novel is

replaced by a "movement in truth" in *The Alexandria Quartet*.

CORTLAND, PETER. "Durrell's sentimentalism." *ER*, XIV (April 1964), 15-19.

He dislikes intellectualism and prefers the body to the mind.

COX, W.O.G. "Another letter to Lawrence Durrell." *The world of Lawrence Durrell,* ed. Harry T. Moore. Southern Illinois UP: Carbondale, 1962. Pp. 112-116.

Space-time in *The Alexandria Quartet*.

CREED, WALTER G. "Contemporary scientific concepts and the structure of Lawrence Durrell's *Alexandria Quartet*." *DAI*, XXX (1969), 1165A (Pa.).

CROWDER, RICHARD. "Durrell, libido and eros." *BSTCF*, III (Winter 1962/63), 34-39.

Opposes "libido", which only demands sexual fulfilment, to "eros", the meaning of which Darley and Clea finally grasp, when they realize that it is art that makes experience understandable.

DARE, H. "The quest for Durrell's Scobie." *MFS*, X (1964/65), 379-383.

Discards the figure of Scobie in *The Alexandria Quartet* as an incredible invention.

DECANCQ, ROLAND. "What lies beyond?: An analysis of Darley's 'quest' in Lawrence Durrell's *Alexandria Quartet*." *RLV,* XXXIV (1968), 134-150.

DE MOTT, BENJAMIN. "Grading the Emanglons." *HudR*, XIII (1960/61), 457-464.

Rev. art. on *The Alexandria Quartet*.

DENNIS, NIGEL. "New four-star king of novelists." *Life,* 21 November 1960, 96-109.

On the reasons for D's success.

DOBREE, BONAMY. "Durrell's Alexandrian series." *SR*, LXIX (1961), 61-79. Repr. in *The world of Lawrence Durrell,* ed. Harry T. Moore. Southern Illinois UP: Carbondale, 1962. Pp. 184-204. Repr. also in *The lamp and the lute. Studies in seven authors*. Cass: London, 1964. Pp. 150-168.

DRESCHER, HORST W. "Raumzeit: Zur Struktur von Lawrence Durrells *Alexandria Quartet.*" *NS*, n.s. XX (1971), 308-318.

DURRELL, LAWRENCE. "Letters from Durrell." *The world of Lawrence Durrell,* ed. Harry T. Moore. Southern Illinois UP: Carbondale, 1962. Pp. 222-239.
Contain remarks on *The Alexandria Quartet* and *The Black Book.*

EDEL, LEON. *The modern psychological novel.* Universal Library: New York, 1964 (rev. ed.). Pp. VIII + 210.
Mainly discussion of Proust, Joyce, Woolf, Faulkner, and Dorothy Richardson. Examines also *The Alexandria Quartet.*

ELLIOTT, GEORGE P. "The other side of the story." *The world of Lawrence Durrell,* ed. Harry T. Moore. Southern Illinois UP: Carbondale, 1962. Pp. 87-94.
The Alexandria Quartet.

ENGELBORGHS, MAURITS. "Nieuwe Engelse romankunst: Lawrence Durrell." *DWB,* CV (1960), 349-360.
The Alexandria Quartet. Bibliographical addenda.

ENRIGHT, D.J. "Alexandrian nights' entertainments: Lawrence Durrell's *Quartet.*" *ILA,* III (1961), 30-39.
Repr. in *Writing in England today. The last fifteen years,* ed. Karl Miller. Penguin Books: Harmondsworth, 1968. Pp. 45-53.
His idea of a four-decker novel in which the sequence of events can be interpreted in various ways is "neither novel nor true".

ESKIN, STANLEY G. "Durrell's themes in the *Alexandria Quartet.*" *TQ,* V (Winter 1962), 43-60.
Personality, causality, rational and moral consciousness, time, and society.

FLINT, R.W. "A major novelist." *Commentary,* XXVII (1959), 353-356.
Praise of *The Alexandria Quartet* as a new kind of novel.

FRAIBERG, LOUIS. "Durrell's dissonant *Quartet.*" *Contemporary British novelists* , ed. Charles Shapiro. Southern Illinois UP: Carbondale, Edwardsville, 1965. Pp. 16-35.

FRASER, G.S. *Lawrence Durrell. A study.* Faber & Faber: London, 1968. Pp. 256.

Traces his background and literary formation. Detailed
discussion of *The Black Book*, D's relations with Greece
and *The Alexandria Quartet*. Short preview of *Tunc*. Contains Alan G. Thomas, "Recollections of a Durrell
collector" and a very extensive bibliography by the
same author.

FRASER, G.S. *Lawrence Durrell*. WTW, 216. Longmans: London,
1970. Pp. 47.

FRICKER, ROBERT. "Lawrence Durrell: *The Alexandria Quartet.*"
Gymnasium Helveticum, XVI (1961/62), 385-399.

FRICKER, ROBERT. "Lawrence Durrell: *The Alexandria Quartet.*"
Der moderne englische Roman. Interpretationen, ed. Horst
Oppel. Schmidt: Berlin, 1971 (rev. ed.). Pp. 401-418.

FRIEDMAN, ALAN WARREN. "Art for love's sake: Lawrence
Durrell and *The Alexandria Quartet.*" *DA*, XXVII (1966),
1365A-1366A (Rochester).

FRIEDMAN, ALAN WARREN. "A 'key' to Lawrence Durrell." *WSCL,*
VIII (1967), 31-42.
The central thesis of *The Alexandria Quartet* that there
is no truth without a referential system is reflected in
Key to Modern British Poetry where Tennyson's "Ulysses"
is compared to Eliot's "Gerontion".

FRIEDMAN, ALAN WARREN. "Place and Durrell's island books."
MFS, XIII (1967/68), 329-341.

FRIEDMAN, ALAN WARREN. *Lawrence Durrell and "The Alexandria
Quartet". Art for love's sake.* Oklahoma UP: Norman, 1970.
Pp. XXV + 221.

GASTER, BERYL. "Lawrence Durrell." *ConR*, CCV (July 1964),
375-379.
On his "prism-sightedness" (*The Alexandria Quartet*).

GERARD, ALBERT. "Lawrence Durrell: Un grand talent de basse
époque." *RGB*, XCVIII (octobre 1962), 15-29.
The defects of *The Alexandria Quartet* make it "ominously
appropriate" to our purposeless age.

GLICKSBERG, CHARLES I. "The fictional world of Lawrence
Durrell." *BuR*, XI (March 1963), 118-133.
On the multiplicity of perspectives in *The Black Book*
and *The Alexandria Quartet*.

GLICKSBERG, CHARLES I. "The relativity of the self: *The Alexandria Quartet*." *The self in modern literature*. Pennsylvania State UP: University Park, 1963. Pp. 89-94.
"... he seeks to communicate not an objective but an artistic truth: namely, that everyone views the universe through the spectrum of his own sensibility."

GODSHALK, WILLIAM LEIGH. "Some sources of Durrell's *Alexandria Quartet*." *MFS*, XIII (1967/68), 361-374.

GORDON, AMBROSE, JR. "Time, space, and eros: *The Alexandria Quartet* rehearsed." *Six contemporary novels. Six introductory essays in modern fiction,* ed. William O.S. Sutherland, Jr. Texas UP: Austin, 1962. Pp. 6-21.

GOSSMAN, ANN. "Some characters in search of a mirror." *Crit,* VIII: 3 (1966), 79-84.
The symbolic value of the mirror in *The Alexandria Quartet*.

GOTTWALD, JOHANNES. "Der Künstlerroman Darleys: Kontinuität in Lawrence Durrells *Alexandria Quartet*." *NS*, n.s. XX (1971), 319-325.

GOULIANOS, JOAN. "Lawrence Durrell and Alexandria." *VQR,* XLV (1969), 664-673.
The view of Egypt in *The Alexandria Quartet* seems to include a contrast with Greece.

GOULIANOS, JOAN. "A conversation with Lawrence Durrell about art, analysis, and politics." *MFS*, XVII (1971/72), 159-166.
Discusses *Nunquam, The Alexandria Quartet*, Henry Miller, colonialism, the present Greek regime, and mystic and oriental philosophy.

GREEN, MARTIN. "Lawrence Durrell, II: A minority report." *YR*, XLIX (1959/60), 496-508. Repr. in *The world of Lawrence Durrell,* ed. Harry T. Moore. Southern Illinois UP: Carbondale, 1962. Pp. 129-145.
His work appeals to the British sensibility which refuses to take modern life seriously.

GROVE, TREVOR. "Now and then." *Spectator*, 28 March 1970, 419-420.
Rev. art. on *Nunquam*.

HAALAND, ARILD. "Flukten fra det gylne skinn: En studie i *Alexandriakvartetten*." *Samtiden,* LXXVII (1968), 617-630.

HAGOPIAN, JOHN V. "The resolution of the *Alexandria Quartet*." *Crit*, VII: 1 (1964), 97-106.

The last episode, the romance of Darley and Clea, contains "the principal features of Durrell's total theme and form".

HAMARD, JEAN-PAUL. "L'espace et le temps dans les romans de Lawrence Durrell." *Critique*, XVI (1960), 387-413.

The theory of relativity is a new myth which fertilizes our aesthetic symbolism. Discussion of "time" in the four novels. Ends with a study of the characters' attitude towards "modern love".

HAMARD, JEAN-PAUL. "Lawrence Durrell: Rénovateur assagi." *Critique*, XVI (1960), 1025-1033.

He has shed his innovating intentions and "rallied to the didactic, puritan and moralizing conception of the novel".

HAMARD, JEAN-PAUL. "Lawrence Durrell: A European writer." *DUJ*, LX (1967/68), 171-181.

The spirit of his work is foreign to contemporary English literature.

HANOTEAU, GUILLAUME. "Lawrence Durrell: Riche et glorieux grâce à quatre femmes." *Paris Match*, 3 décembre 1960, 38-41, 43-46, 49.

On his way of life and the writing of *The Alexandria Quartet*; illustrated.

HARTT, JULIAN N. *The lost image of man*. Louisiana State UP: Baton Rouge, 1963. Pp. XI + 131.

Contains passages on "the decline of the erotic image as the normative representation of health, beauty, and creative power" in *The Alexandria Quartet* (63-67).

HAUGE, INGVAR. "Lawrence Durrell fram til *Alexandriakvartetten*." *Samtiden*, LXXI (1962), 220-226.

HAWKINS, JOANNA LYNN. "A study of the relationship of point of view to the structure of *The Alexandria Quartet* by Lawrence Durrell." *DA*, XXVI (1965), 3338-3339 (Northwestern).

HIGHET, GILBERT. "The Alexandrians of Lawrence Durrell." *Horizon*, II (March 1960), 113-118.

Proustian and exotic elements combine with relativity theory to search out truth.

HOOPS, WIKLEF. "Lawrence Durrell." *Englische Literatur der Gegenwart in Einzeldarstellungen*, ed. Horst W. Drescher. Kröner: Stuttgart, 1970. Pp. 250-280.

His place in literature is difficult to find particularly because of his synthesis of symbolic philosophy and pan-eroticism. There are relations to Lawrence, the French symbolists, Hesse, Yeats, and Proust, but he has found a style of his own in his "vitalist metaphysics". Short biography. Bibliography.

HOWARTH, HERBERT. "A segment of Durrell's *Quartet*." *UTQ*, XXXII (1962/63), 282-293.

HOWARTH, HERBERT. "Lawrence Durrell and some early masters." *BA*, XXXVII (1963), 5-11.

His works show direct and indirect influences of Rémy de Gourmont, Petronius, E.A. Poe, and Stendhal.

HUTCHENS, ELEANOR N. "The heraldic universe in *The Alexandria Quartet*." *CE*, XXIV (1962/63), 56-61.

Relationship to *The Waste Land*.

ISERNHAGEN, HARTWIG. *Sensation, vision, and imagination. The problem of unity in Lawrence Durrell's novels.* Diss. Freiburg, 1969. Pp. 245. Summary in *EASG*, II (1970), 86-88.

Examines the individual novels (*Pied Piper of Lovers, Panic Spring, The Black Book, The Dark Labyrinth,* and *The Alexandria Quartet*) as parts of a continuous and explicit analysis of reality. Extensive bibliography.

JEAN, RAYMOND. "Lawrence Durrell ou le temps délivré." *CS*, L (1960), 445-448. Repr. in *La littérature et le réel. De Diderot au 'Nouveau roman'*. Michel: Paris, 1965. Pp. 172-177.

He has succeeded in treating the most difficult of all subjects: love, because of the symphonic structure of *The Alexandria Quartet*.

JENS, WALTER. "Ein Anwärter auf den Nobelpreis." *Zeit*, 21 November 1958, 9.

Rev. art. on the German translation of *Justine*. D. is regarded as one of the greatest living writers and *Justine* as an excellent novel.

JOHNSON, ANN SCHWERTFEGER. "Lawrence Durrell's 'prism-sightedness': The structure of *The Alexandria Quartet*." *DA*, XXIX (1968), 264A (Pa.).

KAMEYAMA, MASAKO. "Lawrence Durrell: A sketch." *Collected essays by the members of the faculty, 11.* Kyoritsu Women's Junior College: Kyoritsu, Japan, 1968. Pp. 32-49.

KATOPE, CHRISTOPHER G. "Cavafy and Durrell's *The Alexandria Quartet.*" *CL*, XXI (1969), 125-137.
His indebtedness to the Greek Alexandrian poet C.P. Cavafy.

KAZIN, ALFRED. "Lawrence Durrell's rosy-finger'd Egypt." *Contemporaries.* Little, Brown: Boston, 1962. Pp. 188-192.
The first three novels in his tetralogy.

KELLY, JOHN C. "Lawrence Durrell: *The Alexandria Quartet.*" *Studies*, LII (1963), 52-68.
The Alexandria Quartet is unromantic, a story of disillusionment.

KELLY, JOHN C. "Lawrence Durrell's style." *Studies,* LII (1963), 199-204.
Completion of previous article.

KERMODE, FRANK. "Romantic agonies." *London Mag,* VI (February 1959), 51-55.
Confesses to having badly misjudged D's work in its early stages.

KERMODE, FRANK. "Fourth dimension." *REL*, I (April 1960), 73-77.
On *The Alexandria Quartet*, dealing mainly with *Clea.*

KERMODE, FRANK. "Durrell and others." *Puzzles and epiphanies. Essays and reviews 1958-1961.* Routledge & Kegan Paul: London, 1962. Pp. 214-227.
Setting out from a general survey of the fiction scene, *The Alexandria Quartet* is passed in review. "... it is an experiment of very great formal interest, a highly serious contribution to modern fiction."

KRUPPA, JOSEPH E. "Durrell's *Alexandria Quartet* and the 'implosion' of the modern consciousness." *MFS*, XIII (1967/68), 401-416.

KVAM, RAGNAR. "Lawrence Durrell." *Vinduet*, XIV: 3 (1960), 232-240.
In *The Alexandria Quartet* all values are exploded or in the process of exploding.

LEBAS, GERARD. "The mechanisms of space-time in *The Alexandria Quartet*." *Caliban,* 7 (1970), 79-97.

LEMON, LEE T. "*The Alexandria Quartet:* Form and fiction." *WSCL,* IV (1963), 327-338.

The Alexandria Quartet embodies the 20th-century's rela-
tivistic vision of reality and truth: limitations of
content by presenting a variety of perversions but ignor-
ing traditional forms of love, marriage and sexual fulfilment.

LEVITT, MORTON P. "From a new point of view: Studies in the contemporary novel." *DA,* XXVI (1966), 6717 (Penn. State).

Contains chaps on The Alexandria Quartet.

LEVITT, MORTON P. "Art and correspondences: Durrell, Miller, and *The Alexandria Quartet*." *MFS,* XIII (1967/68), 299-318.

LITTLEJOHN, DAVID. "Lawrence Durrell: The novelist as enter-
tainer." *Motive,* XXIII (November 1962), 14-16.

The Alexandria Quartet is seen as "refreshing" as compared
to the sordidness of many contemporary novelists.

LITTLEJOHN, DAVID. "The anti-realists." *Daedalus,* XCII (1963), 250-264.

D. is said to subvert plot to emotional impact. Others
are Joyce, Kafka, Beckett.

LITTLEJOHN, DAVID. "The permanence of Durrell." *ColQ,* XIV (1965/66), 63-71.

His creative imagination makes him the best metaphoric
prose writer in present-day British fiction. The
permanence of The Alexandria Quartet, however, is uncertain.

LUND, MARY GRAHAM. "Submerge for reality: The new novel form of Lawrence Durrell." *SWR,* XLIV (1959), 229-235.

Justine, Balthazar.

LUND, MARY GRAHAM. "Eight aspects of Melissa." *Forum,* III (Winter 1961), 18-22.

Melissa is said to be a woman with a "will to give",
Justine has a "will to possess" and Clea has the "desire
to surrender, to assert".

LUND, MARY GRAHAM. "The Alexandrian projection." *AR,* XXI (1961/62), 193-204.

Compares D's technique with Mercator's projection.

LUND, MARY GRAHAM. "Durrell: Soft focus on crime." *PrS*,
XXXV (1961/62), 339-344.

In his world "things are grotesque reflections of deep
psychological realities."

LUND, MARY GRAHAM. "The big rock crystal mountain." *Four
Quarters*, XI (May 1962), 15-18.

D's images are not constructed but "crystallized".

LYONS, EUGENE & HARRY ANTRIM. "An interview with Lawrence
Durrell." *Shenandoah*, XXII (Winter 1971), 42-58.

D. discusses his novels, his subject matter and its
sources, his interest in Spengler, etc.

LYTLE, ANDREW. "Impressionism, the ego, and the first person." *Daedalus*, XCII (1963), 281-296.

Extensive reference to D.

MACKWORTH, CECILY. "Lawrence Durrell and the new romanti-
cism." *TC*, CLXVII (1960), 203-213. Repr. in *The world of
Lawrence Durrell*, ed. Harry T. Moore. Southern Illinois
UP: Carbondale, 1962. Pp. 24-37.

Detailed analysis of *The Alexandria Quartet*.

MANZALAOUI, MAHMOUD. "Curate's egg: An Alexandrian opinion
of Durrell's *Quartet*." *EA*, XV (1962), 248-260.

MAYNE, RICHARD. "Travel with sintourist." *Encounter*,
XXXI (August 1968), 79-80.

Rev. art. on *Tunc*.

MICHOT, PAULETTE. "Lawrence Durrell's *Alexandria Quartet*."
RLV, XXVI (1960), 361-367.

MILLER, HENRY. "The Durrell of the *Black Book* days." *The
world of Lawrence Durrell*, ed. Harry T. Moore. Southern
Illinois UP: Carbondale, 1962. Pp. 95-99.

MILLER, KARL. "Poet's novel." *Listener*, 25 June 1959,
1099-1100.

On the present state of the novel. D. is thought to be
overrated; *The Alexandria Quartet* is regarded as "deca-
dent".

MITCHELL, JULIAN & GENE ANDREWSKI. "Lawrence Durrell."
Writers at work. The Paris Review interviews. Second
Series, ed. George Plimpton, introd. Van Wyck Brooks.
Viking: New York, 1963. Pp. 257-282.

Biographical account, his writing habits, influences, the
theme of *The Alexandria Quartet*.

MOORE, HARRY T. "Durrell's *Black Book*." *The world of Lawrence
Durrell*, ed. Harry T. Moore. Southern Illinois UP: Carbondale, 1962. Pp. 100-102.

MORCOS, MONA LOUIS. "Elements of the autobiographical in *The
Alexandria Quartet*." *MFS*, XIII (1967/68), 343-359.

MORGAN, THOMAS B. "The autumnal arrival of Lawrence Durrell."
Esquire, LIV (September 1960), 108-111.
Anecdotal.

NEIFER, LEO J. "Durrell's method and purpose of art." *WisSL*,
3 (1966), 99-103.

NEUHAUS, VOLKER. "Lawrence Durrell *The Alexandria Quartet*."
Typen multiperspektivischen Erzählens. Böhlau: Köln, 1971.
Pp. 150-159.

O'BRIEN, R.A. "Time, space and language in Lawrence Durrell."
WatR, VI (Winter 1961), 16-24.
The distinction between clocktime and psychological time
is pointed out *(The Alexandria Quartet)*.

OZANA, ANNA. "Auf dem Wege zum modernen Roman: Gedanken bei
der Lektüre der Romane Lawrence Durrells." *WuW*, XIV (1959),
237-242.

PERLES, ALFRED. *Art and outrage. A correspondence about Henry
Miller between Alfred Perlès and Lawrence Durrell*. Putnam:
London, 1959. Pp. 63.

PERLES, ALFRED. *My friend Lawrence Durrell. An intimate
memoir on the author of "The Alexandria Quartet". With a
bibliography by Bernard Stone*. Scorpion Press: Northwood,
1961. Pp. 62.
Record of their personal friendship, not a literary study.

PRITCHETT, V.S. "Alexandrian hothouse." *The working novelist*.
Chatto & Windus: London, 1965. Pp. 30-35.

PROSER, MATTHEW N. "Darley's dilemma: The problem of structure in Durrell's *Alexandria Quartet*." *Crit*, IV: 2 (1961),
18-28.

RAMBURES, JEAN-LOUIS DE. "Le livre du mois: *Tunc* de Lawrence Durrell." *Réalités*, 280 (mai 1969), 5-15. Interview and an excerpt from the book.

READ, PHYLLIS J. "The illusion of personality: Cyclical time in Durrell's *Alexandria Quartet*." *MFS*, XIII (1967/68), 389-399.

REXROTH, KENNETH. "Lawrence Durrell." *Assays*. Loughlin: Norfolk, 1961. Pp. 118-130. General survey.

ROBINSON, W.R. "Intellect and imagination in *The Alexandria Quartet*." *Shenandoah*, XVIII (Summer 1967), 55-68. *The Alexandria Quartet* "confutes established cliches about alienation and dehumanization as the artist's, and man's, inescapable condition in the twentieth century."

ROMBERG, BERTIL. "*The Alexandria Quartet*." *Studies in the narrative technique of the first-person novel*. Almqvist & Wiksell: Stockholm, 1962. Pp. 277-308.

RUSSO, JOHN PAUL. "Love in Lawrence Durrell." *PrS*, XLIII (1969/70), 396-407. *The Alexandria Quartet* as "an investigation of modern love".

S., W.G. "Lawrence Durrell: Is he the only great novelist of the fifties?" *B&B*, (May 1960), 8-9. Interview.

SCHOLES, ROBERT. "Return to Alexandria: Lawrence Durrell and western narrative tradition." *VQR*, XL (1964), 411-420. Repr. in *The Fabulators*. Oxford UP: New York, 1967. Pp. 17-28. On the structure of *The Alexandria Quartet*.

SERPIERI, ALESSANDRO. "*Il Quartetto di Alessandria* di Lawrence Durrell." *Ponte*, XVIII (1962), 48-57.

SERTOLI, GIUSEPPE. "Lawrence Durrell e il *Quartetto di Alessandria*." *EM*, XVIII (1967), 207-256.

SERVOTTE, HERMAN. "*The Alexandria Quartet* van Lawrence Durrell." *DWB*, CVIII (1963), 646-658. Repr. in *Literatuur als levenskunst. Essays over hedendaagse Engelse literatuur*. Nederlandsche Boekhandel: Antwerpen, 1966. Pp. 52-66.

SMYTH, W.F. "Lawrence Durrell: Modern love in chamber pots and space time." *Edge*, II (1964), 105-116.

He tries to find complex ways to describe simple things and takes writing as a word game. In *The Alexandria Quartet* the word "chamber-pot" occurs every few pages.

STEINER, GEORGE. "Lawrence Durrell, I: The baroque novel." *YR*, XLIX (1959/60), 488-495. Repr. in *The world of Lawrence Durrell*, ed. Harry T. Moore. Southern Illinois UP: Carbondale, 1962. Pp. 13-23.

The Alexandria Quartet excludes real political and social facts. Its strength and meaning spring from a renewal of the richness of language.

SULLIVAN, NANCY. "Lawrence Durrell's epitaph for the novel." *Person*, XLIV (1963), 79-88.

SYKES, GERALD. "One vote for the sun." *The world of Lawrence Durrell*, ed. Harry T. Moore. Southern Illinois UP: Carbondale, 1962. Pp. 146-155.

The Alexandria Quartet: structure and style.

TAYLOR, CHET. "Dissonance and digression: The ill-fitting fusion of philosophy and form in Lawrence Durrell's *Alexandria Quartet*." *MFS*, XVII (1971/72), 167-179.

TOYNBEE, PHILIP. "Mediterranean kaleidoscope." *Observer*, 7 February 1960, 20.

Rev. art. on *The Alexandria Quartet*.

TOYNBEE, PHILIP. "*Tunc* by Lawrence Durrell." *London Mag*, n.s. VIII (April 1968), 80-82.

Rev. art.

TRILLING, LIONEL. "*The Quartet:* Two reviews." *The world of Lawrence Durrell*, ed. Harry T. Moore. Southern Illinois UP: Carbondale, 1962. Pp. 49-65.

"Mr. Durrell is the first contemporary novelist in a long time to captivate my imagination to the extent of leading me to believe that he is telling me something new ..."

TRUCHLAR, LEO. "Versuch über Lawrence Durrell." *NS*, n.s. XX (1971), 289-308.

General survey.

UNTERECKER, JOHN. "The Protean world of Lawrence Durrell." *On contemporary literature. An anthology of critical*

essays on the major movements and writers of contemporary
literature, ed. Richard Kostelanetz. Avon Books: New York,
1964. Pp. 322-329.

UNTERECKER, JOHN. Lawrence Durrell. CEMW, 6. Columbia UP:
New York, 1964. Pp. 48.

VALLETTE, JACQUES. "Lettres Anglo-Saxonnes: Justine, Balthazar, et Lawrence Durrell." MdF, 1143 (1958), 536-540.
Compares his presentation of Alexandria to Tolstoy's
description of Russia.

VALLETTE, JACQUES. "Lettres Anglo-Saxonnes: Note sur Clea."
MdF, 1163 (1960), 535-537.
Theme and characters.

WEATHERHEAD, A.K. "Romantic anachronism in The Alexandria
Quartet." MFS, X (1964/65), 128-136.
"Durrell's novel is set apart from the dominating ideas
of the last forty years." Comparison with Hemingway's
The Sun Also Rises.

WEIGEL, JOHN A. Lawrence Durrell. TEAS, 29. Twayne:
New York, 1965. Pp. 174.

WEIGEL, JOHN A. "Lawrence Durrell's first novel." TCL,
XIV (1968/69), 75-83.
Pied Piper of Lovers.

WENSBERG, ERIK. "I've been reading." CUF, III (Fall 1960),
38-42.
Realizing, in a skeptical way, that "no one knows the
whole truth about anything", D. turns to the fantastic.

WEYERGANS, FRANZ. "Clea de Lawrence Durrell." RevN,
XXXII (1960), 94-98.
Refers to all four novels of The Alexandria Quartet.

WICKES, GEORGE. "An exchange of letters between Henry Miller
and Lawrence Durrell." Paris Rev, VIII (Winter-Spring
1963), 133-159.
Letters dating from January 1937 to October 1949.

WICKES, GEORGE, ed. Lawrence Durrell and Henry Miller. A
private correspondence. Faber & Faber: London, 1963.
Pp. XV + 400.
"The correspondence traces two of the most lively literary
careers over the course of a quarter century" (August 1935

to January 1959). Contains a chronology of their lives and works. Index with explanatory notes.

WOTTON, G.E. "A letter to Lawrence Durrell." *The world of Lawrence Durrell*, ed. Harry T. Moore. Southern Illinois UP: Carbondale, 1962. Pp. 103-111.

Refers to *The Alexandria Quartet*.

YOUNG, KENNETH. "A dialogue with Durrell." *Encounter*, XIII (December 1959), 61-68.

Topics discussed are the reasons for his success, especially in Germany and France, the space-time continuum in *The Alexandria Quartet*, etc.

EDELMAN, MAURICE (1911)

A Trial of Love, 1951; *Who Goes Home*, 1953; *A Dream of Treason*, 1954; *The Happy Ones*, 1957; *A Call on Kuprin*, 1959; *The Minister*, 1961; *The Fratricides*, 1963; *The Prime Minister's Daughter*, 1964; *Shark Island*, 1967; *All on a Summer's Night*, 1969.

ANON. "Chequered careers." *TLS*, 29 October 1954, 694.

Contains rev. of *A Dream of Treason*.

ANON. "The parliamentary novel." *TLS*, 17 August 1956, XVIII.

Mentions, among others, E. and Aldridge *(The Diplomat)* as writers of political novels.

ANON. "Reasons of the heart." *TLS*, 15 February 1957, 93.

Contains rev. of *The Happy Ones*.

ANON. "Who goes home?" *TLS*, 29 May 1959, 317.

Rev. art. on *A Call on Kuprin*.

ANON. "Indiscretion." *TLS*, 28 July 1961, 461.

Rev. art. on *The Minister*.

ANON. "Political positions." *TLS*, 15 March 1963, 181.

Rev. art. on *The Fratricides*.

ANON. "Sex-politic." *TLS,* 1 October 1964, 893.

Rev. art. on *The Prime Minister's Daughter.* Refers also to *The Minister*.

ANON. "Dove's côte." *TLS*, 6 April 1967, 281.

Rev. art. on *Shark Island*.

ANON. "Locked horns." *TLS*, 10 July 1969, 745.

Rev. art. on *All on a Summer's Night*.

D'AVIGDOR-GOLDSMID, HENRY. "Public faces: The political novels of Maurice Edelman." *London Mag*, n.s. IV (January 1965), 87-90.

"... he is a political novelist without a political point of view: he still has time to find one."

JOHNSON, PAUL. "No sex for Johnnie." *New Statesman*, 28 July 1961, 120-121.

Mentions *The Minister* with regard to the English political novel.

NEWQUIST, ROY. "Maurice Edelman." *Counterpoint*. Allen & Unwin: London, 1965. Pp. 167-177.

Interview (1963).

FIELDING, GABRIEL (1916)

Brotherly Love, 1954; *In the Time of Greenbloom,* 1956; *Eight Days,* 1958; *Through Streets Broad and Narrow,* 1960; *The Birthday King,* 1962; *Gentlemen in Their Season,* 1966.

ANON. "Tales of young blood." *TLS*, 6 July 1956, 405.

Contains rev. of *In the Time of Greenbloom*. Refers also to *Brotherly Love*.

ANON. "Suffering and renewal." *TLS*, 28 November 1958, 685.

Contains rev. of *Eight Days*.

ANON. "A place for everything." *TLS*, 11 November 1960, 721.

Contains rev. of *Through Streets Broad and Narrow*.

ANON. "A horrifying normality." *TLS*, 12 October 1962, 797.

Rev. art. on *The Birthday King*.

ANON. "Itch and Incense." *TLS*, 23 June 1966, 549. Repr. in *T.L.S. Essays and reviews from The Times Literary Supplement. 1966.* Oxford UP: London, 1967. Pp. 69-71.

Rev. art. on *Gentlemen in Their Season*. Refers also to *The Birthday King*.

BALLIETT, WHITNEY. "The Blaydon boy." *NY*, 23 September 1961, 174-179.

Rev. art. on *Brotherly Love, In the Time of Greenbloom* and *Through Streets Broad and Narrow*.

BOWERS, FREDERICK. "The unity of Fielding's *Greenbloom*."
Renascence, XVIII (1965/66), 147-155.

Philosophical attitude in *In the Time of Greenbloom*; the
novel considered as a major work.

BOWERS, FREDERICK. "Gabriel Fielding's *The Birthday King*."
QQ, LXXIV (1967), 149-158.

CAVALLO, EVELYN. "Gabriel Fielding: A portrait." *Critic*,
XIX (December 1960/January 1961), 19-20, 84-85.

Autobiography in his novels.

FURBANK, P.N. "John Bull in the German garden." *Encounter*,
XXII (April 1964), 85-91.

The last part of this article is on *The Birthday King*,
on Bedford's *A Legacy* and Hughes's *The Fox in the Attic*.
These novels cover the last hundred years of German
history.

GRANDE, LUKE M. "Gabriel Fielding: New master of the Catholic classic?" *CathW*, CXCVII (June 1963), 172-179.

Praises his originality, sense of drama and narrative
technique in *The Birthday King*.

KUNKEL, FRANCIS L. "Clowns and saviors: Two contemporary
novels." *Renascence*, XVIII (1965/66), 40-44.

Günter Grass, *Katz und Maus*, and *The Birthday King*. Both
novels are set in Nazi Germany.

NEWQUIST, ROY. "Gabriel Fielding." *Counterpoint*. Allen &
Unwin: London, 1965. Pp. 195-207.

Interview (1963).

SEYMOUR-SMITH, MARTIN. "Burgess's wake." *Spectator*,
24 June 1966, 794.

Contains rev. of *Gentlemen in Their Season*.

STANFORD, DEREK. "Gabriel Fielding and the Catholic novel."
Month, CCXII (1961), 352-356.

TOWNE, FRANK. "The tragicomic moment in the art of Gabriel
Fielding." *To find something new. Studies in contemporary
literature*, ed. Henry Grosshans. Washington State UP:
Pullman, 1969. Pp. 102-116.

FITZGIBBON, CONSTANTINE (1919)
The Arabian Bird, 1948; *The Iron Hoop*, 1950; *Cousin Emily*, 1952; *The Holiday*, 1953; *In Love and War*, 1956; *Watcher in Florence*, 1959; *When the Kissing Had to Stop*, 1960; *Going to the River*, 1963; *High Heroic*, 1969.

ANON. "Fact and fantasy." *TLS*, 12 May 1950, 289.
  Contains rev. of *The Iron Hoop*.

ANON. "The wheel of fortune." *TLS*, 2 October 1953, 625.
  Contains rev. of *The Holiday*.

ANON. "Trial and error." *TLS*, 3 August 1956, 461.
  Contains rev. of *In Love and War*.

ANON. "The innocent zany." *TLS*, 6 May 1960, 285.
  Contains rev. of *When the Kissing Had to Stop*.

ANON. "Behind the headlines." *TLS*, 17 May 1963, 361.
  Contains rev. of *Going to the River*. "Mr. FitzGibbon's undoubted talents are politico-sociological-analytic rather than creative."

FITZGIBBON, CONSTANTINE. "Politics and the novel: A letter to Patrick O'Donovan." *Encounter*, XVI (June 1961), 71-73.
  Comments on adverse reviews of *When the Kissing Had to Stop*.

FLEMING, IAN (1908-1964)
Casino Royale, 1953; *Live and Let Die*, 1954; *Moonraker*, 1955; *Diamonds Are Forever*, 1956; *From Russia, with Love*, 1957; *Dr. No*, 1958; *Goldfinger*, 1959; *Thunderball*, 1961; *The Spy Who Loved Me*, 1962; *On Her Majesty's Secret Service*, 1963; *You Only Live Twice*, 1964; *The Man with the Golden Gun*, 1965.

ANON. "On the shady side." *TLS*, 20 May 1955, 265.
  Contains rev. of *Moonraker*.

ANON. "On the seamy side." *TLS*, 3 April 1959, 198.
  Contains rev. of *Goldfinger*.

ANON. "Mighty nonsense." *TLS*, 31 March 1961, 206.
  Contains rev. of *Thunderball*.

ANON. "Strictly for thrills." *TLS*, 5 April 1963, 229.
  Contains rev. of *On Her Majesty's Secret Service*.

ANON. "When clues give way to clobberings." *TLS*, 8 April 1965, 280.

Contains rev. of *The Man with the Golden Gun*.

ANON. "An Englishman's Bond." *TLS*, 27 May 1965, 408. Repr. in *T.L.S. Essays and reviews from The Times Literary Supplement. 1965*. Oxford UP: London, 1966. Pp. 120-125.

Rev. art. on Kingsley Amis's *The James Bond dossier*.

AMIS, KINGSLEY. "Literary agents." *New Statesman,* 20 March 1964, 452-453.

Contains rev. of *You Only Live Twice*.

AMIS, KINGSLEY. "M for murder." *New Statesman,* 2 April 1965, 540-541.

Rev. art. on *The Man with the Golden Gun*.

AMIS, KINGSLEY. *The James Bond dossier*. Pan Books: London, 1966. Pp. 157.

Defence of F. against his critics. Sympathetic study of various subjects in the Bond books. His place in literature is at the side of Jules Verne and Conan Doyle.

AMIS, KINGSLEY. "A new James Bond." *What became of Jane Austen? and other questions*. Cape: London, 1970. Pp. 65-77.

Places F. in the company of Conan Doyle, Wells, Jules Verne, and Buchan.

BERGONZI, BERNARD. "The case of Mr. Fleming." *TC*, CLXIII (1958), 220-228.

"Total lack of any ethical frame of reference" in his novels.

BOND, MARY WICKHAM. *How 007 got his name*. Collins: London, 1966. Pp. 62.

Humorous story of an ornithologist who is constantly being confused with F's famous character.

BOYD, ANN S. "James Bond: Modern-day dragonslayer." *ChCen,* LXXXII (1965), 644-647.

The Bond series is the saga of a modern Philistine, a knight of faith, fighting the demons that attack contemporary mankind.

BOYD, ANN S. *The devil with James Bond!* John Knox Press: Richmond, 1967. Pp. 123.

With bibliography.

BUCH, HANS CHRISTOPH. "James Bond oder Der Kleinbürger in
Waffen." *Monat*, XVII (August 1965), 39-49. Repr. in *Der
Kriminalroman. Zur Theorie und Geschichte einer Gattung*,
ed. Jochen Vogt. Fink: München, 1971. Vol. I, pp. 227-250.
Analyses the success of F's novels.

BUONO, ORESTE DEL & UMBERTO ECO, eds. *Il caso Bond. Le
origini, la natura, gli effetti del fenomeno 007*.
Bompiani: Milano, 1965. Pp. 259.
Eight studies on thematic, structural and sociological
aspects of the James Bond novels. Author bibliography.
Translations into English (1966) and German (1966).

CARPENTER, RICHARD C. "007 and the myth of the hero." *JPC*,
I (Fall 1967), 79-89.

COMFORT, ALEX. "The rape of Andromeda." *L&P*, X (1960),
14-28. Repr. in *Darwin and the naked lady. Discursive
essays on biology and art*. Routledge & Kegan Paul: London, 1961. Pp. 74-99, 167.
Discusses among other things F's "erotic comic-books for
literate adults".

CONNOLLY, CYRIL. *Bond strikes camp*. Shenval Press: London,
1963. Pp. 116.

COOK, BRUCE. "007: The gentleman in decline." *CathW*,
CCIII (June 1966), 169-174.

DAVIS, CURTIS CARROLL. "The figure behind the landscape: The
emergence of the secret agent in British belles-lettres."
SHR, I (1967), 223-235.
Sherlock Holmes and James Bond revive the superman.

ECO, UMBERTO. "Le strutture narrative in Fleming." *L'analisi
del racconto*. Bompiani: Milano, 1969. Pp. 123-162. Repr.
in *Der Kriminalroman. Zur Theorie und Geschichte einer Gattung*, ed. Jochen Vogt. Fink: München, 1971. Vol. I,
pp. 250-293.

EWART, GAVIN. "Bondage." *London Mag*, n.s. V (June 1965),
92-96.
Rev. art. on Kingsley Amis's *The James Bond dossier*.

FLEMING, IAN. "Raymond Chandler." *London Mag*, VI
(December 1959), 43-54.

Exchange of letters between F. and Chandler and a personal recollection.

FURNAS, J.C. "Limey howlers." *New Statesman*, 6 September 1958, 316, 318.
On the failure of English writers to grasp American spoken idioms. Offences abound in F.

GANT, RICHARD. *Ian Fleming. The man with the golden pen.* Mayflower Books: London, 1966. Pp. 172.

GRELLA, GEORGE. "James Bond: Culture hero." *NewR*, 30 May 1964, 17-18, 20.
The spy as a hero of myth and legend, a "Renaissance man".

HARTLEY, ANTHONY. "A hero of our time." *Spectator*, 12 April 1957, 493.
Rev. art. on *From Russia, with Love*.

JONES, D.A.N. "Bondage." *NYRB*, 14 October 1965, 18, 27-28.
Rev. art. on *The Man with the Golden Gun* and Kingsley Amis's *The James Bond dossier*.

LANE, SHELDON, ed. *For Bond lovers only*. Panther Books: London, 1965. Pp. 172.
Various essays on James Bond.

MUGGERIDGE, MALCOLM. "James Bond: The myth and its master." *Observer*, 30 May 1965, 21.

MUIR, P.H. "Ian Fleming: A personal memoir." *BC*, XIV (1965), 24-33.

NEWQUIST, ROY. "Ian Fleming." *Counterpoint*. Allen & Unwin: London, 1965. Pp. 209-216.
Interview (1963).

ORMEROD, DAVID & DAVID WARD. "The Bond game." *London Mag*, n.s. V (May 1965), 41-55.
On the use of ancient mythological motifs and the Freudian structure in the Bond novels.

PEARSON, JOHN. *The life of Ian Fleming*. Cape: London, 1966. Pp. 351.
Detailed biography. Argues that the Bond novels represent his "undercover autobiography".

PLOMER, WILLIAM. "Ian Fleming remembered." *Encounter,* XXIV (January 1965), 64-66.
His novels have a sort of "boyish innocence".

PRICE, JAMES. "Our man in the torture chamber: The novels
of Ian Fleming." *London Mag*, n.s. II (July 1962), 67-70.
"James Bond is essentially an English phenomenon."

RAVEN, SIMON. "You simply can't die." *Spectator*, 20 March
1964, 389.
Rev. art. on *You Only Live Twice*.

RAVEN, SIMON. "Young Adam." *Spectator*, 2 October 1964, 444-
445.
Bond as an archetype.

RAVEN, SIMON. "Vale." *Spectator*, 2 April 1965, 447.
Rev. art. on *The Man with the Golden Gun*.

RAVEN, SIMON. "Amis and the eggheads." *Spectator*, 28 May
1965, 694-695.
Rev. art. on Kingsley Amis's *The James Bond dossier*;
general remarks on F.

RAVEN, SIMON. "The natural man." *Spectator*, 28 October 1966,
552, 554.
Rev. of John Pearson's *The life of Ian Fleming*; general
remarks on F.

RICHLER, MORDECAI. "James Bond unmasked." *Commentary*, XLVI
(1968), 74-81.

SMUDA, MANFRED. "Variation und Innovation: Modelle literari-
scher Möglichkeiten der Prosa in der Nachfolge Edgar Allan
Poes." *Poetica*, III (1970), 165-187. Repr. in *Der Kriminal-
roman. Zur Theorie und Geschichte einer Gattung*, ed. Jochen
Vogt. Fink: München, 1971. Vol. I, pp. 33-63.
Concludes with a discussion of F's spy novels.

SNELLING, O.F. *Double O seven, James Bond. A report*. Spear-
man & Holland Press: London, 1964. Pp. 160.
Tries to explain the appeal and success of the Bond novels.

STARKEY, LYCURGUS MONROE. *James Bond's world of values*.
Abingdon Press: Nashville, 1966. Pp. 96.
Methodist view.

TANNER, WILLIAM. *The book of Bond, or every man his own 007*.
Pan Books: London, 1966. Pp. 111.

TARR, JOEL A. "Goldfinger, the gold conspiracy, and the
Populists." *MASJ*, VII (Fall 1966), 49-52.
Goldfinger bears striking similarities to the 'Goldbug'
villain in Populist fiction.

WEBB, BERNICE LARSON. "James Bond as literary descendant of
Beowulf." *SAQ*, LXVII (Winter 1968), 1-12.
Parallels between Beowulf and the hero in *The Man with the
Golden Gun*.

FOWLES, JOHN (1926)
The Collector, 1963; *The Magus*, 1966; *The French Lieutenant's
Woman*, 1969.

ANON. "Miranda removed." *TLS*, 17 May 1963, 353.
Rev. art. on *The Collector*.

ANON. "No wise." *TLS*, 5 May 1966, 381.
Rev. art. on *The Magus*.

ANON. "Victorian author." *TLS*, 12 June 1969, 629.
Rev. art. on *The French Lieutenant's Woman*.

ALLEN, WALTER. "The achievement of John Fowles." *Encounter*,
XXXV (August 1970), 64-67.
On *The Collector, The Magus* and extensively on *The French
Lieutenant's Woman* as a "remarkably solid historical novel".

AUCHINCLOSS, EVE. "Pop art." *NYRB*, 6 November 1963, 17-18.
Rev. art. on *The Collector*.

BERGONZI, BERNARD. "Bouillabaisse." *NYRB*, 17 March 1966,
20-22.
Contains rev. of *The Magus*.

BOSTON, RICHARD. "John Fowles: Alone but not lonely." *NYTBR*,
9 November 1969, 2, 52, 54.
Biographical article.

BRADBURY, MALCOLM. "John Fowles's *The Magus*." *Sense and
sensibility in twentieth-century writing. A gathering in
memory of William Van O'Connor. With a preface by Harry
T. Moore*, ed. Brom Weber. Southern Illinois UP: Carbondale; Feffer & Simons: London, 1970. Pp. 26-38.

BYROM, BILL. "Puffing and blowing." *Spectator*, 6 May 1966, 574.

Contains rev. of *The Magus*.

CHURCHILL, THOMAS. "Waterhouse, Storey, and Fowles: Which way out of the room?" *Crit*, X:3 (1968), 72-87.

On the "claustrophobic dilemma of the 1960's" as shown in *Billy Liar* and *Jubb*, in *This Sporting Life*, and in *The Collector* and *The Magus*.

CULLIGAN, GLENDY. "The magician and the bore." *Reporter*, 24 February 1966, 56, 58.

Rev. art. on *The Magus*.

DETWEILER, ROBERT. "The unity of John Fowles's fiction." *NCL*, I (March 1971), 3-4.

EDWARDS, LEE R. "Changing our imagination." *MR*, XI (1970), 604-608.

The French Lieutenant's Woman.

FOWLES, JOHN. "Notes on an unfinished novel." *Afterwords. Novelists on their novels,* ed. Thomas McCormack. Harper & Row: New York, 1969. Pp. 160-175.

On his writing habits and the writing of *The French Lieutenant's Woman* then in process.

GRAY, PAUL EDWARD. "New novels in review." *YR*, LIX (1969/70), 430-438.

Contains rev. of *The French Lieutenant's Woman* (430-432).

HALPERN, DANIEL. "A sort of exile in Lyme Regis." *London Mag*, n.s. X (March 1971), 34-46.

Interview.

HICKS, GRANVILLE. "A Caliban with butterflies." *SatR*, 27 July 1963, 19-20.

Rev. art. on *The Collector*.

MOORE, BRIAN. "Too much hocus in the pocus." *NYHTBR*, 9 January 1966, 4.

Rev. art. on *The Magus*.

MUDRICK, MARVIN. "'Evelyn, get the horseradish'." *HudR*, XIX (1966/67), 304-318.

Contains rev. of *The Magus* (305-307).

MURRAY, MICHELE. "A twentieth-century parable." *Commonweal*,
1 November 1963, 172-173.
The Collector.

NEWQUIST, ROY. "John Fowles." *Counterpoint*. Allen & Unwin:
London, 1965. Pp. 217-225.
Interview (1963).

PRYCE-JONES, ALAN. "Obsession's prisoners." *NYTBR*, 28 July
1963, 4, 12.
The Collector.

RICKS, CHRISTOPHER. "The unignorable real." *NYRB*, 12 February
1970, 24.
Rev. art. on *The French Lieutenant's Woman*.

SCOTT, J.D. "Seeing things on Phraxos." *NYTBR*, 9 January
1966, 4-5.
Rev. art. on *The Magus*.

STOLLEY, RICHARD B. "The French lieutenant's woman's man:
Novelist John Fowles." *Life*, 29 May 1970, 67-72.
Biographical article.

TRACY, HONOR. "Love under chloroform." *NewR*, 3 August 1963,
20-21.
The Collector.

WATT, IAN. "*The French Lieutenant's Woman* by John Fowles."
NYTBR, 9 November 1969, 1, 74-75.
Rev. art.

WOLFE, PETER. "*The French Lieutenant's Woman* by John
Fowles." *SatR*, 22 November 1969, 85.
Rev. art.

FRAYN, MICHAEL (1933)
The Tin Men, 1965; *The Russian Interpreter,* 1966; *Towards
the End of the Morning,* 1967; *A Very Private Life,* 1968.

ANON. "A fun atmosphere." *TLS*, 21 January 1965, 41.
Rev. art. on *The Tin Men*.

ANON. "From Russia with Frayn." *TLS*, 31 March 1966, 257.
Rev. art. on *The Russian Interpreter*. Refers also to *The
Tin Men*.

ANON. "Time, gentlemen, please." *TLS*, 8 June 1967, 501.
Rev. art. on *Towards the End of the Morning*.

ANON. "What it's like outside." *TLS*, 3 October 1968, 1097.
Repr. in *T.L.S. Essays and reviews from The Times Literary Supplement. 1968.* Oxford UP: London, 1969.
Pp. 177-180.
Rev. art. on *A Very Private Life*. Refers also to *The Tin Men*, *The Russian Interpreter* and *Towards the End of the Morning*. See also correspondence (*TLS*, 7 November 1968, 1251).

BRONZWAER, W.J.M. *Tense in the novel. An investigation of some potentialities of linguistic criticism.* Wolters-Noordhoff: Groningen, 1970. Pp. IX + 160.
Contains material from *A Very Private Life*.

CAPITANCHIK, MAURICE. "Rich and rare." *Spectator*, 4 October 1968, 476, 478.
Contains rev. of *A Very Private Life*.

FREEMAN, GILLIAN
The Liberty Man, 1955; *Fall of Innocence,* 1956; *Jack Would Be a Gentleman,* 1959; *The Campaign,* 1963; *The Leader,* 1965; *The Alabaster Egg,* 1970.

ANON. "Points of pressure." *TLS*, 10 May 1963, 337.
Contains rev. of *The Campaign*.

ANON. "Sub-Hitler." *TLS*, 2 September 1965, 749.
Rev. art. on *The Leader*.

ANON. "Puzzle of the past." *TLS*, 16 October 1970, 1183.
Rev. art. on *The Alabaster Egg*.

BROPHY, BRIGID. "The novels of Gillian Freeman." *London Mag*, n.s. III (May 1963), 78-81.
From *The Liberty Man* to *The Campaign*.

FULLER, ROY (1912)

Savage Gold, 1946; *With My Little Eye*, 1948; *The Second Curtain*, 1953; *Fantasy and Fugue*, 1954; *Image of a Society*, 1956; *The Ruined Boys*, 1959; *The Father's Comedy*, 1961; *The Perfect Fool*, 1963; *My Child, My Sister*, 1965; *Catspaw*, 1966; *The Carnal Island*, 1970.

ANON. "Nonage and verbiage." *TLS*, 20 March 1959, 166.
Contains rev. of *The Ruined Boys*.

ANON. "Refusal to exaggerate." *TLS*, 2 June 1961, 337.
Rev. art. on *The Father's Comedy*. Refers also to *Image of a Society* and *The Ruined Boys*.

ANON. "Half in love with failure." *TLS*, 19 July 1963, 521.
Rev. art. on *The Perfect Fool*.

ANON. "Leaf's flushed autumn." *TLS*, 7 October 1965, 892.
Rev. art. on *My Child, My Sister*.

ANON. "The poet at home." *TLS*, 25 September 1970, 1075.
Rev. art. on *The Carnal Island*.

DURRELL, LAWRENCE. *"Image of a Society* by Roy Fuller."
London Mag, IV (April 1957), 64.
Rev. art.

FULLER, ROY. "From Blackheath to Oxford." *London Mag*, n.s.
VIII (March 1969), 24-31.
Answers questions about the relation of his poems to his novels, his main pleasures outside literature, his writing habits, etc.

MCGUINNESS, FRANK. "The novels of Roy Fuller." *London Mag*,
n.s. III (November 1963), 73-78.
From *The Second Curtain* to *The Perfect Fool*.

WALL, STEPHEN. *"My Child, My Sister* by Roy Fuller." *London Mag*, n.s. V (December 1965), 97-99.
Rev. art.

GLANVILLE, BRIAN (1931)

The Reluctant Dictator, 1952; *Henry Sows the Wind*, 1954;
Along the Arno, 1956; *The Bankrupts*, 1958; *After Rome,
Africa*, 1959; *Diamond*, 1962; *The Rise of Gerry Logan*, 1963;
A Second Home, 1965; *A Roman Marriage*, 1966; *The Artist
Type*, 1967; *The Olympian*, 1969; *A Cry of Crickets*, 1970.

ANON. "In the news." *TLS*, 11 June 1954, 379.
Contains rev. of *Henry Sows the Wind*.

ANON. "Bitter sweet." *TLS*, 21 March 1958, 157.
Contains rev. of *The Bankrupts*.

ANON. "On the move." *TLS*, 6 April 1962, 229.
Rev. art. on *Diamond*.

ANON. "On the ball." *TLS*, 30 August 1963, 661.
Rev. art. on *The Rise of Gerry Logan*.

ANON. "Character acting." *TLS*, 4 November 1965, 986.
Rev. art. on *A Second Home*.

ANON. "Italian style." *TLS*, 29 September 1966, 906.
Rev. art. on *A Roman Marriage*.

ANON. "Laid out." *TLS*, 26 October 1967, 1005.
Rev. art. on *The Artist Type*.

ANON. "Run for your life." *TLS*, 17 July 1969, 783.
Rev. art. on *The Olympian*.

ANON. "Crrreak, crrreak!" *TLS*, 23 April 1970, 456.
Rev. art. on *A Cry of Crickets*. The central character's
"smugness towards Americans" recalls *One Fat Englishman*
by Amis.

ROSS, ALAN. "*The Olympian* by Brian Glanville." *London Mag,*
n.s. IX (September 1969), 119-120.
Rev. art.

GOLDING, WILLIAM (1911)

Lord of the Flies, 1954; *The Inheritors*, 1955; *Pincher
Martin*, 1956; *Free Fall*, 1959; *The Spire*, 1964; *The
Pyramid*, 1967.

BILES, JACK I. "A William Golding checklist." *TCL*, XVII
(1971), 107-121.

ANON. "Bending over backwards." *TLS*, 23 October 1959, 608.
Repr. in *William Golding's "Lord of the Flies". A source
book*, ed. William Nelson. Odyssey Press: New York, 1963.
Pp. 55-60.
Rev. art. on *Free Fall*. Refers also to his previous novels.

ANON. "The cost of a vision." *TLS*, 16 April 1964, 310. Repr.
in *T.L.S. Essays and reviews from The Times Literary
Supplement. 1964.* Oxford UP: London, 1965. Pp. 35-41.
Rev. art. on *The Spire*.

ANON. "Down to earth." *TLS*, 1 June 1967, 481. Repr. in
*T.L.S. Essays and reviews from The Times Literary Supple-
ment. 1967.* Oxford UP: London, 1968. Pp. 109-112.
Rev. art. on *The Pyramid*.

ADRIAENS, MARK. "Style in W. Golding's *The Inheritors*." *ES*,
LI (1970), 16-30.

ALI, NASOOD AMJAD. "*The Inheritors*: An experiment in technique." *Venture*, V (1968/69), 123-130.
The inexpressible is expressed through the sub-rational of
the Neanderthal man: a daring aesthetic experiment.

AXTHELM, PETER M. "The search for a reconstructed order:
Koestler and Golding." *The modern confessional novel*.
Yale College Series. Yale UP: New Haven, 1967. Pp. 97-127.

BABB, HOWARD S. "On the ending of *Pincher Martin*." *EIC*,
XIV (1964), 106-108.

BABB, HOWARD S. "Four passages from William Golding's fic-
tion." *MinnR*, V (1965), 50-58.
*Lord of the Flies, The Inheritors, Pincher Martin, Free
Fall*.

BABB, HOWARD S. *The novels of William Golding*. Ohio State
UP: Columbus, 1970. Pp. 210.
Attempts to make clear, "through fairly strict formal
analyses, the ways in which the novels develop as stories
and dramatize their meanings."

BAKER, JAMES R. "Why it's no go: A study of William Golding's
Lord of the Flies." *AQ*, XIX (1963), 293-305.

BAKER, JAMES R. *William Golding. A critical study*. St.
Martin's Press: New York, 1965. Pp. XIX + 106.

A detailed study of the five novels from *Lord of the Flies*
to *The Spire* relating them to the early lyric poems, the
play *(Brass Butterfly)*, G's interviews and essays, and his
biography. Stresses the influence of the Greek tragedians
and refutes the picture of G. as a "rigid Christian moralist". Criticizes his achievement modestly: "Golding himself must finally admit us into the reality beyond innocence and ignorance." Annotated bibliography and index.

BAKER, JAMES R. "The decline of *Lord of the Flies*." *SAQ*,
LXIX (1970), 446-460.

BAKER, JAMES R. & ARTHUR P. ZIEGLER, JR., eds. *William
Golding's "Lord of the Flies"*. Casebook Edition. Putnam's
Sons: New York, 1964. Pp. XXIV + 291.

Full text of the novel, an interview by James Keating, an
introduction to *Lord of the Flies* by E.M. Forster, an
article entitled "Simon" by Donald R. Spangler, reminis-
cences by J.T.C. Golding, a brother of the author, another
introduction by Ian Gregor and Mark Kinkead-Weekes, and
various other previously published articles. Extensive
bibliography.

BILES, JACK I. "Piggy: Apologia pro vita sua." *SLitI*, I
(October 1968), 83-109.

In *Lord of the Flies*, Piggy is the most complex of the
four main characters.

BILES, JACK I. "Editor's comment." *SLitI*, II (October 1969),
1-3.

Introductory notes to a "William Golding Miscellany".

BILES, JACK I. *Talk. Conversations with William Golding*.
Harcourt, Brace, Jovanovich: New York, 1970. Pp. XII + 112.
Explores his ideas, life and books.

BILES, JACK I. & CARL R. KROPF. "The cleft rock of conversion: *Robinson Crusoe* and *Pincher Martin*." *SLitI*, II
(October 1969), 17-43.

BLAKE, IAN. "*Pincher Martin*: William Golding and 'Taffrail'."
N&Q, n.s. IX (1962), 309-310.

Parallels and contrasts between *Pincher Martin* and H.T.
Dorling's story *Pincher Martin, O.D.*, published in 1916.

BOYLE, TED E. "The denial of the spirit: An explication of
William Golding's *Free Fall*." *WascanaR*, I:1 (1966), 3-10.

BRAYBROOKE, NEVILLE. "The return of Pincher Martin." *Commonweal*, 25 October 1968, 115-118.
Argues that G's third novel is his most complex.

BRAYBROOKE, NEVILLE. "Two William Golding novels: Two aspects of his work." *QQ*, LXXVI (1969), 92-100.
Lord of the Flies, Pincher Martin.

BROBERG, BRITTA. "Connections between William Golding's first two novels." *MSpr*, LXIII (1969), 1-24.

BROES, ARTHUR T. "The two worlds of William Golding." *Lectures on modern novelists*. Carnegie Series in English, 7. Carnegie Institute of Technology, Department of English: Pittsburgh, 1963. Pp. 1-14.
Good and evil in his novels.

BUFKIN, E.C. "The novels of William Golding: A descriptive and analytic study." *DA*, XXV (1964), 469-470 (Vanderbilt).

BUFKIN, E.C. "*Lord of the Flies*: An analysis." *GaR*, XIX (1965), 40-57.

BUFKIN, E.C. "The ironic art of William Golding's *The Inheritors*." *TSLL*, IX (1967/68), 567-578.

BUFKIN, E.C. "*Pincher Martin*: William Golding's morality play." *SLitI*, II (October 1969), 5-16.

CIXOUS, HELENE. "William Golding." *LanM*, LX (1966), 528-541.
Various aspects of his novels: manifestations of evil, absence of God, allegorical method, etc.

CIXOUS-BERGER, HELENE. "L'allégorie du mal dans l'oeuvre de William Golding." *Critique*, XXII (1966), 309-320.

CLARK, GEORGE. "An illiberal education: William Golding's pedagogy." *Seven contemporary authors. Essays on Cozzens, Miller, West, Golding, Heller, Albee, and Powers*, ed. Thomas B. Whitbread. Texas UP: Austin, 1966. Pp. 73-95.
Detailed study of *Lord of the Flies* and *Pincher Martin* with special emphasis on the process of enlightenment of protagonist and reader. Christopher Martin's "purgatorial experience on the rock is as basically pedagogical as Ralph's experience on the island."

COHN, ALAN M. "The Berengaria allusion in *Lord of the Flies*." *N&Q,* n.s. XIII (1966), 419-420.

COLEMAN, JOHN. "Boys will be beasts." *New Statesman*, 31
  July 1964, 159.
  Film version of *Lord of the Flies*.

COOK, ALBERT. *Prisms. Studies in modern literature.* Indiana
  UP: Bloomington, 1967. Pp. XII + 196.
  Lord of the Flies, The Inheritors, Free Fall (120-127).

COSKREN, THOMAS MARCELLUS. "Is Golding Calvinistic?: A more
  optimistic interpretation of the symbolism found in *Lord
  of the Flies*." *America*, 16 July 1963, 18-20.

COX, C.B. "*Lord of the Flies*." *CritQ*, II (1960), 112-117.
  Repr. in *William Golding's "Lord of the Flies". A source
  book*, ed. William Nelson. Odyssey Press: New York, 1963.
  Pp. 82-88.

COX, C.B. "William Golding's *Pincher Martin*." *Listener*, 12
  March 1964, 430-431.
  From a talk in the Third Programme. Refers also to
  Lord of the Flies and *The Inheritors*.

CRANE, JOHN K. "Crossing the bar twice: Post-mortem consciousness in Bierce, Hemingway, and Golding." *SSF*, VI
  (1968/69), 361-376.
  Refers to *Pincher Martin*.

CROMPTON, D.W. "*The Spire*." *CritQ*, IX (1967), 63-79.

CURTIS, J.-LOUIS. "L'anti-Robinson." *NRF*, XXVI (1965), 507-
  512.
  Peter Brook's film of *Lord of the Flies* shows clearly that
  the book is a reverse image of *Robinson Crusoe*.

DAVIES, CECIL W. "The novels foreshadowed: Some recurring
  themes in early poems by William Golding." *English*, XVII
  (1968), 86-89.

DAVIS, DOUGLAS M. "Golding, the optimist, belies his somber
  pictures and fiction." *National Observer*, 17 September
  1962, 17.
  Report of an interview.

DAVIS, DOUGLAS M. "A conversation with Golding." *NewR*, 4 May
  1963, 28-30.
  General talk.

DAVIS, W. EUGENE. "Mr. Golding's optical delusion." *ELN*, III
(1965/66), 125-126.
Piggy's visual defect in *Lord of the Flies*.

DELBAERE-GARANT, JEANNE. "The evil plant in William Golding's
The Spire." *RLV*, XXXV (1969), 623-631.

DELBAERE-GARANT, JEANNE. "William Golding's *Pincher Martin*."
ES, LI (1970), 538-544.

DELBAERE-GARANT, JEANNE. "From the cellar to the rock: A
recurrent pattern in William Golding's novels." *MFS*, XVII
(1971/72), 501-512.
Childhood obsessions and the attempt to escape from them
are considered the underlying theme in and an important
key to his novels. It is from this source that G's permanent concern with the human condition gains coherence and
achieves full emotional impact.

DEWSNAP, TERENCE. *Review notes and study guide to Golding's
"Lord of the Flies" and "The Inheritors", "Pincher Martin",
"Free Fall"*. Monarch Review Notes and Study Guides, 616.
Monarch Press: New York, 1964. Pp. 85.

DEWSNAP, TERENCE. *Golding's "Pincher Martin"*. Monarch Notes
and Study Guides, 892-O. Monarch Press: New York, 1966.
Pp. 61.

DEWSNAP, TERENCE. *Golding's "The Inheritors", and "Free
Fall"*. Monarch Notes and Study Guides, 893-8. Monarch
Press: New York, 1966. Pp. 74.

DICK, BERNARD F. "'The novelist is a displaced person': An
interview with William Golding." *CE*, XXVI (1964/65),
480-482.
Topics discussed are poetry, Freud and Greek tragedy.

DICK, BERNARD F. *William Golding*. TEAS, 57. Twayne: New York,
1967. Pp. 119.

DICK, BERNARD F. "*The Pyramid:* Mr. Golding's 'new' novel."
SLitI, II (October 1969), 83-95.

DICK, BERNARD F. & RAYMOND J. PORTER. "Jocelin and Oedipus."
Cithara, VI (November 1966), 43-48.
Comparison of Jocelin (*The Spire*) and Oedipus.

DIERICKX, J. "Le thème de la chute dans les romans de W.
Golding." *EA*, XVI (1963), 230-242.
His preoccupation with the Fall; innocence is lost and
evil triumphant.

DILLISTONE, FREDERICK W. "The Fall: Christian truth and
literary symbol." *CLS*, II (1965), 349-362. Repr. in
Mansions of the spirit. Essays in literature and religion,
ed. George A. Panichas. Hawthorn Books: New York, 1967.
Pp. 137-154.
Contains a passage on *Free Fall* and *The Spire*.

DOLBIER, MAURICE. "Running J.D. Salinger a close second: An
interview with William Golding." *NYHTBR*, 20 May 1962, 6,
15.

DONOGHUE, DENIS. "The ordinary universe." *NYRB*, 7 December
1967, 21-24.
Contains extensive rev. of *The Pyramid*.

DREW, PHILIP. "Second reading." *CamR,* 27 October 1956, 79-84.
Repr. in *William Golding's "Lord of the Flies". A source
book,* ed. William Nelson. Odyssey Press: New York, 1963.
Pp. 9-17.
Lord of the Flies.

DREW, PHILIP. "Man on a cold wet rock." *CamR*, 4 May 1957,
538-539.
Pincher Martin.

DUNCAN, KIRBY L. "William Golding and Vardis Fisher: A study
in parallels and extensions." *CE*, XXVII (1965/66), 232-235.
Fisher's *The Golden Rooms* as a possible source for *The
Inheritors*.

ELMEN, PAUL. *William Golding. A critical essay.* Contemporary
Writers in Christian Perspective. Eerdmans: Grand Rapids,
Mich., 1967. Pp. 47.
"Golding turns impatiently from any premature resolution
of the human predicament - from psychology, from sociology,
from Marxism, from philosophy, from religion - on the
grounds that the raw experience of life cannot be cate-
gorized and hence overcome by any of man's abstractions."
Selected bibliography.

ENGELBORGHS, MAURITS. "De romans van William Golding." *DWB*, CV (1960), 515-527.
From *Lord of the Flies* to *Free Fall*. Bibliographical note.

EPSTEIN, E.L. "A biographical and critical note." William Golding, *Lord of the Flies*. Capricorn Books: New York, 1959. Pp. 249-255.

ESCH, ARNO. "William Golding: *Lord of the Flies*." *Der moderne englische Roman. Interpretationen,* ed. Horst Oppel. Schmidt: Berlin, 1971 (rev. ed.). Pp. 330-345.

FACKLER, HERBERT V. "Paleontology and paradise lost: A study of Golding's modifications of fact in *The Inheritors*." *BSUF,* X (Summer 1969), 64-66.

FLECK, A.D. "The golden bough: Aspects of myth and ritual in *Lord of the Flies*." *On the novel. A present for Walter Allen on his 60th birthday from his friends and colleagues,* ed. B.S. Benedikz. Dent: London, 1971. Pp. 189-205.

FORSTER, E.M. "Introduction." William Golding, *Lord of the Flies*. Coward-McCann: New York, 1962. Pp. IX-XII.

FREEDMAN, RALPH. "The new realism: The fancy of William Golding." *Perspective,* X (1958/59), 118-128. Repr. in *William Golding's "Lord of the Flies". A source book,* ed. William Nelson. Odyssey Press: New York, 1963. Pp. 43-53.
His novels are variations on the theme of the "opposition between individual identity, obtained through reason and memory, and a dim, pre-historic consciousness".

FREEHOF, SOLOMON B. "Nostalgia for the middle ages: William Golding's *The Spire*." *Carnegie Magazine,* XXXIX (January 1965), 13-16.

GALLAGHER, MICHAEL P. "The human image in William Golding." *Studies,* LIV (1965), 197-216.

GASKIN, J.C.A. "Beelzebub." *HJ*, LXVI (1967/68), 58-61.
Lord of the Flies.

GINDIN, JAMES. "'Gimmick' and metaphor in the novels of William Golding." *MFS,* VI (1960/61), 145-152. Repr. in *Postwar British fiction. New accents and attitudes.* Cambridge UP: London, 1962. Pp. 196-206. Repr. also in

William Golding's "Lord of the Flies". A source book, ed.
William Nelson. Odyssey Press, New York, 1963.
Pp. 132-140.
The function of the final chaps in the first four novels.

GORDON, ROBERT C. "Classical themes in *Lord of the Flies*."
MFS, XI (1965/66), 424-427.

GRANDE, LUKE M. "The appeal of Golding." *Commonweal,*
25 January 1963, 457-459. Repr. in *William Golding's "Lord*
of the Flies". A source book, ed. William Nelson. Odyssey
Press: New York, 1963. Pp. 156-159.
"Golding has struck the note to which the strings of the
twentieth-century youth are attuned."

GREEN, MARTIN. "Distaste for the contemporary." *Nation,*
21 May 1960, 451-454. Repr. in *William Golding's "Lord of*
the Flies". A source book, ed. William Nelson. Odyssey
Press: New York, 1963. Pp. 75-82.
Attempts to prove that G. is overrated both individually
and stylistically.

GREEN, PETER. "The world of William Golding." *REL*, I (April
1960), 62-72.
Discusses *Lord of the Flies, The Inheritors, Pincher*
Martin, and the short satirical novella *Envoy Extraordi-*
nary. "Golding is, primarily, a religious novelist... the
symbolism of his novels is, in essence, theological."

GREEN, PETER. "The world of William Golding." *EDH*, XXXII
(1963), 37-57. Repr. in *William Golding's "Lord of the*
Flies". A source book, ed. William Nelson. Odyssey Press:
New York, 1963. Pp. 170-189.
Expanded version of the *REL* article.

GREGOR, IAN & MARK KINKEAD-WEEKES. "The strange case of Mr.
Golding and his critics." *TC*, CLXVII (1960), 115-125.
Repr. in *William Golding's "Lord of the Flies". A source*
book, ed. William Nelson. Odyssey Press: New York, 1963.
Pp. 60-70.
Discusses hostile reviews of *Free Fall*.

GREGOR, IAN & MARK KINKEAD-WEEKES. "Introduction." William
Golding, *Lord of the Flies*. Faber Educational Editions.
Faber & Faber: London, 1962. Pp. I-XII.

GREGOR, IAN & MARK KINKEAD-WEEKES. "Introduction." William
   Golding, *The Inheritors*. Faber Educational Editions. Faber
   & Faber: London, 1964. Pp. 11-18.

GULBIN, SUZANNE. "Parallels and contrasts in *Lord of the
   Flies* and *Animal Farm*." *EJ*, LV (1966), 86-90, 92.

GUTWILLIG, ROBERT. "*Lord of the Flies*." *Vogue*, (May 1963),
   154-157, 200-202.

HAINSWORTH, J.D. "William Golding." *HJ*, LXIV (1965/66),
   122-123.
   His novels attack optimistic scientific rationalism.

HAMPTON, T. "An error in *Lord of the Flies*." *N&Q*, n.s. XII
   (1965), 275.
   Piggy's visual defect.

HARRIS, WENDELL V. "Golding's *Free Fall*." *Expl*, XXIII
   (1964/65), 76.
   The naming of Mountjoy, Beatrice, Halde.

HASAN, R. *A linguistic study of contrasting features in the
   style of two contemporary English prose writers, William
   Golding and Angus Wilson*. Diss. Edinburgh, 1963/64.

HENRY, AVRIL. "William Golding: *The Pyramid*." *SoRA*, III
   (1968/69), 5-31.

HENTIG, HARTMUT VON. "'Jus' you wait!': Beobachtungen zu
   William Goldings *Herr der Fliegen*." *NSammlung*, VII (1967),
   383-429. Repr. in *Spielraum und Ernstfall. Gesammelte Auf-
   sätze zu einer Pädagogik der Selbstbestimmung*. Klett:
   Stuttgart, 1969. Pp. 107-131.

HERNDL, GEORGE C. "Golding and Salinger: A clear choice."
   WiseR, 502 (Winter 1964/65), 309-322.
   Contrasting views on evil, man and society.

HINDMARSH, RONALD. "William Golding." *Englische Dichter der
   Moderne. Ihr Leben und Werk. Unter Mitarbeit zahlreicher
   Fachgelehrter*, eds. Rudolf Sühnel & Dieter Riesner.
   Schmidt: Berlin, 1971. Pp. 546-559.
   Biographical and literary essay. Selected bibliography.

HODSON, LEIGHTON. *William Golding*. Writers and Critics.
   Oliver & Boyd: Edinburgh, 1969. Pp. 116.

HOLLAHAN, EUGENE. "Running in circles: A major motif in
  Lord of the Flies." *SIN*, II (1970), 22-30.

HURT, JAMES R. "Grendel's point of view: *Beowulf* and
  William Golding." *MFS*, XIII (1967/68), 264-265.
  Parallels between the Old English poem and *The Inheritors*.

HYNES, SAMUEL. "Novels of a religious man." *Commonweal*, 18
  March 1960, 673-675. Repr. in *William Golding's "Lord of
  the Flies"*. *A source book,* ed. William Nelson. Odyssey
  Press: New York, 1963. Pp. 70-75.
  G's first three novels are religious, his last one deals
  with ordinary modern English society and is therefore a
  failure.

HYNES, SAMUEL. *William Golding*. CEMW, 2. Columbia UP: New
  York, 1964. Pp. 48.

JACKSON, FREDERICK J. *Lord of the Flies*. *Notes*. Coles Notes,
  935. Coles: Toronto, 1970. Pp. 94.
  Technique, style, meaning, character, plot, reprint of
  critical commentaries, etc.

JOSIPOVICI, GABRIEL. "Golding: The hidden source." *The world
  and the book. A study of modern fiction*. MacMillan: London,
  1971. Pp. 236-255.
  Analyses how the "novels mime their own creation by the
  author and their recreation by the reader."

KAHRMANN, BERND. "William Golding." *Die englische Literatur
  der Gegenwart in Einzeldarstellungen,* ed. Horst W. Drescher. Kröner: Stuttgart, 1970. Pp. 306-326.
  His subject is man whom he depicts by allegories. Short
  biography. Bibliography.

KEARNS, FRANCIS E. "Golding revisited." *William Golding's
  "Lord of the Flies"*. *A source book,* ed. William Nelson.
  Odyssey Press: New York, 1963. Pp. 165-169.
  A rejoinder to the comments of Luke M. Grande in *Common-
  weal*, 22 February 1963, 570-571.

KEARNS, FRANCIS E. "Salinger and Golding: Conflict on the
  campus." *America*, 26 January 1963, 136-139. Repr. in
  William Golding's "Lord of the Flies". *A source book,* ed.
  William Nelson. Odyssey Press: New York, 1963. Pp. 148-155.

Ranks G. as a pessimist and a conservative as opposed to
the liberal-humanistic tradition represented by Salinger.

KEARNS, FRANCIS E. & LUKE M. GRANDE. "An exchange of views:
'The appeal of Golding'." *Commonweal*, 22 February 1963,
569-571. Repr. in *William Golding's "Lord of the Flies"*.
A source book, ed. William Nelson. Odyssey Press: New
York, 1963. Pp. 160-164.
Controversy over the question whether there is hope in the
world of *Lord of the Flies* or not.

KERMODE, FRANK. "Coral islands." *Spectator*, 22 August 1958,
257. Repr. in *William Golding's "Lord of the Flies"*. *A
source book*, ed. William Nelson. Odyssey Press: New York,
1963. Pp. 39-42.
Compares Ballantyne's *The Coral Island* to *Lord of the Flies*.

KERMODE, FRANK. "The meaning of it all." *B&B*, (October 1959),
9-10.
Interview mainly pertaining to *Lord of the Flies*; broad-
cast on the BBC Third Programme.

KERMODE, FRANK. "The novels of William Golding." *ILA*, III
(1961), 11-29. Repr. in *Puzzles and epiphanies. Essays and
reviews 1958-1961*. Routledge & Kegan Paul: London, 1962.
Pp. 198-213. Repr. in *William Golding's "Lord of the Flies"*.
A source book, ed. William Nelson. Odyssey Press: New York,
1963. Pp. 107-120. Repr. in *On contemporary literature. An
anthology of critical essays on the major movements and
writers of contemporary literature*, ed. Richard Kostelanetz. Avon Books: New York, 1964. Pp. 366-381. Repr. in
Writing in England today. The last fifteen years, ed. Karl
Miller. Penguin Books: Harmondsworth, 1968. Pp. 131-146.
A novel-by-novel account up to *Free Fall*. He is regarded
as a writer of myths dealing with the basic issues con-
fronting man.

KERMODE, FRANK. "The case for William Golding." *NYRB*, 30
April 1964, 3-4. Repr. in *On contemporary literature. An
anthology of critical essays on the major movements and
writers of contemporary literature*, ed. Richard Kostelanetz. Avon Books: New York, 1964. Pp. 381-387. Repr. in
Continuities. Routledge & Kegan Paul: London, 1968.
Pp. 186-194.

Rev. art. on *The Spire*. Refers to previous novels.

KINKEAD-WEEKES, MARK & IAN GREGOR. *William Golding. A critical study*. Faber & Faber: London, 1967. Pp. 257.

A novel-by-novel approach from *Lord of the Flies* to *The Spire*. The last chap. relates the five novels discussed to the terms "fable", "history" and "myth".

KORT, WESLEY. "The groundless glory of Golding's spire." *Renascence*, XX (1967/68), 75-78.

KVAM, RAGNAR. "William Golding." *Vinduet*, XIII (1959), 292-298.

Particular reference to *Lord of the Flies*.

LACHANCE, PAUL R. "*Pincher Martin*: The essential dilemma of modern man." *Cithara*, VIII (May 1969), 55-60.

LASS, ABRAHAM, H., ed. "*Lord of the Flies* by William Golding (1911-)." *A student's guide to 50 British novels*. Washington Square Press: New York, 1966. Pp. 350-357.

Plot outline, character analysis, critical evaluation.

LEDERER, RICHARD H. "Student reactions to *Lord of the Flies*." *EJ*, LIII (1964), 575-579.

LEED, JACOB. "Golding's *Lord of the Flies*, chapter 7." *Expl*, XXIV (1965/66), 8.

LEVITT, LEON. "Trust the tale: A second reading of *Lord of the Flies*." *EJ*, LVIII (1969), 521-522, 533.

Evil rests in Western society, not in man.

LODGE, DAVID. "William Golding." *Spectator*, 10 April 1964, 489-490.

Rev. art. on *The Spire*; general remarks on his work.

MCCOMBIE, FRANK. "Introduction." William Golding, *Free Fall*. Faber Educational Editions. Faber & Faber: London, 1968. Pp. I-XVIII.

MCGUINNESS, FRANK. "*The Spire* by William Golding." *London Mag*, n.s. IV (August 1964), 84-88.

Rev. art.

MACLURE, MILLAR. "William Golding's survivor stories." *TamR*, 4 (Summer 1957), 60-67.

MACLURE, MILLAR. "Allegories of innocence." *DR*, XL (1960/61), 144-156.

Not exclusively on G., extends also to Faulkner's *Absalom, Absalom!* and Camus' *La Chute*. "Innocence" is something we do not remember but merely believe.

MACSHANE, FRANK. "The novels of William Golding." *DR*, XLII (1962/63), 171-183.

Traces the novels from *Lord of the Flies* to *Free Fall*.

MALIN, IRVING. "The elements of William Golding." *Contemporary British novelists*, ed. Charles Shapiro. Southern Illinois UP: Carbondale, Edwardsville, 1965. Pp. 36-47.

MARCUS, STEVEN. "The novel again." *PR*, XXIX (1962), 171-195. Repr. in *The novel. Modern essays in criticism*, ed. Robert Murray Davis. Prentice-Hall: Englewood Cliffs, 1969. Pp. 266-289.

G's first four novels evidence the general tendency of contemporary fiction: poetic compression in both style and structure.

MARTIN, JEROME. "Symbol hunting: Golding's *Lord of the Flies*." *EJ*, LVIII (1969), 408-413.

MASSEY, IRVING. "An end to innocence." *QQ*, LXXII (1965), 178-194.

Refers to *Lord of the Flies*.

MICHEL-MICHOT, PAULETTE. "The myth of innocence." *RLV*, XXVIII (1962), 510-520. Repr. in *Englische Literatur von Oscar Wilde bis Samuel Beckett*, ed. Willi Erzgräber. Interpretationen, 9. Fischer Bücherei: Frankfurt, 1970. Pp. 316-328 (German translation).

Lord of the Flies.

MITCHELL, CHARLES. "The lord of the flies and the escape from freedom." *ArQ*, XXII (1966), 27-40.

MITCHELL, JULIET. "Concepts and techniques in William Golding." *NLR*, 15 (May-June 1962), 63-71.

His novels are easy to overestimate.

MOODY, PHILIPPA. *A critical commentary on William Golding's "Lord of the Flies"*. Macmillan Critical Commentaries. Macmillan: London; St. Martin's Press: New York, 1968. Pp. 57.

MORGAN, EDWIN. "*Pincher Martin* and *The Coral Island.*" *N&Q*,
n.s. VII (1960), 150.

MUZINA, MATEJ. "William Golding: Novels of extreme situations." *SRAZ*, 27-28 (July-December 1969), 43-66.
Lord of the Flies, The Inheritors, Pincher Martin.

MUZINA, MATEJ. "William Golding: The world of perception and
the world of cognition." *SRAZ*, 27-28 (July-December 1969),
107-127.
The Inheritors, Free Fall.

NELSON, WILLIAM, ed. *William Golding's "Lord of the Flies".*
A source book. Odyssey Press: New York, 1963. Pp. X + 291.
Consists of three parts: a collection of thirty-one previously published articles on Golding, extracts from related readings and questions for documented papers and
essays.

NIEMEYER, CARL. "*The Coral Island* revisited." *CE*, XXII
(1960/61), 241-245. Repr. in *William Golding's "Lord of
the Flies". A source book*, ed. William Nelson. Odyssey
Press: New York, 1963. Pp. 88-94.
Argues that G., in contrast to Ballantyne (*The Coral Island*),
sees the beast in man which is only held at bay by civili-
zation.

NOSSEN, EVON. "The beast-man theme in the work of William
Golding." *BSUF*, IX (Spring 1968), 60-69.

O'HARA, J.D. "Mute choirboys and angelic pigs: The fable in
Lord of the Flies." *TSLL*, VII (1965/66), 411-420.

OAKLAND, JOHN. "Satiric technique in *Lord of the Flies.*"
MSpr, LXIV (1970), 14-18.

OLDSEY, BERNARD S. & STANLEY WEINTRAUB. "*Lord of the Flies*:
Beelzebub revisited." *CE*, XXV (1963/64), 90-99.

OLDSEY, BERNARD S. & STANLEY WEINTRAUB. *The art of William
Golding.* Harcourt, Brace & World: New York, 1965. Pp. 178.
Discusses the novels from *Lord of the Flies* to *The Spire.*
Bibliography of his major publications.

PEARSON, ANTHONY. "H.G. Wells and *Pincher Martin.*" *N&Q*, n.s.
XII (1965), 275-276.
Parallels between the novel and Wells's short story, "The
Remarkable Case of Davidson's Eyes" (1895).

PEMBERTON, CLIVE. *William Golding*. WTW, 210. Longmans, Green: London, 1969. Pp. 30.

PENDRY, E.D. "William Golding and 'mankind's essential illness'." *MSpr*, LV (1961), 1-7.
Both he and Murdoch are literary newcomers, but in their endeavours to evaluate society they do not differ from their predecessors.

PETER, JOHN. "The fables of William Golding." *KR*, XIX (1957), 577-592. Repr. (with a postscript) in *William Golding's "Lord of the Flies". A source book*, ed. William Nelson. Odyssey Press: New York, 1963. Pp. 21-34.
Discusses modern fable on the basis of *Lord of the Flies*, *The Inheritors* and *Pincher Martin*.

PIRA, GISELA. "Die Macht des Bösen in Goldings Roman *Lord of the Flies*." *NS*, n.s. XVIII (1969), 67-73.

PITTOCK, M.J.W. & J.G. ROBERTS. "Michael Roberts and William Golding." *ES*, LII (1971), 442-443.
Certain features in *Lord of the Flies* and *Pincher Martin* derive from two poems by Roberts, "The Child" and "Rockall".

PRAWER, SIEGBERT S. "William Golding: *Lord of the Flies*." *Zeitgenössische englische Dichtung. Einführung in die englische Literaturbetrachtung mit Interpretationen, II: Prosa*, ed. Werner Hüllen. Hirschgraben: Frankfurt, 1966. Pp. 115-122.

PRITCHETT, V.S. "Secret parables." *New Statesman*, 2 August 1958, 146-147. Repr. in *William Golding's "Lord of the Flies". A source book*, ed. William Nelson. Odyssey Press: New York, 1963. Pp. 35-39. Also repr. in *The working novelist*. Chatto & Windus: London, 1965. Pp. 56-61.
Lord of the Flies, *The Inheritors* and *Pincher Martin* are regarded as romance.

QUINN, MICHAEL. "An unheroic hero: William Golding's *Pincher Martin*." *CritQ*, IV (1962), 247-256.

RICHTER, IRMGARD. "Betrachtungen zu William Goldings *Lord of the Flies*." *NS*, n.s. XIV (1965), 332-336.

RICHTER, RICHARD H. "William Golding." *Praxis*, XVII (1970), 62-68.
Biographical data; short discussion of the novels.

ROCCO-BERGERA, N. "William Golding." *RLMC*, XXII (1969), 204-229.

ROPER, DEREK. "Allegory and novel in Golding's *The Spire*." *WSCL*, VIII (1967), 19-30.

ROSENBERG, BRUCE A. "Lord of the fireflies." *CentR*, XI (1967), 128-139.
Fire as structural skeleton and literary symbol in *Lord of the Flies*.

ROSENFIELD, CLAIRE. "'Men of a smaller growth': A psychological analysis of William Golding's *Lord of the Flies*." *L&P*, XI (1961), 93-101. Repr. in *William Golding's "Lord of the Flies". A source book*, ed. William Nelson. Odyssey Press: New York, 1963. Pp. 121-132. Repr. in *Hidden patterns. Studies in psychoanalytic literary criticism*, eds. Leonard & Eleanor Manheim. Macmillan: New York, 1966. Pp. 259-274.

SERVOTTE, HERMAN. "William Golding: Religieus romancier zonder dogma's." *DWB*, CVIII (1963), 437-444. Repr. in *Literatuur als levenskunst. Essays over hedendaagse Engelse literatuur*. Nederlandsche Boekhandel: Antwerpen, 1966. Pp. 82-89.

SERVOTTE, HERMAN. "Sterfelijkheid en licht." *DWB*, CIX (1964), 590-595. Repr. in *Literatuur als levenskunst. Essays over hedendaagse Engelse literatuur*. Nederlandsche Boekhandel: Antwerpen, 1966. Pp. 90-96.
Rev. art. on *The Spire*.

SEYMOUR-SMITH, MARTIN. "Golding's pyramid." *Spectator*, 30 June 1967, 768-769.
Rev. art on *The Pyramid*. Refers also to his previous novels.

SKILTON, DAVID. "Golding's *The Spire*." *SLitI*, II (October 1969), 45-56.

SPECTOR, ROBERT D. "Islands of good and evil: *Tom Sawyer* and *Lord of the Flies*." Samuel L. Clemens, *The Adventures of Tom Sawyer*. Bantam Books: New York, 1966. Pp. 243-245.

SPITZ, DAVID. "Power and authority: An interpretation of Golding's *Lord of the Flies*." *AR*, XXX (1970/71), 21-33.

STERNLICHT, SANFORD. "A source for Golding's *Lord of the Flies: Peter Pan*?" *ER*, XIV (December 1963), 41-42.

STERNLICHT, SANFORD. "Pincher Martin: A Freudian Crusoe." *ER*, XV (April 1965), 2-4.

STERNLICHT, SANFORD. "The sin of pride in Golding's *The Spire*." *MinnR*, V (1965), 59-60.

STERNLICHT, SANFORD. "Songs of innocence and songs of experience in *Lord of the Flies* and *The Inheritors*." *MQ*, IX (1967/68), 383-390.

SULLIVAN, WALTER. "William Golding: The fables and the art." *SR*, LXXI (1963), 660-664.

SULLIVAN, WALTER. "The long chronicle of guilt: William Golding's *The Spire*." *HC*, I (June 1964), 1-12.

SUTHERLAND, RAYMOND CARTER. "Mediaeval elements in *The Spire*." *SLitI*, II (October 1969), 57-65.

TALON, HENRI. "Le mal dans l'œuvre de William Golding." *ALM*, 73 (1966), 3-88.
Mainly on *Lord of the Flies* and its chief characters Jack, Roger and Simon.

TALON, HENRI. "Irony in *Lord of the Flies*." *EIC*, XVIII (1968), 296-309.

TAYLOR, HARRY H. "The case against William Golding's Simon-Piggy." *ConR*, CCIX (September 1966), 155-160.

TEMPLE, E.R.A. "William Golding's *The Spire*: A critique." *Renascence*, XX (1967/68), 171-173.

THOMSON, GEORGE H. "The real world of William Golding." *Alphabet*, IX (November 1964), 26-33.
His view of reality in *The Inheritors* and *Lord of the Flies*.

THOMSON, GEORGE H. "William Golding: Between God-darkness and God-light." *Cresset*, XXXII (June 1969), 8-12.
Seen as an orthodox Christian whose novels explore the concepts of pride and grace.

TURCK, SUSANNE. *An interpretation of William Golding's "Lord of the Flies"*. Diesterwegs neusprachliche Bibliothek, 416. Diesterweg: Frankfurt a.M., 1970. Pp. 68.

VEIDEMANIS, GLADYS. "*Lord of the Flies* in the classroom: No passing fad." *EJ*, LIII (1964), 569-574.

WAIN, JOHN. "Lord of the agonies." *Aspect*, 3 (April 1963), 56-67.
Surveys G's first four novels.

WALKER, MARSHALL. "William Golding: From paradigm to pyramid." *SLitI*, II (October 1969), 67-82.
Traces the structural and thematic development from "certitude" to "process".

WALTERS, MARGARET. "Two fabulists: Golding and Camus." *MCR*, IV (1961), 18-29. Repr. in *William Golding's "Lord of the Flies". A source book,* ed. William Nelson. Odyssey Press: New York, 1963. Pp. 95-107.
Lord of the Flies and *The Plague* as fables.

WARNER, OLIVER. "Mr. Golding and Marryat's *Little Savage.*" *REL*, V (January 1964), 51-55.
A comparison between two island stories: *Lord of the Flies* and *The Little Savage.*

WASSERSTROM, WILLIAM. "Reason and reverence in art and science." *L&P*, XII (1962), 2-5.
Comments on Claire Rosenfield's article in *L&P*, XI (1961), 93-101.

WATSON, KENNETH. "A reading of *Lord of the Flies.*" *English,* XV (1964/65), 2-7.
The novel works in moral and socio-political, not religious or theological terms. The children are a microcosm of the adult world.

WHITE, ROBERT J. "Butterfly and beast in *Lord of the Flies.*" *MFS*, X (1964/65), 163-170.
The novel shows the interaction between man and society. Since evil is inherent in man it is also a force in society.

WHITEHEAD, LEE M. "The moment out of time: Golding's *Pincher Martin.*" *ConL*, XII (1971), 18-41.

WHITLEY, JOHN S. *Golding: "Lord of the Flies".* Studies in English Literature, 42. Arnold: London, 1970. Pp. 64.
Analysis and evaluation of the novel with ample quotations.

WICHT, WOLFGANG. "'Oh, the continent of a man!': Das Men-
schenbild in William Goldings Romanen *Free Fall*, *The
Spire* und *The Pyramid*." *ZAA*, XVIII (1970), 59-70.

WILLIAMS, H.M. "The art of William Golding." *BDEC*, III:
3/4 (1962), 20-31.

YOUNG, WAYLAND. "Letter from London." *KR*, XIX (1957), 477-
482. Repr. in *William Golding's "Lord of the Flies". A
source book*, ed. William Nelson. Odyssey Press: New York,
1963. Pp. 18-21.
  G's first three novels and the "tricky ending" device of
  their final chaps.

GRAY, SIMON (1936)
Colmain, 1963; *Simple People*, 1965; *Little Portia*, 1967.

ANON. "Small-town send-up." *TLS*, 30 August 1963, 661.
  Rev. art. on *Colmain*.

ANON. "A Canuck at Cambridge." *TLS*, 11 March 1965, 189.
  Rev. art. on *Simple People*.

ANON. "What went wrong." *TLS*, 27 April 1967, 364.
  Rev. art. on *Little Portia*. See also correspondence (*TLS*,
  18 May 1967, 424).

CHURCHILL, THOMAS. "Simon Gray's *Simple People*." *Crit*,
VIII:1 (1965), 94-97.

HANLEY, GERALD (1916)
The Consul at Sunset, 1951; *The Year of the Lion*, 1953;
Drinkers of Darkness, 1955; *Without Love*, 1957; *The Journey
Homeward*, 1961; *Gilligan's Last Elephant*, 1962; *See You in
Yasukuni*, 1969.

ANON. "Imperial themes." *TLS*, 19 January 1951, 33.
  Contains rev. of *The Consul at Sunset*.

ANON. "Colonial questions." *TLS*, 28 January 1955, 53.
  Contains rev. of *Drinkers of Darkness*.

ANON. "Tradition and race." *TLS*, 24 March 1961, 189.
  Contains rev. of *The Journey Homeward*.

ANON. "Last of the big-game hunters." *TLS*, 17 August 1962,
621.
  Rev. art. on *Gilligan's Last Elephant*.

HUFFAKER, ROBERT. "Gerald Hanley's *The Consul at Sunset:
Epilogue of Empire.*" *SHR*, V (1971), 377-386.

HEPPENSTALL, RAYNER (1911)
The Blaze of Noon, 1939; *Saturnine*, 1943; *The Lesser
Infortune*, 1953; *The Greater Infortune*, 1960 (rev. ed. of
Saturnine); *The Connecting Door*, 1962; *The Woodshed*, 1962;
The Shearers, 1969.

ANON. "That year of grace." *TLS*, 29 April 1960, 269.
  Rev. art. on *The Greater Infortune*.

ANON. "An English anti-novel." *TLS*, 2 February 1962, 69.
  Rev. art. on *The Connecting Door*. See also correspondence
  (*TLS*, 23 March 1962, 201; 30 March 1962, 217).

ANON. "Return journey." *TLS*, 28 September 1962, 757.
  Rev. art. on *The Woodshed* and *The Blaze of Noon* (reissue).

ANON. "Unmodish iniquities." *TLS*, 24 July 1969, 807.
  Rev. art. on *The Shearers*.

COOK, BRUCE A. "A literary gent." *Commonweal*,
23 February 1962, 560-562.
  Seen as a literary amateur whose "work is in some sense
  autobiographical".

LERNER, LAURENCE. "New novels." *Listener*, 18 October 1962,
630.
  Contains rev. of *The Woodshed* and *The Blaze of Noon*
  (reissue).

LUCAS, BARBARA. "*The Greater Infortune* by Rayner Heppenstall." *TC*, CLXVIII (1960), 281-284.
  Rev. art.

MONOD, SYLVERE. "Rayner Heppenstall and the *Nouveau roman*."
*Imagined worlds. Essays on some English novels and novel-
ists in honour of John Butt*, eds. Maynard Mack & Ian
Gregor. Methuen: London, 1968. Pp. 461-475.

His two "anti-novels" *The Connecting Door* and *The Wood-shed*; "... original approach to story-telling and characterization."

WALL, BERNARD. "Rayner Heppenstall - lone wolf." *London Mag,*
n.s. II (March 1963), 58-64.
Biographical and literary essay.

HINDE, THOMAS (Sir Thomas Chitty, Bart., 1926)

Mr. Nicholas, 1952; *Happy as Larry,* 1957; *For the Good of the Company,* 1961; *A Place Like Home,* 1962; *The Cage,* 1962; *Ninety Double Martinis,* 1963; *The Day the Call Came,* 1964; *Games of Chance,* 1965; *The Village,* 1966; *High,* 1968; *Bird,* 1970.

ANON. "Inside the effigy." *TLS,* 26 May 1961, 321.
Rev. art. on *For the Good of the Company.*

ANON. "Fumbling towards reality." *TLS,* 12 January 1962, 21.
Rev. art. on *A Place Like Home.*

ANON. "Dangerous ground." *TLS,* 24 August 1962, 637.
Rev. art. on *The Cage.*

ANON. "A spoiled weekend." *TLS,* 18 October 1963, 821.
Rev. art. on *Ninety Double Martinis.*

ANON. "A dangerous neighbour." *TLS,* 11 June 1964, 505. Repr.
in *T.L.S. Essays and reviews from The Times Literary Supplement. 1964.* Oxford UP: London, 1965. Pp. 107-109.
Rev. art. on *The Day the Call Came.*

ANON. "No dice." *TLS,* 14 October 1965, 912.
Rev. art. on *Games of Chance.*

ANON. "Forms of insanity." *TLS,* 27 October 1966, 973.
Rev. art. on *The Village.* Refers also to *The Day the Call Came.*

ANON. "Ulterior egos." *TLS,* 7 November 1968, 1245. Repr.
in *T.L.S. Essays and reviews from The Times Literary Supplement. 1968.* Oxford UP: London, 1969. Pp. 190-192.
Rev. art. on *High.*

ANON. "Lilo." *TLS*, 11 September 1970, 989.

Rev. art. on *Bird*. Refers also to *Mr. Nicholas* and *The Day the Call Came*.

BERGONZI, BERNARD. "New fiction." *NYRB*, 22 April 1965, 15-16.

Contains rev. of *The Day the Call Came*.

BERGONZI, BERNARD. "Catch-31." *NYRB*, 18 January 1968, 30-32.

Contains rev. of *Games of Chance*.

BROOKE, JOCELYN. "New fiction." *Listener*, 25 October 1963, 667.

Contains rev. of *Ninety Double Martinis*.

DENNIS, NIGEL. "'Late again,' he groaned." *NYRB*, 23 March 1967, 12-13.

Contains rev. of *The Village*.

MCGUINNESS, FRANK. "*Games of Chance* by Thomas Hinde." *London Mag*, n.s. V (December 1965), 89-91.

Rev. art.

PODHORETZ, NORMAN. "The new nihilism and the novel." *PR*, XXV (1958), 576-590.

Happy as Larry provides "a good illustration of how the new nihilism is being treated in England."

VANSITTART, PETER. "Ominous chords." *Spectator*, 28 October 1966, 560.

Contains rev. of *The Village*.

HOWARD, ELIZABETH JANE (1923)
The Beautiful Visit, 1950; *The Long View,* 1956; *The Sea Change,* 1959; *After Julius,* 1965; *Something in Disguise,* 1969.

ANON. "Points of view." *TLS*, 23 March 1956, 179.

Contains rev. of *The Long View*.

ANON. "A moral climate." *TLS*, 20 November 1959, 673.

Rev. art. on *The Sea Change*.

ANON. "Unquiet weekend." *TLS*, 4 November 1965, 973.

Rev. art. on *After Julius*.

ANON. "Sweet and sour." *TLS*, 6 November 1969, 1273.

Rev. art. on *Something in Disguise*. Refers also to *The Long View*.

HUMPHREYS, EMYR (1919)

The Little Kingdom, 1946; *The Voice of a Stranger*, 1949; *A Change of Heart*, 1951; *Hear and Forgive*, 1952; *A Man's Estate*, 1955; *The Italian Wife*, 1957; *A Toy Epic*, 1958; *The Gift*, 1963; *Outside the House of Baal*, 1965.

ANON. "Emyr Humphreys: *A Change of Heart*." *TLS*, 9 March 1951, 145.

Short rev.

ANON. "Daily rounds." *TLS*, 3 October 1952, 641.

Contains rev. of *Hear and Forgive*.

ANON. "Troubled waters." *TLS*, 11 November 1955, 669.

Contains rev. of *A Man's Estate*.

ANON. "Tempered in the fire." *TLS*, 28 November 1958, 685.

Contains rev. of *A Toy Epic*. Refers also to *The Little Kingdom*, *A Change of Heart* and *A Man's Estate*.

ANON. "In character." *TLS*, 18 January 1963, 37.

Rev. art. on *The Gift*.

ANON. "Wales under stress." *TLS*, 27 May 1965, 409.

Rev. art. on *Outside the House of Baal*.

BURGESS, EVE. "New novels." *Punch*, 9 June 1965, 870.

Contains rev. of *Outside the House of Baal*.

REES, GORONWY. "A Welsh elegy." *Spectator*, 14 May 1965, 641.

Rev. art. on *Outside the House of Baal*.

HYAMS, EDWARD (1910)

A Time to Cast Away, 1939; *The Wings of the Morning*, 1939; *William Medium*, 1947; *Not in Our Stars*, 1949; *The Astrologer*, 1950; *Sylvester*, 1951; *Gentian Violet*, 1953; *The Slaughter-house Informer*, 1955; *Into the Dream*, 1957; *Taking It Easy*, 1958; *All We Possess*, 1961; *A Perfect Stranger*, 1964; *The Last Poor Man*, 1966; *The Mischief Makers*, 1968; *The Death Lottery*, 1971.

ANON. "A private world." *TLS*, 30 November 1951, 761.
   Contains rev. of *Sylvester*.

ANON. "No joking matter." *TLS*, 3 June 1955, 297.
   Contains rev. of *The Slaughterhouse Informer*.

ANON. "The times we live in." *TLS*, 18 July 1958, 414.
   Contains rev. of *Taking It Easy*.

ANON. "Half and half." *TLS*, 21 April 1961, 243.
   Rev. art. on *All We Possess*.

ANON. "Pride and a fall." *TLS*, 24 September 1964, 873.
   Rev. art. on *A Perfect Stranger*.

ANON. "Cottage spy." *TLS*, 10 November 1966, 1028.
   Rev. art. on *The Last Poor Man*.

ANON. "Edward Hyams: *The Death Lottery*." *TLS*, 31 December
   1971, 1638.
   Short rev.

JOHNSON, B.S. (1933)
Travelling People, 1963; *Albert Angelo*, 1964; *Trawl*, 1966;
The Unfortunates, 1969; *House Mother Normal*, 1971.

ANON. "Other new novels." *TLS*, 26 April 1963, 292.
   Short rev. of *Travelling People*.

ANON. "Author as obstacle." *TLS*, 6 August 1964, 680.
   Rev. art. on *Albert Angelo*.

ANON. "The shallow end." *TLS*, 10 November 1966, 1017.
   Rev. art. on *Trawl*.

ANON. "Shake well before use." *TLS*, 20 February 1969, 175.
   Rev. art. on *The Unfortunates*.

ANON. "Marking time." *TLS*, 11 June 1971, 667.
   Rev. art. on *House Mother Normal*.

DANIEL, JOHN. "Novel novel." *Spectator*, 26 April 1963,
   544-545.
   Rev. art. on *Travelling People*.

HEARSUM, JOHN. "Random times nine." *London Mag*, n.s. IX
   (June 1969), 98-102.
   Contains rev. of *The Unfortunates*.

JOHNSON, PAMELA HANSFORD (1912)
This Bed Thy Centre, 1935; *Blessed Above Women*, 1936; *Here
To-Day*, 1937; *World's End*, 1937; *The Monument*, 1938; *Girdle
of Venus*, 1939; *Too Dear for My Possessing*, 1940; *The
Family Pattern*, 1942; *Winter Quarters*, 1943; *The Trojan
Brothers*, 1944; *An Avenue of Stone*, 1947; *A Summer to
Decide*, 1948; *The Philistines*, 1949; *Catherine Carter*, 1952
(rev. ed. 1968); *An Impossible Marriage*, 1954; *The Last
Resort*, 1956; *The Unspeakable Skipton*, 1959; *The Humbler
Creation*, 1959; *An Error of Judgement*, 1962; *Night and
Silence Who Is Here?*, 1963; *Cork Street, Next to the
Hatter's*, 1965; *The Survival of the Fittest*, 1968; *The
Honours Board*, 1970.

ANON. "Career on the stage." *TLS*, 1 February 1952, 89.
   Rev. art. on *Catherine Carter*.

ANON. "Courtship in Clapham." *TLS*, 2 April 1954, 213.
   Rev. art. on *An Impossible Marriage*.

ANON. "A Corvo of our day." *TLS*, 9 January 1959, 18.
   Rev. art. on *The Unspeakable Skipton*. Refers also to *An
   Avenue of Stone*, *A Summer to Decide* and *The Last Resort*.

ANON. "Finding the centre." *TLS*, 25 September 1959, 541.
   Rev. art. on *The Humbler Creation*.

ANON. "The road to hell?" *TLS*, 20 July 1962, 521.
   Rev. art. on *An Error of Judgement*.

ANON. "Cold on the campus." *TLS*, 31 May 1963, 385.
   Rev. art. on *Night and Silence Who Is Here?*. Refers also
   to *The Unspeakable Skipton*.

ANON. "Mockery or plea?" *TLS*, 30 September 1965, 850.
   Rev. art. on *Cork Street, Next to the Hatter's*.

ANON. "Once upon a time." *TLS*, 16 May 1968, 497.
   Rev. art. on *The Survival of the Fittest*.

ANON. "Growing down." *TLS*, 14 August 1970, 893.
  Rev. art. on *The Honours Board*.

HOUGH, GRAHAM. "New novels." *Listener*, 1 October 1959, 542.
  Contains rev. of *The Humbler Creation*.

IVASHEVA, V. "Tvorcheskii put' P. Khensford Dzhonson." *VMU*,
  I (1968), 18-32.

JOHNSON, PAMELA HANSFORD. "An author's special problems."
  JOL, 8 February 1962, 123-124.
  Her own work and narrative technique.

NEWQUIST, ROY. "Pamela Hansford Johnson." *Counterpoint*.
  Allen & Unwin: London, 1965. Pp. 365-373.
  Interview (1963).

QUIGLY, ISABEL. *Pamela Hansford Johnson*. WTW, 203. Longmans,
  Green: London, 1968. Pp. 48.

KING, FRANCIS (1923)
To the Dark Tower, 1946; *Never Again*, 1947; *An Air That
Kills*, 1948; *The Dividing Stream*, 1951; *The Dark Glasses*,
1954; *The Firewalkers*, 1956 (as Frank Cauldwell); *The Widow*,
1957; *The Man on the Rock*, 1958; *The Custom House*, 1961; *The
Last of the Pleasure Gardens*, 1965; *The Waves Behind the
Boat*, 1967; *A Domestic Animal*, 1970.

ANON. "Flashes of insight." *TLS*, 22 June 1951, 385.
  Contains rev. of *The Dividing Stream*.

ANON. "Away from home." *TLS*, 28 September 1956, 565.
  Contains rev. of *The Firewalkers*.

ANON. "The will to live." *TLS*, 12 April 1957, 221.
  Contains rev. of *The Widow*.

ANON. "Preoccupations in Greece." *TLS*, 31 January 1958, 66.
  Contains rev. of *The Man on the Rock*.

ANON. "Seen from the outside." *TLS*, 22 September 1961, 625.
  Rev. art. on *The Custom House*.

ANON. "Creations large and small." *TLS*, 14 October 1965, 912.
  Contains rev. of *The Last of the Pleasure Gardens*.

ANON. "Minimelodramatics." *TLS*, 11 May 1967, 404.

Rev. art. on *The Waves Behind the Boat*.

ANON. "Ravaged." *TLS*, 23 October 1970, 1213.

Rev. art. on *A Domestic Animal*.

GEORGE, DANIEL. "New novels." *Spectator*, 5 April 1957, 457-459.

Contains rev. of *The Widow*.

LARKIN, PHILIP (1922)
Jill, 1946; *A Girl in Winter*, 1947.

BERGONZI, BERNARD. "A part of our time." *NYRB*,
19 November 1964, 12-14.
Contains rev. of *Jill* (reissue).

COX, C.B. "Philip Larkin." *CritQ*, I (1959), 14-17.
His position in literature, mainly as a poet; discussion
of his standing in comparison to Wain and Amis.

CRANSTON, MAURICE. "The young and the established."
Encounter, VII (November 1956), 80-84.
Contains rev. of *A Girl in Winter* (reissue).

CRISPIN, EDMUND. "An Oxford group." *Spectator*,
17 April 1964, 525.
Rev. art. on the reissue of *Jill*.

HAMILTON, IAN. "Four conversations." *London Mag*, n.s.
IV (November 1964), 64-85.
Contains interview with L. (71-77), mainly concerned with
his poems. One question refers to his novels and why he
has not written any more.

WAIN, JOHN. "Engagement or withdrawal? Some notes on the
work of Philip Larkin." *CritQ*, VI (1964), 167-178.
Includes discussions of *Jill* and *A Girl in Winter*.

WELZ, DIETER. "Philip Larkin." *Englische Literatur der Gegenwart in Einzeldarstellungen,* ed. Horst W. Drescher. Kröner: Stuttgart, 1970. Pp. 579-589.
Discussion of his work and development. Short biography.
Bibliography.

LE CARRE, JOHN (David John Moore Cornwell, 1931)
Call for the Dead, 1961; *A Murder of Quality*, 1962; *The Spy Who Came in from the Cold*, 1963; *The Looking-Glass War*, 1965; *A Small Town in Germany*, 1968; *The Naive and Sentimental Lover*, 1971.

ANON. "Skills and thrills." *TLS*, 31 August 1962, 661.
   Contains rev. of *A Murder of Quality*.

ANON. "Limits of control." *TLS*, 13 September 1963, 693.
   Rev. art. on *The Spy Who Came in from the Cold*.

ANON. "Twenty years after." *TLS*, 24 June 1965, 533.
   Rev. art. on *The Looking-Glass War*.

ANON. "Labyrinthine ways." *TLS*, 31 October 1968, 1218.
   Rev. art. on *A Small Town in Germany*.

ANON. "Wishful thinking." *TLS*, 24 September 1971, 1138.
   Rev. art. on *The Naive and Sentimental Lover*. Refers also to his spy stories and *The Spy Who Came in from the Cold*, a "masterly thriller".

ADAMS, ROBERT M. "Couldn't put it down." *NYRB*, 5 March 1964, 13-14.
   Contains rev. of *The Spy Who Came in from the Cold*.

AMIS, KINGSLEY. "A new James Bond." *What became of Jane Austen? and other questions*. Cape: London, 1970. Pp. 65-77.
   Contains a note on L. and Deighton.

CRUTCHLEY, LEIGH. "The fictional world of espionage." *Listener*, 14 April 1966, 548-549.
   Interview with the author of *The Spy Who Came in from the Cold*.

ENZENBERGER, HOWARD. "Up the circus." *Spectator*, 25 June 1965, 827.
   Rev. art. on *The Looking-Glass War*.

MARCUS, STEVEN. "Grand illusions." *NYRB*, 5 August 1965, 20-21.
   Contains extensive rev. of *The Looking-Glass War*.

SAINT-PHALBE, THERESE DE. "John Le Carré: L'écrivain qui venait d'ailleurs." *RdP*, LXXIII (janvier 1966), 149-152.

LESSING, DORIS (1919)

The Grass Is Singing, 1950; *Children of Violence: Martha Quest*, 1952, *A Proper Marriage*, 1954, *A Ripple from the Storm*, 1958, *Landlocked*, 1965, *The Four-Gated City*, 1969. *Retreat to Innocence*, 1956; *The Golden Notebook*, 1962; *Briefing for a Descent into Hell*, 1971.

BURKOM, SELMA R. "A Doris Lessing checklist." *Crit*, XI:1 (1968), 69-81.

ANON. "Doris Lessing: *The Grass Is Singing*." *TLS,* 14 April 1950, 225.
Short rev.

ANON. "Searchings and findings." *TLS*, 24 October 1952, 689.
Contains rev. of *Martha Quest*.

ANON. "The fog of war." *TLS*, 27 April 1962, 280.
Rev. art. on *The Golden Notebook*. includes general remarks on her work.

ANON. "Engaged women -." *TLS*, 24 June 1965, 533.
Rev. art. on *Landlocked*. Refers also to *A Ripple from the Storm*.

ANON. "The wrong members in control." *TLS*, 3 July 1969, 720.
Rev. art. on *The Four-Gated City*. Includes general remarks on *Children of Violence*.

ANON. "Extra-sensory experiments." *TLS*, 16 April 1971, 437.
Rev. art. on *Briefing for a Descent into Hell*.

ALLEN, WALTER. "Doris Lessing: Her early novels." *On contemporary literature. An anthology of critical essays on the major movements and writers of contemporary literature,* ed. Richard Kostelanetz. Avon Books: New York, 1964. Pp. 400-401.

BERGONZI, BERNARD. "In pursuit of Doris Lessing." *NYRB*, 11 February 1965, 12-14.
Rev. art. on *Children of Violence*.

BREWER, JOSEPH E. "The anti-hero in contemporary literature." *IEY*, 12 (1967), 55-60.
L., Updike, Heller, Roth.

BREWSTER, DOROTHY. *Doris Lessing*. TEAS, 21. Twayne: New York, 1965. Pp. 173.

BRITTON, ANNE. "Doris Lessing's whirlwind." *B&B*,
(August 1962), 53-54.
The Golden Notebook.

BURKOM, SELMA R. "'Only connect': Form and content in the
works of Doris Lessing." *Crit*, XI:1 (1968), 51-68.
Offers an explanation of her writings as aesthetic wholes.

CAREY, FATHER ALFRED AUGUSTINE. "Doris Lessing: The search
for reality. A study of the major themes in her novels."
DA, XXVI (1965), 3297 (Wis.).

COLE, BARRY. "More is less." *Spectator*, 5 July 1969, 18.
Contains rev. of *The Four-Gated City*.

GARIS, ROBERT. "Lawrence of Africa." *PR*, XXXIII (1966),
302-305.
Rev. art. on *African Stories*; mentions *The Golden Notebook*.

GRAUSTEIN, GOTTFRIED. "Entwicklungstendenzen im Schaffen
Doris Lessings." *WZUL*, XII (1963), 529-533.

GRAUSTEIN, GOTTFRIED. *Entwicklungstendenzen im Schaffen Doris
Lessings*. Diss. Leipzig, 1963. Pp. 262.
*The Grass Is Singing, Retreat to Innocence, The Golden Note-
book,* and the first three volumes of *Children of Violence*.
Selected bibliography listing various reviews and transla-
tions of her novels.

HARTWIG, DOROTHEA. "Die Widerspieglung afrikanischer Probleme
im Werk Doris Lessings." *WZUR*, XII (1963), 87-104.
Discussion of *The Grass Is Singing* and the short novels
The Antheap and *Hunger*.

HOWARD, RICHARD. "The Lessing report." *PR*, XXXI (1964),
117-120.
Rev. art. on *A Man and Two Women*; mentions her novels.

HOWE, FLORENCE. "Doris Lessing's free women." *Nation*,
11 January 1965, 34-37.
Rev. art. on *Children of Violence*.

HOWE, FLORENCE. "A talk with Doris Lessing." *Nation*,
6 March 1967, 311-313.
Mainly on *The Golden Notebook*.

KAMPF, LOUIS. *On modernism. The prospects for literature and freedom*. M.I.T. Press: Cambridge, 1967. Pp. VIII + 338.

Contains discussion of *The Golden Notebook*.

KARL, FREDERICK R. "Doris Lessing in the sixties: The new anatomy of melancholy." *ConL*, XIII (1972), 15-33.

The Golden Notebook, The Four-Gated City; parallels with Powell.

LEBOWITZ, NAOMI. *Humanism and the absurd in the modern novel*. Northwestern UP: Evanston, 1971. Pp. XIII + 141.

Contains discussion of *The Golden Notebook* (130-134).

MCDOWELL, FREDERICK W.P. "The fiction of Doris Lessing: An interim view." *ArQ*, XXI (1965), 315-345.

First lengthy study dealing with all her novels published so far. She surpasses her contemporaries Snow, Powell and Durrell.

NEWQUIST, ROY. "Doris Lessing." *Counterpoint*. Allen & Unwin: London, 1965. Pp. 413-424.

Interview (1963).

RABAN, JONATHAN. "Mrs. Lessing's diary." *London Mag*, n.s. IX (September 1969), 111-115.

Rev. art. on *The Four-Gated City*.

RASKIN, JONAH. "Doris Lessing at Stony Brook: An interview." *New American Review*, 8 (January 1970), 166-179.

"Dialogue between the two generations of radicals", on students and black power, writer and politics, drugs, liberals, and the old left.

SCHEER-SCHÄZLER, BRIGITTE. "Doris Lessing." *Englische Literatur der Gegenwart in Einzeldarstellungen*, ed. Horst W. Drescher. Kröner: Stuttgart, 1970. Pp. 86-103.

Discusses her merits in the field of the *Bildungsroman*, her narrative technique, her psychological and realistic drawing of character. Short biography. Bibliography.

SCHLUETER, PAUL. "Doris Lessing: The free woman's commitment." *Contemporary British novelists*, ed. Charles Shapiro. Southern Illinois UP: Carbondale, Edwardsville, 1965. Pp. 48-61.

126

SCHLUETER, PAUL. "A study of the major novels of Doris Lessing." *DA*, XXIX (1969), 3619A-3620A (So. Ill.).

TAUBMAN, ROBERT. "Near zero." *New Statesman*, 8 November 1963, 653-654.

Treatment of character in *The Golden Notebook* and the stories of *A Man and Two Women*.

LINDSAY, JACK (1900)

Cressida's First Lover, 1932; *Rome for Sale*, 1934; *Caesar Is Dead*, 1934; *Storm at Sea*, 1935; *Last Days with Cleopatra*, 1935; *Despoiling Venus*, 1935; *The Wanderings of Wenamen*, 1936; *Sue Verney*, 1937; *Adam of a New World*, 1937; *To Arms!*, 1938; *1649*, 1938; *Lost Birthright*, 1939; *Brief Light*, 1939; *Hannibaal Takes a Hand*, 1941; *Light in Italy*, 1941; *The Stormy Violence*, 1941; *We Shall Return*, 1942; *Beyond Terror*, 1943; *Hullo Stranger!*, 1945; *The Barriers Are Down*, 1945; *Time to Live*, 1946; *The Subtle Knot*, 1948; *Men of Forty-Eight*, 1948; *Fires in Smithfield*, 1950; *The Passionate Pastoral*, 1951; *Betrayed Spring*, 1953; *Rising Tide*, 1953; *The Moment of Choice*, 1955; *The Great Oak*, 1957; *A Local Habitation*, 1957; *The Revolt of the Sons*, 1960; *All on the Never-Never*, 1961; *The Way the Ball Bounces*, 1962; *Masks and Faces*, 1963; *Choice of Times*, 1964; *Thunder Underground*, 1965.

KLOTZ, GÜNTHER. "Eine erste Bibliographie der bisher erschienenen Werke Jack Lindsays." *ZAA*, III (1955), 122-127.

ANON. "History and imagination." *TLS*, 14 April 1950, 225.
Contains rev. of *Fires in Smithfield*.

ANON. "The path of honour." *TLS*, 28 September 1951, 617.
Contains rev. of *The Passionate Pastoral*.

ANON. "Jack Lindsay: *Choice of Times*." *TLS*, 23 April 1964, 361.
Rev. art.

BRÜNING, EBERHARD. "Jack Lindsay: *Betrayed Spring & Rising Tide*." *ZAA*, III (1955), 191-196.
Rev. art. on two of his *Novels of the British Way*.

JACQUE, VALENTINA. "Jack Lindsay and Soviet readers." *SovL*,
2 (1966), 170-173.
Major Soviet critical attitudes.

KLOTZ, GÜNTHER. "Lindsay über die Achtundvierziger Revolution." *ZAA*, II (1954), 337-341.
Rev. art. on the German translation of *Men of Forty-Eight*.

MILNER, IAN. "Novels of the British way." *Overland*, 5
(Spring 1955), 29.
Rev. art. on *The Moment of Choice*.

RIVKIS, JA. "Postigaja zakony istorii: O tvorčestve Džeka
Lindseja." *VLit*, 11 (November 1964), 174-188.
L's fiction is in full accord with his theoretical inves-
tigations.

VANSITTART, PETER. "All the conspirators." *Spectator*, 21 May
1965, 669.
Contains rev. of *Thunder Underground*.

WEST, ALICK. *The mountain in the sunlight. Studies in conflict and unity.* Lawrence & Wishart: London, 1958. Pp. 208.
Contains an essay on L. (195-208).

LODGE, DAVID (1935)
The Picturegoers, 1960; *Ginger, You're Barmy*, 1962; *The
British Museum Is Falling Down*, 1965; *Out of the Shelter*,
1970.

ANON. "How to wear a mask." *TLS*, 12 August 1960, 509.
Contains rev. of *The Picturegoers*.

ANON. "On parade." *TLS*, 9 November 1962, 853.
Rev. art. on *Ginger, You're Barmy*.

ANON. "Bucking for Pope." *TLS*, 2 December 1965, 1097.
Rev. art. on *The British Museum Is Falling Down*.

ANON. "Anglo-American encounter." *TLS*, 9 October 1970, 1155.
Repr. in *T.L.S. Essays and reviews from The Times Literary
Supplement. 1970.* Oxford UP: London, 1971. Pp. 188-190.
Rev. art. on *Out of the Shelter*.

BERGONZI, BERNARD. "David Lodge." *Alta*, II (Winter 1968/69), 15-19.

Interview for the BBC radio series "Novelists of the Sixties".

MACINNES, COLIN (1914)

June in Her Spring, 1952; *City of Spades*, 1957; *Absolute Beginners*, 1959; *Mr. Love and Justice*, 1960; *All Day Saturday*, 1966; *Westward to Laughter*, 1969; *Three Years to Play*, 1970.

ANON. "At odds with society." *TLS*, 20 September 1957, 557.

Contains rev. of *City of Spades*.

ANON. "Making a day of it." *TLS*, 18 August 1966, 737.

Rev. art. on *All Day Saturday*. Refers also to *June in Her Spring*, *City of Spades* and *Absolute Beginners*.

ANON. "Reconstructions." *TLS*, 11 September 1969, 993.

Rev. art. on *Westward to Laughter*.

ANON. "The bawdy limit." *TLS*, 23 April 1970, 456.

Rev. art. on *Three Years to Play*.

LEVIDOVA, INNA. "The monologue of Colin MacInnes." *SovL*, 10 (1963), 196-200.

His novels are a kind of monologue in which the author speaks out about problems facing present-day British society.

MORTIMER, JOHN. "Novels." *Encounter*, IX (December 1957), 84-88.

Contains rev. of *City of Spades*.

MOSSMAN, JAMES, JAMES BALDWIN & COLIN MACINNES. "Race, hate, sex, and colour: A conversation." *Encounter*, XXV (July 1965), 55-60.

M's London trilogy deals with aspects of Negro life.

RAVEN, SIMON. "Mother and son." *Spectator*, 4 September 1964, 316, 318.

Rev. art. on *June in Her Spring*, *City of Spades*, *Absolute Beginners*, *Mr. Love and Justice*.

REES, GORONWY. "The teen-age thing." *Encounter*, XIII
(October 1959), 71-73.
Rev. art. on *Absolute Beginners*.

TUBE, HENRY. "In the know." *Spectator*, 13 September 1969,
338, 340.
Rev. art. on *Westward to Laughter*.

WATERHOUSE, KEITH. "Cats among the pigeons." *New Statesman*,
5 September 1959, 283-284.
Rev. art. on *Absolute Beginners*.

WYNDHAM, FRANCIS. "New novels." *Spectator*, 13 September
1957, 348.
Contains rev. of *City of Spades*.

WYNDHAM, FRANCIS. "*Mr. Love and Justice* by Colin MacInnes."
London Mag, VII (September 1960), 70-73.
Rev. art. Refers to the London trilogy and earlier novels.

MIDDLETON, STANLEY (1919)

A Short Answer, 1958; *Harris's Requiem*, 1960; *A Serious
Woman*, 1961; *The Just Exchange*, 1962; *Two's Company*, 1963;
Him They Compelled, 1964; *Terms of Reference*, 1966; *The
Golden Evening*, 1968; *Wages of Virtue*, 1969; *Apple of the
Eye*, 1970; *Brazen Prison*, 1971.

ANON. "Local boys make good." *TLS*, 3 June 1960, 349.
Contains rev. of *Harris's Requiem*.

ANON. "Growing and ingrowing pains." *TLS*, 14 June 1963, 417.
Contains rev. of *Two's Company*.

ANON. "Life's long haul." *TLS*, 8 October 1964, 923.
Rev. art. on *Him They Compelled*.

ANON. "Much-married love." *TLS*, 16 June 1966, 529.
Rev. art. on *Terms of Reference*.

ANON. "Bogged down." *TLS*, 15 August 1968, 865.
Short rev. of *The Golden Evening*.

ANON. "No joy." *TLS*, 29 May 1969, 575.
Rev. art. on *Wages of Virtue*.

ANON. "Time and place." *TLS*, 28 May 1971, 609.
Rev. art. on *Brazen Prison*.

MITCHELL, JULIAN (1935)
Imaginary Toys, 1961; *As Far as You Can Go*, 1963; *The White Father*, 1964; *A Circle of Friends*, 1966; *The Undiscovered Country*, 1968.

ANON. "Four voices." *TLS*, 14 April 1961, 229.
Rev. art. on *Imaginary Toys*.

ANON. "Go west, young man." *TLS*, 18 January 1963, 37.
Contains rev. of *As Far as You Can Go*.

ANON. "The eyes of a stranger." *TLS*, 9 April 1964, 285.
Rev. art. on *The White Father*.

ANON. "Skilful shadows." *TLS*, 22 September 1966, 873.
Rev. art. on *A Circle of Friends*.

ANON. "Look, two hands." *TLS*, 15 February 1968, 149. Repr. in *T.L.S. Essays and reviews from The Times Literary Supplement. 1968*. Oxford UP: London, 1969. Pp. 61-63.
Rev. art. on *The Undiscovered Country*.

LERNER, LAURENCE. "New novels." *Listener*, 17 January 1963, 133.
Contains rev. of *As Far as You Can Go*.

MOORE, BRIAN (1921)
Judith Hearne, 1955; *The Feast of Lupercal*, 1957; *The Luck of Ginger Coffey*, 1960; *An Answer from Limbo*, 1962; *The Emperor of Ice-Cream*, 1965; *I Am Mary Dunne*, 1968; *Fergus*, 1970.

ANON. "Four women." *TLS*, 17 June 1955, 335.
Contains rev. of *Judith Hearne*.

ANON. "Local chaps." *TLS*, 2 September 1960, 557.
Contains rev. of *The Luck of Ginger Coffey*.

ANON. "Self-sacrifice." *TLS*, 29 March 1963, 221.
Contains rev. of *An Answer from Limbo*.

ANON. "Bombing around Belfast." *TLS*, 3 February 1966, 77.
  Rev. art. on *The Emperor of Ice-Cream.*

ANON. "But who am I?" *TLS*, 24 October 1968, 1192.
  Rev. art. on *I Am Mary Dunne.*

ANON. "How to get on with your ghosts." *TLS*, 9 April 1971,
  413.
  Rev. art. on *Fergus*; refers to M's previous novels.

BRYDEN, RONALD. "Dubliner displaced." *Spectator*, 26 August
  1960, 316.
  Contains rev. of *The Luck of Ginger Coffey.*

BUCKEYE, ROBERT. "Brian Moore: *The Emperor of Ice-Cream.*"
  DR, XLVI (1966/67), 135-139.
  Rev. art.

CRONIN, JOHN. "Ulster's alarming novels." *Eire-Ireland*, IV
  (Winter 1969), 27-34.
  Contains discussion of *Judith Hearne, The Feast of Lupercal*
  and *The Emperor of Ice-Cream.*

DAHLIE, HALLVARD. "Brian Moore's broader vision: *The Emperor
  of Ice-Cream.*" *Crit*, IX:1 (1966), 43-55.
  Concludes with a bibliography (51-55) of works by and on M.

DAHLIE, HALLVARD. "Moore's new perspective." *CanL*, 38
  (Autumn 1968), 81-84.
  Rev. art. on *I Am Mary Dunne.*

DAHLIE, HALLVARD. "Interviews Brian Moore." *TamR*, 46 (Winter
  1968), 7-29.
  On his basic theme: "the different selves we are at
  different times of our life".

DAHLIE, HALLVARD. "The novels of Brian Moore." *DA*, XXIX
  (1968), 255A (U. of Wash.).

DAHLIE, HALLVARD. *Brian Moore*. Studies in Canadian Literature, 2. Copp Clark: Toronto, 1969. Pp. VI + 130.
  Novel-by-novel discussion, notes, bibliography of works by
  and about M.

FOSTER, JOHN WILSON. "Crisis and ritual in Brian Moore's
  Belfast novels." *Eire-Ireland*, III (Autumn 1968), 66-74.
  *Judith Hearne, The Feast of Lupercal, The Emperor of
  Ice-Cream.*

FOSTER, JOHN WILSON. "Passage through limbo: Brian Moore's North American novels." *Crit*, XIII:1 (1970), 5-18.

FRENCH, PHILIP. "The novels of Brian Moore." *London Mag*, n.s. V (February 1966), 86-91.
Judith Hearne, The Feast of Lupercal, The Luck of Ginger Coffey, An Answer from Limbo, The Emperor of Ice-Cream.

FULFORD, ROBERT. "Interviews Brian Moore." *TamR*, 23 (Spring 1962), 5-18.
Discussion of his novels and literary opinions.

GIRSON, ROCHELLE. "Interviews Brian Moore." *SatR*, 13 October 1962, 20.

HORCHLER, RICHARD. "A wrench of pity." *Commonweal*, 12 July 1957, 380-381.
Rev. art. on *The Feast of Lupercal*.

HORNYANSKY, MICHAEL. "Countries of the mind." *TamR*, 26 (Winter 1963), 58-68.
Rev. art. on *An Answer from Limbo*.

KATTAN, NAIM. "Brian Moore." *CanL*, 18 (Autumn 1963), 30-39.
His novels show the smothering of the individual's *élan* by the conventions and traditions of society.

KATTAN, NAIM. "Montreal and French-Canadian culture: What they mean to English-Canadian novelists." *TamR*, 40 (Summer 1966), 40-53.
Contains references to M.

KERSNOWSKI, FRANK L. "Exit the anti-hero." *Crit*, X:3 (1968), 60-71.
M. chronicles the exit of the anti-hero of the 1920's.

LUDWIG, JACK. "Fiction for the majors." *TamR*, 17 (Autumn 1960), 65-71.
Rev. art. on *The Luck of Ginger Coffey*.

LUDWIG, JACK. "A mirror of Moore." *CanL*, 7 (Winter 1961), 18-23.
Each of his first three novels contains a scene in which a character faces a mirror and seeks the truth about himself.

LUDWIG, JACK. "Brian Moore: Ireland's loss, Canada's novelist." *Crit*, V:1 (1962), 5-13.

Close analysis of *Judith Hearne, The Feast of Lupercal* and *The Luck of Ginger Coffey*.

LUDWIG, JACK. "Exile from the emerald isle." *Nation*, 15 March 1965, 287-288.

Parallels between M. and Joyce.

PROSKY, MURRAY. "The crisis of identity in the novels of Brian Moore." *Eire-Ireland*, VI (Fall 1971), 106-118.

Refers to his first six novels.

RICKS, CHRISTOPHER. "The simple excellence of Brian Moore." *New Statesman*, 18 February 1966, 227-228.

Short discussion of *Judith Hearne, The Emperor of Ice-Cream* and *An Answer from Limbo*.

SALE, RICHARD B. "An interview in London with Brian Moore." *SIN*, I (1969), 67-80.

STEDMOND, JOHN. "Introduction." Brian Moore, *Judith Hearne*. New Canadian Library: Toronto, 1964. Pp. V-VIII.

MORTIMER, PENELOPE (1918)

A Villa in Summer, 1954; *The Bright Prison,* 1956; *Daddy's Gone A-Hunting,* 1958; *The Pumpkin Eater,* 1962; *My Friend Says It's Bullet-Proof,* 1967; *The Home,* 1971.

ANON. "The loved ones." *TLS*, 17 October 1958, 589.

Contains rev. of *Daddy's Gone A-Hunting,* "a remarkably fine novel".

ANON. "'Be a man, Mrs. Evans.'" *TLS*, 5 October 1962, 773.

Rev. art. on *The Pumpkin Eater.*

ANON. "She alone." *TLS*, 12 October 1967, 953. Repr. in *T.L.S. Essays and reviews from The Times Literary Supplement. 1967.* Oxford UP: London, 1968. Pp. 204-206.

Rev. art. on *My Friend Says It's Bullet-Proof.* Refers also to *The Pumpkin Eater.*

ANON. "Casualty of marriage." *TLS*, 24 September 1971, 1137.

Rev. art. on *The Home.*

LERNER, LAURENCE. "New novels." *Listener*, 18 October 1962, 630.

Contains rev. of *The Pumpkin Eater.*

MOSLEY, NICHOLAS (1923)

Spaces of the Dark, 1951; *The Rainbearers*, 1955; *Corruption*, 1957; *Meeting Place*, 1962; *Accident*, 1965; *Assassins*, 1966; *Impossible Object*, 1968; *Natalie Natalia*, 1971.

ANON. "Nicholas Mosley: *Spaces of the Dark*." *TLS*, 2 February 1951, 65.
   Short rev.

ANON. "Vile bodies." *TLS*, 16 November 1962, 869.
   Contains rev. of *Meeting Place*.

ANON. "Exploiting Anna." *TLS*, 14 January 1965, 21.
   Rev. art. on *Accident*.

ANON. "The wise child." *TLS*, 27 October 1966, 974.
   Rev. art. on *Assassins*.

ANON. "Cross words." *TLS*, 17 October 1968, 1171.
   Rev. art. on *Impossible Object*.

ANON. "Obscure ambitions." *TLS*, 9 July 1971, 797.
   Rev. art. on *Natalie Natalia*.

TUBE, HENRY. "True valour." *Spectator*, 27 September 1968, 435-436.
   Contains rev. of *Impossible Object*.

MURDOCH, IRIS (1919)

Under the Net, 1954; *The Flight from the Enchanter*, 1955; *The Sandcastle*, 1957; *The Bell*, 1958; *A Severed Head*, 1961; *An Unofficial Rose*, 1962; *The Unicorn*, 1963; *The Italian Girl*, 1964; *The Red and the Green*, 1965; *The Time of the Angels*, 1966; *The Nice and the Good*, 1968; *Bruno's Dream*, 1969; *A Fairly Honourable Defeat*, 1970; *An Accidental Man*, 1971.

BALDANZA, FRANK. "The Murdoch manuscripts at the University of Iowa: An addendum." *MFS*, XVI (1970/71), 201-202.

CULLEY, ANN & JOHN FEASTER. "Criticism of Iris Murdoch: A selected checklist." *MFS*, XV (1969/70), 449-457.

MURRAY, WILLIAM M. "A note on the Iris Murdoch manuscripts in the University of Iowa Libraries." *MFS*, XV (1969/70), 445-448.

WIDMANN, R.L. "An Iris Murdoch checklist." *Crit*, X:1 (1967), 17-29.

ANON. "Perpetual motion." *TLS*, 6 April 1956, 205.
Rev. art. on *The Flight from the Enchanter*.

ANON. "Out of school." *TLS*, 10 May 1957, 285.
Rev. art. on *The Sandcastle*.

ANON. "In the heart or in the head?" *TLS*, 7 November 1958, 640.
Rev. art. on *The Bell*; describes M's development as a writer by passing her previous novels in review.

ANON. "Leisured philanderings." *TLS*, 16 June 1961, 369.
Rev. art. on *A Severed Head*.

ANON. "Stretching the net." *TLS*, 8 June 1962, 425.
Rev. art. on *An Unofficial Rose*.

ANON. "Observer profile: Iris Murdoch." *Observer*, 17 June 1962, 23.

ANON. "Fable mates." *TLS*, 6 September 1963, 669. Repr. in *T.L.S. Essays and reviews from The Times Literary Supplement. 1963.* Oxford UP: London, 1964. Pp. 176-178.
Rev. art. on *The Unicorn*.

ANON. "Speaking of writing, XII: Iris Murdoch." *Times*, 13 February 1964, 15.

ANON. "Enter someone." *TLS*, 10 September 1964, 837.
Rev. art. on *The Italian Girl*.

ANON. "Republic and private." *TLS*, 14 October 1965, 912.
Repr. in *T.L.S. Essays and reviews from The Times Literary Supplement. 1965.* Oxford UP: London, 1966. Pp. 40-41.
Rev. art. on *The Red and the Green*.

ANON. "Picking up the pieces." *TLS*, 8 September 1966, 798.
Repr. in *T.L.S. Essays and reviews from The Times Literary Supplement. 1966.* Oxford UP: London, 1967. Pp. 33-36.
Rev. art. on *The Time of the Angels*.

ANON. "Characters in love." *TLS*, 25 January 1968, 77. Repr.
in *T.L.S. Essays and reviews from The Times Literary
Supplement. 1968.* Oxford UP: London, 1969. Pp. 58-61.
Rev. art. on *The Nice and the Good.*

ANON. "Spiders and flies." *TLS*, 16 January 1969, 53.
Rev. art. on *Bruno's Dream.*

ANON. "Re-run for the enchanter." *TLS*, 29 January 1970, 101.
Repr. in *T.L.S. Essays and reviews from The Times Literary
Supplement. 1970.* Oxford UP: London, 1971. Pp. 183-186.
Rev. art. on *A Fairly Honourable Defeat.*

ANON. "I'll move mine if you move yours." *TLS*, 22 October
1971, 1305.
Rev. art. on *An Accidental Man.*

AHLIN, LARS. "'Den berusade båten.'" *BLM*, XXX (1961),
280-286.
Discusses "Against Dryness" which was published in the
March issue of *BLM*.

ARNAUD, PIERRE. "Les vertus du chiffre sept et le mythe de
la dame à la licorne: Essai d'interprétation de *The
Unicorn*, d'Iris Murdoch." *LanM*, LXII (1968), 206-210.

AUCHINCLOSS, EVE. "Oxford Gothic." *NYRB*, 12 September 1963,
38-39.
Rev. art. on *The Unicorn*; mentions M's previous novels.

BALDANZA, FRANK. "Iris Murdoch and the theory of personal-
ity." *Criticism*, VII (1965), 176-189.
Compares her theory with her practice (mainly on *A
Severed Head*).

BALDANZA, FRANK. "Iris Murdoch." *WSCL*, VIII (1967), 454-458.
Rev. of two books (A.S. Byatt; Peter Wolfe) on M.

BALDANZA, FRANK. "*The Nice and the Good*." *MFS*, XV (1969/70),
417-428.

BARROWS, JOHN. "Iris Murdoch." *JOL*, 4 May 1961, 498.
Her writing makes for "sheer *intellectual* enjoyment".

BATCHELOR, BILLIE. "Revision in Iris Murdoch's *Under the
Net*." *BI*, 8 (April 1968), 30-36.

BERGONZI, BERNARD. "Nice but not good." *NYRB*, 11 April 1968, 36-38.

Contains extensive rev. of *The Nice and the Good*.

BERTHOFF, WARNER. "The enemy of freedom is fantasy." *MR*, VIII (1967), 580-584.

The Time of the Angels.

BERTHOFF, WARNER. "Fortunes of the novel: Muriel Spark and Iris Murdoch." *MR*, VIII (1967), 301-332.

Themes, influences and contrasts as shown by the works of these two writers of the honourable second rank.

BRADBURY, MALCOLM. "Iris Murdoch's *Under the Net*." *CritQ*, IV (1962), 47-54.

BRADBURY, MALCOLM. "The romantic Miss Murdoch." *Spectator*, 3 September 1965, 293.

"Miss Murdoch's position has its paradoxes."

BREDELLA, LOTHAR. *Die entstellte Wirklichkeit. Eine Analyse der Romane und theoretischen Schriften von Iris Murdoch*. Diss. Frankfurt a.M., 1968. Pp. 256. Summary in *EASG*, I (1969), 78-81.

Her novels present "a world which is distorted by power, possession, and self-deception" and give "psychological and social reasons" for this. Selected bibliography.

BRONZWAER, W.J.M. *Tense in the novel. An investigation of some potentialities of linguistic criticism*. Wolters-Noordhoff: Groningen, 1970. Pp. IX + 160.

Contains chap. on *The Italian Girl* and a selected bibliography of Murdoch criticism.

BRUGIERE, BERNARD. "L'univers romanesque d'Iris Murdoch." *MdF*, CCCLII (1964), 699-711.

BRYDEN, RONALD. "Talking to Iris Murdoch." *Listener*, 4 April 1968, 433-434.

In her fiction she sees two modes: the mythological and the psychological, and the realistic.

BYATT, A.S. *Degrees of freedom. The novels of Iris Murdoch*. Chatto & Windus: London, 1965. Pp. 224.

Examines the first seven novels. Deals with her theory of the novel, especially with her distinction between the "crystalline" and the "journalistic" type of novel. A final chap. evaluates her achievement and puts her work in a historical context. Bibliography.

BYATT, A.S. "Kiss and make up." *New Statesman*, 26 January 1968, 113-114.
Rev. art. on *The Nice and the Good*.

CLAYRE, ALASDAIR. "Common cause: A garden in the clearing." *TLS*, 7 August 1959, XXX-XXXI.
A certain British philosophical tradition and a certain tradition in the novel are illustrated in *The Bell*: negation of one absolute system, understanding of the human reason and moral interpretation from experience.

CULLEY, ANN. "Theory and practice: Characterization in the novels of Iris Murdoch." *MFS*, XV (1969/70), 335-345.
Parallels between her philosophy of personality and her technique of characterization.

DE MOTT, BENJAMIN. "Dirty words?" *HudR*, XVIII (1965/66), 31-44.
Contains a passage on the "theme of silence" in *Under the Net*.

DICK, BERNARD F. "The novels of Iris Murdoch: A formula for enchantment." *BuR*, XIV (May 1966), 66-81.
"Enchantment" as opposed to freedom is her favourite theme.

EMERSON, DONALD. "Violence and survival in the novels of Iris Murdoch." *TWA*, LVII (1969), 21-28.

ENGELBORGHS, M. "John Wain en Iris Murdoch." *DWB*, CIII (1958), 50-56.
Under the Net, The Flight from the Enchanter, Hurry on Down, Living in the Present.

EVERETT, BARBARA. "*A Severed Head* by Iris Murdoch." *CritQ*, III (1961), 270-271.
Rev. art.

FELHEIM, MARVIN. "Symbolic characterization in the novels of Iris Murdoch." *TSLL*, II (1960/61), 189-197.
Mainly on the women in her first four novels.

FIEDLER, LESLIE A. "The novel in the post-political world." *PR*, XXIII (1956), 358-365.
Contains rev. of *The Flight from the Enchanter*.

FRASER, G.S. "Iris Murdoch: The solidity of the normal." *ILA*, II (1959), 37-54.

Short discussion of *Under the Net, The Sandcastle* and *The Bell*. Emphasis is on *The Bell*.

FRIES, UDO. "Iris Murdoch, *Under the Net*: Ein Beitrag zur Erzähltechnik im Ich-Roman." *NS*, n.s. XVIII (1969), 449-459.

FURBANK, P.N. "*The Italian Girl* by Iris Murdoch." *Encounter*, XXIII (November 1964), 88-90.
Mentions her previous novels.

FYTTON, FRANCIS. "*The Red and the Green* by Iris Murdoch." *London Mag*, n.s. V (November 1965), 99-100.
Rev. art.

GATHORNE-HARDY, JONATHAN. "*The Nice and the Good* by Iris Murdoch." *London Mag*, n.s. VII (February 1968), 97-99.
Rev. art.

GERARD, ALBERT. "Lettres anglaises: Iris Murdoch." *RevN*, XXXIX (1964), 633-640.
M. in the tradition of Jane Austen, George Eliot and E.M. Forster.

GERMAN, HOWARD. "Allusions in the early novels of Iris Murdoch." *MFS*, XV (1969/70), 361-377.
Allusive material (literary classics, myths, biographies, etc.) in her first five novels.

GERMAN, HOWARD. "The range of allusions in the novels of Iris Murdoch." *JML*, II (1971/72), 57-85.

GINDIN, JAMES. "Images of illusion in the work of Iris Murdoch." *TSLL*, II (1960/61), 180-188. Repr. in *Postwar British fiction. New accents and attitudes*. Cambridge UP: London, 1962. Pp. 178-195 (enlarged).
Discusses her first four (five) novels.

GREGOR, IAN. "Towards a Christian literary criticism." *Month*, CCXIX (1965), 239-249.
A Severed Head and Lawrence's *Women in Love*.

GUSTAFSSON, LARS. "Ord för drömmar, termer för beslut." *BLM*, XXX (1961), 286-288.
Discusses "Against Dryness" which was published in the March issue of *BLM*.

HALL, JAMES. "Blurring the will: The growth of Iris Murdoch."
ELH, XXXII (1965), 256-273. Repr. in *The lunatic giant in
the drawing room. The British and American novel since
1930*. Indiana UP: Bloomington, 1968. Pp. 181-212 (consider-
ably enlarged).
She "has become important through the intensity of her
effort to reconcile will and sensitivity."

HALL, WILLIAM. "'The third way': The novels of Iris Murdoch."
DR, XLVI (1966/67), 306-318.
On her attempt to write novels which avoid the shortcomings
both of naturalism and symbolism.

HALL, WILLIAM. "*Bruno's Dream*: Technique and meaning in the
novels of Iris Murdoch." *MFS*, XV (1969/70), 429-443.

HEYD, RUTH. "An interview with Iris Murdoch." *UWR*, I (Spring
1965), 138-143.

HICKS, GRANVILLE. "Literary horizons." *SatR*, 18 January 1969,
32.
Rev. art. on *Bruno's Dream*.

HOBSON, HAROLD. "Lunch with Iris Murdoch." *Sunday Times*,
11 March 1962, 28.

HOFFMAN, FREDERICK J. "Iris Murdoch: The reality of persons."
Crit, VII:1 (1964), 48-57.
Her technique of depicting characters in her first seven
novels.

HOFFMAN, FREDERICK J. "The miracle of contingency: The
novels of Iris Murdoch." *Shenandoah*, XVII (Autumn 1965),
49-56.
Relates *The Italian Girl* to her previous novels.

HOPE, FRANCIS. "The novels of Iris Murdoch." *London Mag*,
n.s. I (August 1961), 84-87. Repr. in *On contemporary
literature. An anthology of critical essays on the major
movements and writers of contemporary literature*, ed.
Richard Kostelanetz. Avon Books: New York, 1964.
Pp. 468-472.
Rev. art. on *A Severed Head*. Refers to her previous
novels.

JACOBSON, DAN. "Farce, totem and taboo." *New Statesman,* 16
June 1961, 956-957.
Rev. art. on *A Severed Head;* deals also with M's narrative
technique.

JONES, DOROTHY. "Introduction." Iris Murdoch, *Under the Net.*
Heritage of Literature Series, 83. Longmans, Green: London,
1966. Pp. 268-292.

JONES, DOROTHY. "Love and morality in Iris Murdoch's *The
Bell.*" *Meanjin,* XXVI (1967), 85-90.

KAEHELE, SHARON & HOWARD GERMAN. "The discovery of reality
in Iris Murdoch's *The Bell.*" *PMLA,* LXXXII (1967), 554-563.

KAHRMANN, BERND. "Iris Murdoch." *Englische Literatur der
Gegenwart in Einzeldarstellungen,* ed. Horst W. Drescher.
Kröner: Stuttgart, 1970. Pp. 281-305.
Her literary theory, her philosophy and her novels are in
the tradition of the European enlightenment. Man is the
subject of her studies. Short biography. Bibliography.

KEMP, PETER. *Fantasy and symbol in the works of Iris
Murdoch.* M. Phil. London (King's College), 1967/68.

KEMP, PETER. "The fight against fantasy: Iris Murdoch's
The Red and the Green." *MFS,* XV (1969/70), 403-415.

KENNEY, ALICE P. "The mythic history of *A Severed Head.*"
MFS, XV (1969/70), 387-401.

KERMODE, FRANK. "Novels of Iris Murdoch." *Spectator,*
7 November 1958, 618.
Rev. art. on *The Bell;* mentions her earlier novels.

KERMODE, FRANK. "The house of fiction: Interviews with
seven English novelists." *PR,* XXX (1963), 61-82.
With M. (62-65).

KOGAN, PAULINE. "Beyond solipsism to irrationalism: A study
of Iris Murdoch's novels." *L&I,* II (1969), 47-69.

KRIEGEL, LEONARD. "Iris Murdoch: Everybody through the
looking-glass." *Contemporary British novelists,* ed.
Charles Shapiro. Southern Illinois UP: Carbondale,
Edwardsville, 1965. Pp. 62-80.

KUEHL, LINDA. "Iris Murdoch: The novelist as magician / The magician as novelist." *MFS*, XV (1969/70), 347-360.
"Combination of pyrotechnics and philosophy" in *The Flight from the Enchanter, A Severed Head, The Unicorn*.

LANE, MARGARET. *"Under the Net* by Iris Murdoch." *London Mag*, I (September 1954), 104-106.
Rev. art.

MCCABE, BERNARD. "The guises of love." *Commonweal*, 3 December 1965, 270-273.
M's heroes as outsiders in search of identity.

MCGINNIS, ROBERT M. "Murdoch's *The Bell.*" *Expl*, XXVIII (1969/70), 1.
Parallelism to Hauptmann's play *Die versunkene Glocke*.

MAES-JELINEK, HENA. "A house for free characters: The novels of Iris Murdoch." *RLV*, XXIX (1963), 45-69.

MARTIN, GRAHAM. "Iris Murdoch and the symbolist novel." *BJA*, V (1965), 296-300.

MARTZ, LOUIS L. "Iris Murdoch: The London novels." *Twentieth-century literature in retrospect*, ed. Reuben A. Brower. Harvard English Studies, 2. Harvard UP: Cambridge, Mass., 1971. Pp. 65-86.
Mainly on *Under the Net, Bruno's Dream, A Fairly Honourable Defeat*.

MAYER, EVA MARIA. *Illusion und Erfahrung in Iris Murdochs Romanwelt*. Diss. Salzburg, 1969. Pp. 130.

MEHTA, VED. *Fly and the fly-bottle. Encounters with British intellectuals*. Weidenfeld & Nicolson: London, 1963. Pp. 214.
Contains an account of a meeting with M. in Oxford (48-51).

MEIDNER, OLGA MCDONALD. "Reviewer's bane: A study of Iris Murdoch's *The Flight from the Enchanter.*" *EIC*, XI (1961), 435-447.

MEIDNER, OLGA MCDONALD. "The progress of Iris Murdoch." *ESA*, IV (1961), 17-38.
On her first four novels which fail to communicate her moral judgements.

MICHA, RENE. "Les romans 'à machines' d'Iris Murdoch."
Critique, XVI (1960), 291-301.
Tragedies in her novels seen as "tranquil catastrophes".

MORRELL, ROY. "Iris Murdoch: The early novels." *CritQ,* IX
(1967), 272-282.

O'CONNOR, WILLIAM VAN. "Iris Murdoch: The formal and the
contingent." *Crit*, III:2 (1960), 34-46. Repr. in *The new
university wits and the end of modernism*. With a preface
by Harry T. Moore. Southern Illinois UP: Carbondale, 1963.
Pp. 54-74, 160.
Discusses her first four novels.

O'CONNOR, WILLIAM VAN. "Iris Murdoch: *A Severed Head." Crit*,
V:1 (1962), 74-77.
Rev. art.

O'SULLIVAN, KEVIN. "Iris Murdoch and the image of liberal
man." *YLM*, CXXXI (December 1962), 27-36.

PAGE, MALCOLM. "Iris Murdoch: *Bruno's Dream." WCR*, IV
(January 1970), 54-56.
Rev. art.

PEARSON, GABRIEL. "Iris Murdoch and the romantic novel." *NLR*,
13-14 (January-April 1962), 137-145.
"Dryness" can be discovered in her own novels.

PONDROM, CYRENA NORMAN. "Iris Murdoch: *The Unicorn." Crit*,
VI:3 (1963), 177-180.
Rev. art.

PONDROM, CYRENA NORMAN. "Iris Murdoch: An existentialist?"
CLS, V (1968), 403-419.
Extensive reference to *An Unofficial Rose*. In her concept
of partial freedom she differs from the existentialists.

PORTER, RAYMOND J. "*Leitmotiv* in Iris Murdoch's *Under the
Net." MFS*, XV (1969/70), 379-385.

RABINOVITZ, RUBIN. *Iris Murdoch*. CEMW, 34. Columbia UP: New
York, 1968. Pp. 48.

RAYMOND, JOHN. "The unclassifiable image." *New Statesman,*
15 November 1958, 697-698.

On the occasion of the publication of *The Bell* M's theory
of art, human nature and society is discussed.

RICKS, CHRISTOPHER. "A sort of mystery novel." *New Statesman*, 22 October 1965, 604-605.

On the occasion of the publication of *The Red and the
Green* M's novel theory and practice are discussed.

RIEGER, VOLKER. *Iris Murdochs "philosophische" Romane*. Diss.
Tübingen, 1969. Pp. 164. Summary in *EASG*, II (1970),
88-90.

Investigation of the "interplay of Iris Murdoch's thought
and art". All her novels from *Under the Net* to *The
Unicorn* are discussed. Selected bibliography.

ROCKEFELLER, LARRY JEAN. "Comedy and the early novels of
Iris Murdoch." *DA*, XXIX (1969), 4018A (Bowling Green).

ROSE, W.K. "An interview with Iris Murdoch." *Shenandoah*,
XIX (Winter 1968), 3-22.

On the dramatization of *A Severed Head* and *The Italian
Girl*. Nearly all of her novels are touched upon.

ROSE, W.K. "Iris Murdoch, informally." *London Mag*, n.s.
VIII (June 1968), 59-73.

Interview, initially sponsored by the American magazine
Shenandoah.

RYAN, MARJORIE. "Iris Murdoch: *An Unofficial Rose*." *Crit*,
V:3 (1963), 117-121.

SCHRICKX, W. "Recente Engelse romankunst: Iris Murdoch."
VlG, XLVI (1962), 516-532.

SEYMOUR-SMITH, MARTIN. "Virtue its own reward." *Spectator*,
26 January 1968, 103-104.

Rev. art. on *The Nice and the Good* (and *The Sovereignty of
Good over Other Concepts*).

SHESTAKOV, DMITRI. "An Iris Murdoch novel in Russian." *SovL*,
7 (1966), 169-175.

Her novels criticize contemporary life in a romantic sense.
Her characters are not angry young men.

SOUVAGE, JACQUES. "The unresolved tension: An interpretation
of Iris Murdoch's *Under the Net*." *RLV*, XXVI (1960),
420-430.

SOUVAGE, JACQUES. "Theme and structure in Iris Murdoch's *The Flight from the Enchanter*." *Spieghel Historiael van de Bond van Gentse Germanisten*, III (June 1961), 73-88.

SOUVAGE, JACQUES. "The novels of Iris Murdoch." *SGG*, IV (1962), 225-252.
Mainly on the philosophical basis of her novels.

SOUVAGE, JACQUES. "Symbol as narrative device: An interpretation of Iris Murdoch's *The Bell*." *ES*, XLIII (1962), 81-96.

STETTLER-IMFELD, BARBARA. *The adolescent in the novels of Iris Murdoch*. Juris: Zürich, 1970. Pp. 158.
Novels and adolescents considered are: Annette (*The Flight from the Enchanter*), Don and Felicity (*The Sandcastle*), Toby (*The Bell*), Miranda and Penn (*An Unofficial Rose*), Flora (*The Italian Girl*), Andrew (*The Red and the Green*), Pierce and Barbara (*The Nice and the Good*). Bibliography.

STIMPSON, CATHARINE ROSLYN. "The early novels of Iris Murdoch." *DA*, XXVIII (1968), 5073A-5074A (Columbia).

STUBBS, P.J.A. *A comparative study of the fiction of Iris Murdoch and Muriel Spark*. M.Phil. London (University College), 1968/69.

TAUBMAN, ROBERT. "L'année dernière at Dungeness." *New Statesman*, 8 June 1962, 836.
An Unofficial Rose is a crypto-comedy of honour and spirituality, a clever, formal *L'Année Dernière à Marienbad*.

TAYLOR, GRIFFIN. "'What doth it profit a man...?': Three British views of the null and the void." *SR*, LXVI (1958), 132-146.
The Sandcastle, Angus Wilson's *Anglo-Saxon Attitudes,* Macaulay's *The Towers of Trebizond*.

TAYLOR, JANE. "Iris Murdoch." *B&B*, (April 1971), 26-27.
Report of an interview.

THOMAS, EDWARD. "Veteran propellors." *London Mag*, n.s. X (April 1970), 100-103.
Contains rev. of *A Fairly Honourable Defeat* (101-103).

THOMSON, P.W. "Iris Murdoch's honest puppetry: The characters of *Bruno's Dream*." *CritQ*, XI (1969), 277-283.

TUBE, HENRY. "Tu quoque." *Spectator*, 24 January 1970,
111-112.
Rev. art. on *A Fairly Honourable Defeat*.

TUCKER, MARTIN. "The odd fish in Iris Murdoch's kettle."
NewR, 5 February 1966, 26-28.
Rev. art. on *The Red and the Green*.

VICKERY, JOHN B. "The dilemmas of language: Sartre's *La
Nausée* and Iris Murdoch's *Under the Net*." *JNT*, I (1971),
69-76.

VIEBROCK, HELMUT. "Iris Murdoch: *Under the Net*." *Der moderne englische Roman. Interpretationen*, ed. Horst Oppel.
Schmidt: Berlin, 1971 (rev. ed.). Pp. 346-360.

WALL, STEPHEN. "The bell in *The Bell*." *EIC*, XIII (1963),
265-273.

WASSON, RICHARD. "Notes on a new sensibility." *PR*, XXXVI
(1969), 460-477.
Partly a discussion of M's "objections to dramatic myth
and unifying metaphor".

WEATHERHEAD, A.K. "Background with figures in Iris Murdoch."
TSLL, X (1968/69), 635-648.
On her art of relating person and environment.

WHITESIDE, GEORGE. "The novels of Iris Murdoch." *Crit*,
VII:1 (1964), 27-47.
"Miss Murdoch is a realist and a realist satirist." Dis-
cusses the novels from *Under the Net* to *The Unicorn*.

WIDMANN, R.L. "Murdoch's *Under the Net*: Theory and practice
of fiction." *Crit*, X:1 (1967), 5-16.

WOLFE, PETER. "Philosophical themes in the novels of Iris
Murdoch." *DA*, XXVI (1965), 3357-3358 (Wis.).

WOLFE, PETER. *The disciplined heart. Iris Murdoch and her
novels*. Missouri UP: Columbia, 1966. Pp. XII + 220.
Discussion of her philosophical essays, especially her
remarks about fiction; followed by a close novel-by-novel
approach: *Under the Net* to *The Italian Girl*. Bibliography.

NEWBY, P.H. (1918)

A Journey to the Interior, 1945; *Agents and Witnesses,* 1947;
Mariner Dances, 1948; *The Snow Pasture,* 1949; *The Young May
Moon,* 1950; *A Season in England,* 1951; *A Step to Silence,* 1952;
The Retreat, 1953; *The Picnic at Sakkara,* 1955; *Revolution and
Roses,* 1957; *A Guest and His Going,* 1959; *The Barbary Light,*
1962; *One of the Founders,* 1965; *Something to Answer For,* 1968.

ANON. "Men in training." *TLS,* 4 April 1952, 233.
   Rev. art. on *A Step to Silence.*

ANON. "P.H. Newby: *The Retreat.*" *TLS,* 13 March 1953, 165.
   Rev. art.

ANON. "Good-will gesture." *TLS,* 19 June 1959, 365.
   Rev. art. on *A Guest and His Going.*

ANON. "A novelist on his own." *TLS,* 6 April 1962, 232.
   Repr. in *T.L.S. 1962. Essays and reviews from The Times
   Literary Supplement.* Oxford UP: London, 1963. Pp. 101-106.
   Rev. art. on *The Barbary Light;* mentions briefly N's
   previous novels.

ANON. "Dark but light." *TLS,* 16 September 1965, 795.
   Rev. art. on *One of the Founders.*

ANON. "Who's who?" *TLS,* 21 November 1968, 1301.
   Rev. art. on *Something to Answer For.*

BUFKIN, E.C. "Quest in the novels of P.H. Newby." *Crit,*
   VIII:1 (1965), 51-62.
   "... the quester moves away from disorder (misunderstand-
   ing) toward order (reconciliation)." Mainly on *A Journey
   to the Interior, The Retreat* and *The Barbary Light.*

DICKERSON, LUCIA. "Portrait of the artist as a Jung man."
   KR, XXI (1959), 58-83.
   N's indebtedness to Jungian myths and archetypes.

LE FRANC, BOLIVAR. "'We're weak animals in a cold and hostile
   universe.'" *B&B,* (July 1969), 30-32.
   Report of an interview.

MATHEWS, F.X. "The fiction of P.H. Newby." *DA,* XXV (1964),
   2515-2516 (Wis.).

MATHEWS, F.X. "Newby on the Nile: The comic trilogy." *TCL*,
XIV (1968/69), 3-16.
The Picnic at Sakkara, Revolution and Roses, A Guest and
His Going.

MATHEWS, F.X. "Witness to violence: The war novels of P.H.
Newby." *TSLL*, XII (1970/71), 121-135.
Aspects of the "witness theme".

POSS, STANLEY. "Manners and myths in the novels of P.H.
Newby." *Crit*, XII:1 (1970), 5-19.
Distinguishes between his romances and his political
comedies.

SPINNER, KASPAR. "P.H. Newby." *Englische Literatur der Gegen-*
wart in Einzeldarstellungen, ed. Horst W. Drescher. Kröner:
Stuttgart, 1970. Pp. 236-249.
All his novels center round the conflict between imagination and reality. Regarded as one of the avant-gardists
of the "realistic novel". Short biography. Bibliography.

WATTS, HAROLD H. "P.H. Newby: Experience as farce." *Perspec-*
tive, X (1958/59), 106-117.
His novels present experience as farce.

O'BRIEN, EDNA (1932)
The Country Girls, 1960; *The Lonely Girl,* 1962; *Girls in*
Their Married Bliss, 1964; *August Is a Wicked Month,* 1965;
Casualties of Peace, 1966; *A Pagan Place,* 1970; *Zee & Co.,*
1971.

ANON. "Women in love." *TLS*, 18 May 1962, 353.
Contains rev. of *The Lonely Girl*. Refers also to *The*
Country Girls.

ANON. "Woman talk." *TLS*, 12 November 1964, 1012.
Rev. art. on *Girls in Their Married Bliss*.

ANON. "Girl meets men." *TLS*, 7 October 1965, 893.
Rev. art. on *August Is a Wicked Month*.

ANON. "Glass widow." *TLS*, 3 November 1966, 997.
Rev. art. on *Casualties of Peace*.

ANON. "Have done with you." *TLS*, 16 April 1970, 401. Repr.
in *T.L.S. Essays and reviews from The Times Literary
Supplement. 1970.* Oxford UP: London, 1971. Pp. 36-38.
Rev. art. on *A Pagan Place;* compares the novel with
Spark's *The Prime of Miss Jean Brodie* and refers also to
O's previous writings.

BERGONZI, BERNARD. "Mixed company." *NYRB*, 3 June 1965, 19-20.
Contains rev. of *August Is a Wicked Month.*

BERGONZI, BERNARD. "Total recall." *NYRB*, 24 August 1967,
37-38.
Contains rev. of *Casualties of Peace.*

MCMAHON, SEAN. "A sex by themselves: An interim report on
the novels of Edna O'Brien." *Eire-Ireland*, II (Spring
1967), 79-87.

SHEEHY, MICHAEL. "Irish literary censorship." *Nation*,
30 June 1969, 833-836.
O. as victim of the Irish censorship board.

SYMONS, JULIAN. "Irish whiskey." *London Mag*, n.s. X (July/
August 1970), 184-186.
Contains rev. of *A Pagan Place.*

POWELL, ANTHONY (1905)
Afternoon Men, 1931; *Venusberg,* 1932; *From a View to a Death,*
1933; *Agents and Patients,* 1936; *What's Become of Waring,*
1939; *A Dance to the Music of Time: A Question of Upbringing,*
1951, *A Buyer's Market,* 1952, *The Acceptance World,* 1955, *At
Lady Molly's,* 1957, *Casanova's Chinese Restaurant,* 1960, *The
Kindly Ones,* 1962, *The Valley of Bones,* 1964, *The Soldier's
Art,* 1966, *The Military Philosóphers,* 1968, *Books Do Furnish
a Room,* 1971.

ANON. "From a chase to a view." *TLS*, 16 February 1951, 100.
Rev. art. on *A Question of Upbringing.*

ANON. "Time marches on." *TLS*, 1 November 1957, 653.
Rev. art. on *At Lady Molly's.*

ANON. "Nick goes to war." *TLS*, 5 March 1964, 189. Repr. in
T.L.S. Essays and reviews from The Times Literary Supple-

ment. 1964. Oxford UP: London, 1965. Pp. 105-107.

Rev. art. on *The Valley of Bones.* Refers also to previous
novels of *The Music of Time* sequence.

ANON. "War games." *TLS,* 15 September 1966, 853. Repr. in
*T.L.S. Essays and reviews from The Times Literary Supple-
ment. 1966.* Oxford UP: London, 1967. Pp. 74-75.

Rev. art. on *The Soldier's Art.*

ANON. "Dancing in the dark." *TLS,* 17 October 1968, 1170.
Repr. in *T.L.S. Essays and reviews from The Times Liter-
ary Supplement. 1968.* Oxford UP: London, 1969.
Pp. 183-185.

Rev. art. on *The Military Philosophers.*

ANON. "Time marches on." *TLS,* 19 February 1971, 199. Repr.
in *T.L.S. Essays and reviews from The Times Literary
Supplement. 1971.* Oxford UP: London, 1972. Pp. 202-204.

Rev. art. on *Books Do Furnish a Room.*

AMIS, KINGSLEY. "Afternoon world." *Spectator,* 13 May 1955,
619-620.

Rev. art. on *The Acceptance World.* Refers also to P's
earlier novels.

BAILEY, PAUL. "Sniffing the scandal." *London Mag,* n.s. XI
(August-September 1971), 147-150.

Rev. art. on *Books Do Furnish a Room.*

BERGONZI, BERNARD. *Anthony Powell.* WTW, 144. Longmans,
Green: London, 1962. Pp. 24-40.

BERGONZI, BERNARD. "At Anthony Powell's." *NYRB,* 8 October
1964, 11-12.

Rev. art. on *The Valley of Bones.*

BERGONZI, BERNARD. "Anthony Powell: 9/12." *CritQ,* XI (1969),
76-86.

The first nine novels of *The Music of Time.*

BJORNSON, BARBARA ANN. "An examination of narrative strategy
in *A la recherche du temps perdu* and *A Dance to the Music
of Time.*" *DA,* XXX (1969), 679A (U. of Wash.).

BROOKE, JOCELYN. "From Wauchop to Widmerpool." *London Mag,*
VII (September 1960), 60-64.

Links between the five pre-war novels and *The Music of Time* novels.

DAVIS, DOUGLAS M. "An interview with Anthony Powell: Frome, England, June 1962." *CE*, XXIV (1962/63), 533-536.
Various topics; *The Music of Time*, character drawing, etc.

FENWICK, J.H. "*The Music of Time*." *London Mag,* n.s. II (July 1962), 63-67.
Rev. art. on *The Kindly Ones*.

FULLER, ROY. "*The Valley of Bones* by Anthony Powell." *London Mag*, n.s. IV (May 1964), 86-88.
Rev. art.

GLAZEBROOK, MARK. "The art of Horace Isbister, E. Bosworth Deacon and Ralph Barnby." *London Mag*, n.s. VII (November 1967), 76-82.
On the imaginary artists in *The Music of Time*; P. evokes the climate of taste in art in the 20s and 30s.

GRANSDEN, K.W. "Taste of the old time: On Anthony Powell." *Encounter*, XXVII (December 1966), 106-108.
Rev. art. on *The Soldier's Art*.

GUTIERREZ, DONALD K. "A critical study of Anthony Powell's *A Dance to the Music of Time*." *DAI*, XXX (1969), 724A (U.C.L.A.).

GUTWILLIG, ROBERT. "A walk around London with Anthony Powell." *NYTBR*, 30 September 1962, 5, 30.
Interview.

HALL, JAMES. "The uses of polite surprise: Anthony Powell." *EIC*, XII (1962), 167-183. Repr. in *The tragic comedians. Seven modern British novelists*. Indiana UP: Bloomington, 1966 (3rd printing). Pp. 129-150 (enlarged).
Discussion of the novels up to *At Lady Molly's* (*EIC*); *Casanova's Chinese Restaurant* (*The tragic comedians*).

HARTLEY, L.P. "Jenkins at war." *Spectator*, 20 March 1964, 383.
Rev. art. on *The Valley of Bones*.

HERRING, H.D. "Anthony Powell: A reaction against determinism." *BSUF*, IX (Winter 1968), 17-21.
The Music of Time.

HYNES, SAM. "Novelist of society." *Commonweal*, 31 July 1958,
396-397.

The Music of Time is "essentially a recollection of and a
meditation on the history of a segment of English society
in the years between the two wars."

KERMODE, FRANK. "The interpretation of the times." *Encounter*,
XV (September 1960), 71-76. Repr. in *Puzzles and epiphanies.*
Essays and reviews 1958-1961. Routledge & Kegan Paul:
London, 1962. Pp. 121-130.

Contains rev. of *Casanova's Chinese Restaurant* which is
regarded as a 'slow-motion' farce "having to do with lost
souls and disordered times".

LARKIN, PHILIP. "Mr. Powell's mural." *New Statesman*,
19 February 1971, 243-244.

The main element lacking in *The Music of Time* is the sense
of time.

LECLAIRE, LUCIEN A. "Anthony Powell: Biographie spirituelle
d'une génération." *EA*, IX (1956), 23-27.

The Music of Time, up to *The Acceptance World.*

LEE, JAMES WARD. "The novels of Anthony Powell." *DA*, XXV
(1965), 5281-5282 (Auburn).

MCCALL, RAYMOND G. "Anthony Powell's gallery." *CE*, XXVII
(1965/66), 227-232.

Characters in *The Music of Time.*

MCLAUGHLIN, RICHARD. "Anthony Powell: *The Music of Time.*"
B&B, (April 1971), 4-8.

MCLEOD, DAN. "The art of Anthony Powell." *DAI*, XXX (1969),
1174A (Claremont).

MCLEOD, DAN. "Anthony Powell: Some notes on the art of the
sequence novel." *SIN*, III (1971), 44-63.

Analyses themes and techniques.

MAES-JELINEK, HENA. "Anthony Powell." *Criticism of society
in the English novel between the wars.* Société d'Editions
"Les Belles Lettres": Paris, 1970. Pp. 499-518.

The Music of Time as a "sad comment on the past".

MAYNE, RICHARD. "Incidental music by Anthony Powell."
New Statesman, 6 July 1962, 17-18.

Rev. art. on *The Kindly Ones.*

MIZENER, ARTHUR. "A dance to the music of time: The novels
of Anthony Powell." *KR,* XXII (1960), 79-92.

MIZENER, ARTHUR. "The novel and nature in the twentieth
century: Anthony Powell and James Gould Cozzens." *The sense
of life in the modern novel.* Houghton Mifflin: Boston, 1964.
Pp. 79-103.
P's novels are "undistorted by doctrine".

MORRIS, ROBERT K. "The early novels of Anthony Powell: A
thematic study." *DA,* XXV (1965), 4152-4153 (Wis.).

MORRIS, ROBERT K. *The novels of Anthony Powell.* Critical
Essays in Modern Literature. Pittsburgh UP: Pittsburgh,
1968. Pp. XI + 253.
Discussion of all novels up to 1968. The struggle between
the power-hungry and the sensualist is discerned as his
central theme.

POWELL, ANTHONY. "Taken from life." *TC,* CLXX (July 1961),
50-53.
Report of an interview conducted by W.J. Weatherby.

PRITCHETT, V.S. "Books in general." *New Statesman,*
28 June 1952, 774-775.
Rev. art. on *A Buyer's Market.* Refers also to the previous
novels of *The Music of Time.*

PRITCHETT, V.S. "The bored barbarians." *The working novelist.*
Chatto & Windus: London, 1965. Pp. 172-180.
P. is a master of farce. His novels also reflect his pre-
occupations with social questions.

QUESENBERY, W.D., JR. "Anthony Powell: The anatomy of decay."
Crit, VII:1 (1964), 5-26.
English society from 1921 to 1939 in *The Music of Time;*
P. deals with time not only in a linear way but also
cyclically.

QUESENBERY, W.D., JR. "Anthony Powell." *ConL,* X (1969),
124-126.
Rev. art. on Robert K. Morris's study.

RADNER, SANFORD. "The world of Anthony Powell." *ClareQ,* X:2
(1963), 41-57.

RADNER, SANFORD. "Powell's early novels: A study in point
of view." *Renascence,* XVI (1963/64), 194-200.

RADNER, SANFORD. "Anthony Powell and *The Valley of Bones.*"
ER, XV (April 1965), 8-9.

RUOFF, GENE W. "Social mobility and the artist in *Manhattan Transfer* and *The Music of Time.*" *WSCL,* V (Winter 1964), 64-76.

RUSSELL, JOHN. "Quintet from the '30s: Anthony Powell." *KR,* XXVII (1965), 698-726.
His early novels *(Afternoon Men, Venusberg, From a View to a Death, Agents and Patients, What's Become of Waring)* are a comedy of manners.

RUSSELL, JOHN. *Anthony Powell. A quintet, sextet, and war.*
Indiana UP: Bloomington, 1970. Pp. XI + 238.
A critical account of his five novels from the 30s and of the nine completed novels in *The Music of Time* sequence. Chap. on stylistic aspects.

SCHLESINGER, ARTHUR L., JR. "Waugh à la Proust." *NewR,*
20 October 1958, 20-21.
P. is profoundly influenced by Proust and continues to rival Waugh.

SEYMOUR-SMITH, MARTIN. "Jenkins marches on." *Spectator,*
16 September 1966, 353.
Rev. art. on *The Soldier's Art.*

SHAPIRO, CHARLES. "Widmerpool and *The Music of Time.*" *Contemporary British novelists,* ed. Charles Shapiro. Southern Illinois UP: Carbondale, Edwardsville, 1965. Pp. 81-94.

STÜRZL, ERWIN. "Anthony Powell." *Englische Literatur der Gegenwart in Einzeldarstellungen,* ed. Horst W. Drescher. Kröner: Stuttgart, 1970. Pp. 65-85.
He does not want to give an all-embracing view of life, but confronts his readers with a panorama, a kaleidoscope of ideas. Short biography. Bibliography.

SYMONS, JULIAN. "Time's laughing stocks." *TLS,* 29 June 1962, 476. Repr. under the title "A long way from Firbank" in *Critical occasions. . .* in Hamilton: London, 1966. Pp. 74-79.
Rev. art. on *The Kindly Ones* and Waugh's *Decline and Fall.*

TUBE, HENRY. "Facing the music." *Spectator,* 18 October 1968, 547-548.
Rev. art. on *The Military Philosophers.*

VINSON, JAMES. "Anthony Powell's *Music of Time*." *Perspective*,
  X (1958/59), 146-152.

VOORHEES, RICHARD J. "Anthony Powell: The first phase." *PrS*,
  XXVIII (1954/55), 337-344.
  The early novels display tragedy and comedy growing out of
  the same materials.

VOORHEES, RICHARD J. "*The Music of Time*: Themes and variations." *DR*, XLII (1962/63), 313-321.
  Relates the novels to his earlier work and analyses some of
  their features (farce, low comedy, etc.).

WAUGH, EVELYN. "Marriage à la mode - 1936." *Spectator*,
  24 June 1960, 919.
  Rev. art. on *Casanova's Chinese Restaurant*. Refers also to
  previous novels of *The Music of Time* sequence.

WAUGH, EVELYN. "Bioscope." *Spectator*, 29 June 1962, 863-864.
  Rev. art. on *The Kindly Ones*.

WOODWARD, A.G. "The novels of Anthony Powell." *ESA*, X (1967),
  117-128.
  The Music of Time "excels in revealing the London of the
  1920's and 30's."

WYNDHAM, FRANCIS. "*The Acceptance World* by Anthony Powell."
  London Mag, II (September 1955), 77-78.
  Rev. art.

ZIGERELL, JAMES J. "Anthony Powell's *Music of Time*: Chronicle
  of a declining establishment." *TCL*, XII (1966/67), 138-146.
  The Valley of Bones presents a comic portrayal of the decline of the upper classes in England.

RAPHAEL, FREDERIC (1931)
Obbligato, 1956; *The Earlsdon Way*, 1958; *The Limits of Love*,
1960; *A Wild Surmise*, 1961; *The Graduate Wife*, 1962; *The
Trouble with England*, 1962; *Lindmann*, 1963; *Darling*, 1965;
Orchestra and Beginners, 1967; *Like Men Betrayed*, 1970; *Who
Were You with Last Night?*, 1971.

ANON. "Frederic Raphael: *A Wild Surmise*." *TLS*, 9 June 1961,
  361.
  Short rev.

ANON. "Man of war." *TLS,* 5 July 1963, 489.

Rev. art. on *Lindmann*.

ANON. "Prep gang." *TLS,* 19 October 1967, 977.

Rev. art. on *Orchestra and Beginners*.

BERGONZI, BERNARD. "Nice but not good." *NYRB,* 11 April 1968, 36-38.

Contains rev. of *Orchestra and Beginners*.

MCDOWELL, FREDERICK P.W. "World within world: Gerda Charles, Frederic Raphael, and the Anglo-Jewish community." *Crit,* VI:3 (1963), 143-150.

Similarities and differences between *The Limits of Love* and Charles's *The Crossing Point*.

MCDOWELL, FREDERICK P.W. "The varied universe of Frederic Raphael's fiction." *Crit,* VIII:1 (1965), 21-50.

Points out the variety of style and subject and deals extensively with all the novels up to 1963.

MUDRICK, MARVIN. "News from nowhere." *NYRB,* 9 July 1964, 19-20.

Contains rev. of *Lindmann*.

WAUGH, AUBERON. "Broken rules." *Spectator,* 7 November 1970, 564-565.

Contains rev. of *Like Men Betrayed*.

YOUNG, JAMES DEAN. "False identity and feeling in Raphael's *Lindmann*." *Crit,* XIII:1 (1970), 59-65.

RAVEN, SIMON (1927)

The Feathers of Death, 1959; *Brother Cain,* 1959; *Doctors Wear Scarlet,* 1960; *Close of Play,* 1962; *Alms for Oblivion: The Rich Pay Late,* 1964, *Friends in Low Places,* 1965, *The Sabre Squadron,* 1966, *Fielding Gray,* 1967, *The Judas Boy,* 1968, *Places Where They Sing,* 1970, *Sound the Retreat,* 1971.

ANON. "Officers and cads." *TLS,* 23 October 1959, 605.

Contains rev. of *Brother Cain.* Refers also to *The Feathers of Death*.

ANON. "Ill will towards all." *TLS,* 8 October 1964, 913.

Rev. art. on *The Rich Pay Late*.

ANON. "Honour bright." *TLS*, 13 October 1966, 933. Repr. in
T.L.S. Essays and reviews from The Times Literary Supplement. 1966. Oxford UP: London, 1967. Pp. 77-80.
Rev. art. on *The Sabre Squadron*.

ANON. "Long, hot adolescence." *TLS*, 14 September 1967, 813.
Repr. in *T.L.S. Essays and reviews from The Times Literary Supplement. 1967.* Oxford UP: London, 1968. Pp. 207-208.
Rev. art. on *Fielding Gray*. Refers also to *The Sabre Squadron*.

ANON. "Rewards and fairies." *TLS*, 3 October 1968, 1097.
Rev. art. on *The Judas Boy*.

ANON. "O'er the infected house." *TLS*, 26 February 1970, 217.
Rev. art. on *Places Where They Sing*.

ANON. "Drably deviant." *TLS*, 22 October 1971, 1340.
Rev. art. on *Sound the Retreat*. Refers also to the *Alms for Oblivion* sequence in general.

BERGONZI, BERNARD. "New fiction." *NYRB*, 22 April 1965, 15-16.
Contains rev. of *The Rich Pay Late*.

BUCHAN, WILLIAM. "Out of school." *Spectator*, 22 September 1967, 328-329.
Contains rev. of *Fielding Gray*.

COLE, BARRY. "Songs of praise." *Spectator*, 7 March 1970, 309-310.
Rev. art. on *Places Where They Sing*.

FYTTON, FRANCIS. "*The Sabre Squadron* by Simon Raven." *London Mag*, n.s. VI (December 1966), 114-118.
Rev. art.

MCGUINNESS, FRANK. "*Friends in Low Places* by Simon Raven." *London Mag*, n.s. V (January 1966), 85-86.
Rev. art.

MCSWEENEY, KERRY. "The novels of Simon Raven." *QQ*, LXXVIII (1971), 106-116.
His novels deal with "moral degeneration and the decline of personal loyalty".

MITCHELL, ADRIAN. "Full toss." *Spectator*, 7 December 1962, 900.
Contains rev. of *Close of Play*.

RAVEN, SIMON. "Reflections of a middle-aged novelist."
Spectator, 24 January 1969, 104.

"... the chief fascination of novels, as of life, lies in
the perception, and the celebration, of human inequalities."

WAUGH, AUBERON. "The modern round." *Spectator*, 27 September
1968, 436-437.

Rev. art. on *The Judas Boy*.

READ, PIERS PAUL (1941)
Game in Heaven with Tussy Marx, 1966; *The Junkers*, 1968;
Monk Dawson, 1969; *The Professor's Daughter*, 1971.

ANON. "Life without father." *TLS*, 2 June 1966, 489.
Rev. art. on *Game in Heaven with Tussy Marx*.

ANON. "Refusal to blame." *TLS*, 20 June 1968, 637. Repr. in
*T.L.S. Essays and reviews from The Times Literary Supple-
ment. 1968*. Oxford UP: London, 1969. Pp. 68-70.
Rev. art. on *The Junkers*.

ANON. "Simply extraordinary." *TLS*, 6 November 1969, 1273.
Repr. in *T.L.S. Essays and reviews from The Times Literary
Supplement. 1969*. Oxford UP: London, 1970. Pp. 60-62.
Rev. art. on *Monk Dawson*.

ANON. "Casualties of the corrupt society." *TLS*, 24 September 1971, 1137.
Rev. art. on *The Professor's Daughter*.

RENAULT, MARY (Mary Challans, 1905)
Purposes of Love, 1939; *Kind Are Her Answers*, 1940; *The
Friendly Young Ladies*, 1944; *Return to Night*, 1947; *North
Face*, 1948; *The Charioteer*, 1953; *The Last of the Wine*, 1956;
The King Must Die, 1958; *The Bull from the Sea*, 1962; *The
Mask of Apollo*, 1966; *Fire from Heaven*, 1970.

ANON. "Defying convention." *TLS*, 30 October 1953, 689.
Contains rev. of *The Charioteer*.

ANON. "Barbaric themes." *TLS*, 29 June 1956, 389.
Contains rev. of *The Last of the Wine*.

ANON. "Theseus and the Hellenes." *TLS*, 19 September 1958, 528.
Rev. art. on *The King Must Die*.

ANON. "King in Athens." *TLS*, 16 March 1962, 181.
Rev. art. on *The Bull from the Sea*.

ANON. "Purely Platonic." *TLS*, 15 December 1966, 1165.
Rev. art. on *The Mask of Apollo*.

ANON. "The conqueror as a boy." *TLS*, 11 December 1970, 1437.
Rev. art. on *Fire from Heaven*.

BURNS, LANDON C., JR. "Men are only men: The novels of Mary Renault." *Crit*, VI: 3 (1963), 102-121.
Regards her as an outstanding historical novelist: *The Last of the Wine, The King Must Die, The Bull from the Sea*.

HERBERT, KEVIN. "The Theseus theme: Some recent versions." *CJ*, LV (1959/60), 173-185.
The King Must Die and Lindsay's long poem *Clue of Darkness*.

MANDEL, SIEGFRIED. "The hero as a young Athenian." *NYTBR*, 13 July 1958, 1.
Rev. art. on *The King Must Die*.

RENAULT, MARY. "Notes on *The King Must Die*." *Afterwords. Novelists on their novels*, ed. Thomas McCormack. Harper & Row: New York, 1969. Pp. 80-87.
The genesis of *The King Must Die*.

WARNER, REX. "*The King Must Die* by Mary Renault." *London Mag*, VI (February 1959), 66-68.
Rev. art.

WOLFE, PETER. *Mary Renault*. TEAS, 98. Twayne: New York, 1969. Pp. 198.

SANSOM, WILLIAM (1912)
The Body, 1949; *The Face of Innocence*, 1951; *A Bed of Roses*, 1954; *The Loving Eye*, 1956; *The Cautious Heart*, 1958; *The Last Hours of Sandra Lee*, 1961; *Goodbye*, 1966; *Hans Feet in Love*, 1971.

ANON. "View of the alcove." *TLS*, 27 April 1951, 257.
Rev. art. on *The Face of Innocence*.

ANON. "Mixed motives." *TLS*, 29 January 1954, 69.
Contains rev. of *A Bed of Roses*.

ANON. "Love in idleness." *TLS*, 16 November 1956, 677.
Contains rev. of *The Loving Eye*.

ANON. "Make-do-and-mend lovers." *TLS*, 5 December 1958, 701.
Contains rev. of *The Cautious Heart*.

ANON. "Party piece." *TLS*, 3 November 1961, 785.
Rev. art. on *The Last Hours of Sandra Lee*.

ANON. "Blind fireworks." *TLS*, 27 October 1966, 973.
Rev. art. on *Goodbye*.

ANON. "Flat feet." *TLS*, 24 September 1971, 1138.
Rev. art. on *Hans Feet in Love*.

BERGONZI, BERNARD. "Total recall." *NYRB*, 24 August 1967,
37-38.
Contains rev. of *Goodbye*.

BODEN, BERTIL. "*The Body*." *BLM*, XIX (1950), 524-527.
Rev. art. on the Swedish translation.

MCGUINNESS, FRANK. "*Goodbye* by William Sansom." *London Mag,*
n.s. VI (October 1966), 115-116.
Rev. art.

MICHEL-MICHOT, PAULETTE. "Franz Kafka and William Sansom
reconsidered." *RLV*, XXXVII (1971), 712-718.
Mainly on the short stories.

MICHEL-MICHOT, PAULETTE. *William Sansom. A critical assessment.*
Bibliothèque de la Faculté de Philosophie et Lettres de
l'Université de Liège, 193. Société d'Edition "Les Belles
Lettres": Paris, 1971. Pp. XXI + 408.
First full-length and detailed study. Part Two discusses
his novels in chronological order. Bibliography of primary
and secondary sources.

NEMEROV, HOWARD. "Sansom's fiction." *KR*, XVII (1955),
130-135.
Rev. art. on *A Bed of Roses* and two collections of his
short stories.

TAYLOR, JANE. "William Sansom." *B&B*, (July 1971), 30-31.
  Interview: mainly on *Hans Feet in Love.*

VICKERY, JOHN B. "William Sansom and logical empiricism."
  Thought, XXXVI (1961), 231-245.

WILSON, ANGUS. "*The Last Hours of Sandra Lee* by William
  Sansom." *London Mag*, n.s. I (December 1961), 89-92.
  Rev. art.

WYNDHAM, FRANCIS. "*A Bed of Roses* by William Sansom." *London
  Mag*, I (March 1954), 87-89.
  Rev. art.

SCOTT, J.D. (1917)
The Cellar, 1947; *The Margin*, 1949; *The Way to Glory*, 1952;
The End of an Old Song, 1954; *The Pretty Penny*, 1963.

ANON. "Interlude in Paris." *TLS*, 23 May 1952, 341.
  Rev. art. on *The Way to Glory.*

ANON. "Against the tide." *TLS*, 9 April 1954, 229.
  Contains rev. of *The End of an Old Song.*

ANON. "Power without glory." *TLS*, 1 November 1963, 881.
  Rev. art. on *The Pretty Penny.*

BROOKE, JOCELYN. "New fiction." *Listener*, 24 October 1963,
  667.
  Contains rev. of *The Pretty Penny.*

SCOTT, PAUL (1920)
Johnnie Sahib, 1952; *The Alien Sky*, 1953; *A Male Child*, 1956;
The Mark of the Warrior, 1958; *The Chinese Love Pavilion*,
1960; *The Birds of Paradise*, 1962; *The Bender*, 1963; *The
Corrida at San Feliu*, 1964; *The Jewel in the Crown*, 1966; *The
Day of the Scorpion*, 1968; *The Towers of Silence*, 1971.

ANON. "Foreign affairs." *TLS*, 25 September 1953, 609.
  Contains rev. of *The Alien Sky.*

ANON. "The seamier side." *TLS*, 16 March 1956, 163.
Contains rev. of *A Male Child*.

ANON. "Pressure points." *TLS*, 14 March 1958, 137.
Contains rev. of *The Mark of the Warrior*. See also S's
letter to the editor (*TLS*, 21 March 1958, 153).

ANON. "Time remembered." *TLS*, 13 April 1962, 245.
Rev. art. on *The Birds of Paradise*.

ANON. "Tensions and despairs." *TLS*, 12 April 1963, 245.
Rev. art. on *The Bender*.

ANON. "Toro Agonistes." *TLS*, 27 August 1964, 761.
Rev. art. on *The Corrida at San Feliu*.

ANON. "The rape of India." *TLS*, 21 July 1966, 629. Repr. in
*T.L.S. Essays and reviews from The Times Literary Supple-
ment. 1966.* Oxford UP: London, 1967. Pp. 71-74.
Rev. art. on *The Jewel in the Crown*.

ANON. "Mighty opposites." *TLS*, 12 September 1968, 975.
Contains rev. of *The Day of the Scorpion*.

ANON. "Decline and fall." *TLS*, 8 October 1971, 1199.
Rev. art. on *The Towers of Silence*.

BROOKE, JOCELYN. "Accent on sex." *Spectator*, 28 August 1964,
282-283.
Contains rev. of *The Corrida at San Feliu*.

DICK, KAY. "Shades of Kipling." *Spectator*, 22 July 1966,
127-128.
Contains rev. of *The Jewel in the Crown*.

SCOTT, PAUL. "India: A post-Forsterian view." *EDH*, XXXVI
(1970), 113-132.
S. examines his own novels about Anglo-India and Anglo-
Indian relations.

SHAW, ROBERT (1927)
The Hiding Place, 1959; *The Sun Doctor*, 1961; *The Flag*, 1965;
The Man in the Glass Booth, 1967; *A Card from Morocco*, 1969.

ANON. "Trouble in the air." *TLS*, 16 October 1959, 589.
Contains rev. of *The Hiding Place*.

ANON. "Leader, healer, actor." *TLS*, 2 June 1961, 337.
  Rev. art. on *The Sun Doctor*.

ANON. "In the red parish." *TLS*, 14 January 1965, 21.
  Rev. art. on *The Flag*.

ANON. "Wounding questions." *TLS*, 12 January 1967, 21.
  Rev. art. on *The Man in the Glass Booth*.

GRIGSON, GEOFFREY. "A question of manner." *Spectator,*
  19 May 1961, 728.
  Contains rev. of *The Sun Doctor*.

JOHNSON, B.S. "Great expectations." *Spectator*, 15 January
  1965, 75.
  Contains rev. of *The Flag*.

NEUMEYER, PETER F. "Arcadia revisited: Arthur Goldman and
  Nicolas Poussin." *UR*, XXXVI (1969/70), 263-267.
  The Man in the Glass Booth.

REES, GORONWY. "Men alone." *Encounter*, XIV (January 1960),
  84-85.
  Contains rev. of *The Hiding Place*.

SILLITOE, ALAN (1928)
Saturday Night and Sunday Morning, 1958; *The General*, 1960;
Key to the Door, 1961; *The Death of William Posters*, 1965;
A Tree on Fire, 1967; *A Start in Life*, 1970; *Travels in
Nihilon*, 1971.

ANON. "A weakness for music." *TLS*, 20 May 1960, 317.
  Rev. art. on *The General*.

ANON. "Scenes from provincial life." *TLS*, 20 October 1961,
  749.
  Rev. art. on *Key to the Door*.

ANON. "Symbolism must merge with realism: An interview with
  Alan Sillitoe." *B&B*, (October 1961), 7-8.

ANON. "Speaking of writing, XI: Alan Sillitoe." *Times,*
  6 February 1964, 15.
  His career as a writer.

ANON. "Hitching out of reality." *TLS*, 13 May 1965, 365.
  Rev. art. on *The Death of William Posters*.

ANON. "Anglo-apocalyptic." *TLS*, 9 November 1967, 1053.
Rev. art. on *A Tree on Fire*.

ANON. "A naturalist no more." *TLS*, 18 September 1970, 1026.
Repr. in *T.L.S. Essays and reviews from The Times Literary Supplement. 1970.* Oxford UP: London, 1971. Pp. 43-45.
Rev. art. on *A Start in Life*.

ANON. "Nothing doing." *TLS*, 17 September 1971, 1105.
Rev. art. on *Travels in Nihilon*.

ALLEN, WALTER. "The fable and the moral." *New Statesman,*
21 May 1960, 765.
Rev. art. on *The General*.

ATHERTON, STANLEY S. "Alan Sillitoe's battleground." *DR*,
XLVIII (1968/69), 324-331.
"His fiction reminds us that the tradition of social commitment in literature is not dead ..."

BAHN, SONJA. "Alan Sillitoe." *Englische Literatur der Gegenwart in Einzeldarstellungen,* ed. Horst W. Drescher. Kröner: Stuttgart, 1970. Pp. 207-223.
The only modern writer to identify himself with the working-class. His writing is typified, but he still attempts to find positive solutions going beyond mere protest. Short biography. Bibliography.

BARROWS, JOHN. "Alan Sillitoe." *JOL*, 30 November 1961,
596-597.
He sees his work as a protest against the impersonality of mass communication.

BIESTER, HANNE-LORE. "Alan Sillitoe und die Sowjetunion."
ZAA, XVII (1969), 60-74.
His working-class heroes.

CAUTE, DAVID. "Breakthrough." *Time and Tide*, 12 October 1961,
1705.
Rev. art. on *Key to the Door*.

COLEMAN, JOHN. "The unthinkables." *New Statesman*, 27 October 1961, 610, 612.
Rev. art. on *Key to the Door*, beginning with a short survey of S's literary career.

CRAIG, DAVID. "Commentary." Alan Sillitoe, *Saturday Night and Sunday Morning*. Heritage of Literature Series, 97. Longmans, Green: London, 1968. Pp. 215-235.

The novel is seen against the background of "working-class literature".

GINDIN, JAMES. "Alan Sillitoe's jungle." *TSLL*, IV (1962/63), 35-48. Repr. in *Postwar British fiction. New accents and attitudes*. Cambridge UP: London, 1962. Pp. 14-33.

Saturday Night and Sunday Morning, The General.

HAJEK, IGOR. "Morning coffee with Alan Sillitoe." *Nation*, 27 January 1969, 122-124.

Interview.

HARCOURT, PETER. "*The General* by Alan Sillitoe." *TC*, CLXVIII (1960), 90-92.

Rev. art. and discussion of previous works.

HOWE, IRVING. "The worker as a young tough." *NewR*, 24 August 1959, 27-28.

Refers mainly to *Saturday Night and Sunday Morning*.

HURRELL, JOHN DENNIS. "Alan Sillitoe and the serious novel." *Crit*, IV:1 (1961), 3-16.

Refers to *Saturday Night and Sunday Morning, The Loneliness of the Long-Distance Runner* and *The General*. Regards S. as a serious novelist who "examines a large segment of contemporary British society, and shows us a character who has found a cure for some of its ills not in any political nostrum but in the rehabilitation of his own heart and mind."

KERMODE, FRANK. "Rammel." *New Statesman*, 14 May 1965, 765-766. Repr. in *Continuities*. Routledge & Kegan Paul: London, 1968. Pp. 227-232.

Rev. art. on *The Death of William Posters;* S. is compared with Mailer.

KLOTZ, GÜNTHER. "Naturalistische Züge in Alan Sillitoes Roman *Saturday Night and Sunday Morning*." *ZAA*, X (1962), 153-161.

KLOTZ, GÜNTHER. "Alan Sillitoe's heroes." *Essays in honour of William Gallacher*. Life and Literature of the Working Class, ed. Anselm Schlösser. Humboldt-Universität: Berlin, 1966. Pp. 259-263.

"Sillitoe remains one of the richest potentials in the new forward-pointing literature of Great Britain." Examines his "proletarian heroes" in *The Loneliness of the Long-Distance Runner* and *Saturday Night and Sunday Morning*.

LE FRANC, BOLIVAR. "Sillitoe at forty." *B&B*, (June 1969),
21-22, 24.
Based on an interview, which raises the question, whether
he is still an "angry writer". Discussion of *A Tree on Fire*.

MCDOWELL, FREDERICK P.W. "Self and society: Alan Sillitoe's
Key to the Door." *Crit*, VI:1 (1963), 116-123.
Rev. art.

MCGUINNESS, FRANK. "*The Death of William Posters* by Alan
Sillitoe." *London Mag*, n.s. V (August 1965), 102-104.
Rev. art.

MCGUINNESS, FRANK. "*A Tree on Fire* by Alan Sillitoe." *London
Mag*, n.s. VII (November 1967), 91-92.
Rev. art.

MALOFF, SAUL. "The eccentricity of Alan Sillitoe." *Contemporary British novelists,* ed. Charles Shapiro. Southern
Illinois UP: Carbondale, Edwardsville, 1965. Pp. 95-113.

MARLAND, MICHAEL, ed. *Alan Sillitoe.* Times Authors, 4. Times
Education Services: London, n.d.
Collection of articles, reviews, autobiography, etc.

OSGERBY, J.R. "Alan Sillitoe's *Saturday Night and Sunday
Morning.*" *Renaissance and modern essays. Presented to
Vivian de Sola Pinto in celebration of his seventieth
birthday,* eds. G.R. Hibbard, George A. Panichas & Allan
Rodway. Routledge & Kegan Paul: London, 1966. Pp. 215-230.

PENNER, ALLEN RICHARD. "Dantesque allegory in Sillitoe's *Key
to the Door.*" *Renascence,* XX (1967/68), 79-85, 103.

PENNER, ALLEN RICHARD. "The political prologue and two parts
of a trilogy: *The Death of William Posters* and *A Tree on
Fire:* A liturgy for revolution." *UR*, XXXV (1968/69), 11-20.

PENNER, ALLEN RICHARD. "Human dignity and social anarchy:
Sillitoe's *The Loneliness of the Long-Distance Runner.*"
ConL, X (1969), 253-265.
Relates him to the Angry Young Men; mentions his novels.

PENNER, ALLEN RICHARD. "*The General*: Exceptional proof of a
critical rule." *SHR*, IV (1970), 135-143.

PRINCE, ROD. *"Saturday Night and Sunday Morning."* *NLR*, 6
(November/December 1960), 14-17.
Novel and film.

ROSSELLI, JOHN. "A cry from the brick streets." *Reporter*,
10 November 1960, 37-42.
S's theme is "rebellion ... against all organized society".

SHESTAKOV, DMITRI. "Alan Sillitoe from Nottingham." *SovL*, 9
(1963), 176-179.
His novels are examinations of environment. One of his
major themes is the uselessness of war and its "imperialist
origin".

SILLITOE, ALAN. "Introduction." *Saturday Night and Sunday
Morning*. Heritage of Literature Series, 97. Longmans,
Green: London, 1968. Pp. VII-XII.
On the author's development into a writer and the origins
of his first novel.

SMITH, HERBERT. "Towards a socialist literature in Britain."
Essays in honour of William Gallacher. Life and Literature
of the Working Class, ed. Anselm Schlösser. Humboldt-Universität: Berlin, 1966. Pp. 248-253.
"... the new literature will ... create the representative
figure of the twentieth century: the proletarian image,
consciously effecting change." *Key to the Door* as a recent
sign of emergence.

STAPLES, HUGH B. *"Saturday Night and Sunday Morning:* Alan
Sillitoe and the White Goddess." *MFS*, X (1964/65), 171-181.
The importance of myth.

STEPHANE, NELLY. "Alan Sillitoe." *Europe*, XLII (janvier-
février 1964), 289-293.
Saturday Night and Sunday Morning, The General.

SNOW, C.P. (1905)
Death under Sail, 1932; *New Lives for Old,* 1933; *The Search,*
1934; *Strangers and Brothers: Strangers and Brothers,* 1940,
The Light and the Dark, 1947, *Time of Hope,* 1949, *The
Masters,* 1951, *The New Men,* 1954, *Homecomings,* 1956, *The Con-
science of the Rich,* 1958, *The Affair,* 1960, *Corridors of
Power,* 1964, *The Sleep of Reason,* 1968, *Last Things,* 1970.

ANON. "Corridors of power." *TLS*, 7 September 1956, 524.
Rev. art. on *Homecomings*.

ANON. "A question of creeds." *TLS*, 28 March 1958, 165.
Rev. art. on *The Conscience of the Rich*.

ANON. "Old friends in new roles." *TLS*, 15 April 1960, 237.
Rev. art. on *The Affair*.

ANON. "Interview with C.P. Snow." *REL*, III (July 1962),
91-108.
Discussion of various topics: the autobiographical elements
in the Lewis Eliot sequence, methods of characterization,
his plans for the future, etc.

ANON. "The realism of the worldly." *TLS*, 5 November 1964,
993. Repr. in *T.L.S. Essays and reviews from The Times
Literary Supplement. 1964.* Oxford UP: London, 1965.
Pp. 100-103.
Rev. art. on *Corridors of Power*. Refers also to *The Masters*
and *The Affair*.

ANON. "Monsters at bay." *TLS*, 31 October 1968, 1217. Repr. in
*T.L.S. Essays and reviews from The Times Literary Supple-
ment. 1968.* Oxford UP: London, 1969. Pp. 175-177.
Rev. art. on *The Sleep of Reason*.

ANON. "The world of power and groups." *TLS*, 23 October 1970,
1223.
Rev. art. on *Last Things*.

ALLEN, WALTER, A.C.B. LOVELL, J.H. PLUMB, DAVID RIESMAN,
BERTRAND RUSSELL, JOHN COCKCROFT & MICHAEL AYRTON. "*The Two
Cultures:* A discussion of C.P. Snow's views." *Encounter*,
XIII (August 1959), 67-73.

BERGONZI, BERNARD. "All decent." *Spectator*, 15 April 1960,
548-549.
Rev. art. on *The Affair*; considered the best novel since
The Masters.

BERGONZI, BERNARD. "The world of Lewis Eliot." *TC*, CLXVII
(1960), 214-225.
Failure in the point of view technique in the *Strangers
and Brothers* sequence. See also P. Fison's article.

BERNARD, KENNETH. "C.P. Snow and modern literature." *UR*,
XXXI (1964/65), 231-233.

BRADBURY, MALCOLM. "Literary culture in England today."
Listener, 9 August 1962, 209.
The Snow-Leavis controversy.

BRADBURY, MALCOLM. "Snow's bleak landscape." *New Statesman*,
30 October 1970, 566-567.
The Sleep of Reason, Last Things.

BUCKLEY, VINCENT. "C.P. Snow: How many cultures?" *MCR*, V
(1962), 102-107.
The Two Cultures.

COOPER, WILLIAM. "The world of C.P. Snow." *Nation*,
2 February 1957, 104-105.

COOPER, WILLIAM. "The committee man and the technician." *TC*,
CLXII (1957), 178-184.
The Two Cultures.

COOPER, WILLIAM. "C.P. Snow." *BBN*, 115 (November 1959), 7-40.
Thematic material, style and basic attitude in his novels.

COOPER, WILLIAM. *C.P. Snow*. WTW, 115. Longmans, Green: London,
1962 (rev. ed.). Pp. 40.

CORNELIUS, DAVID K. & EDWIN ST. VINCENT, eds. *Cultures in
conflict. Perspectives on the Snow-Leavis controversy*.
Scott, Foresman: Chicago, 1964. Pp. 179.
Part One presents the main outline of the "Snow-Leavis
controversy" by reprinting S's views and the main reactions.

DAVIS, ROBERT GORHAM. *C.P. Snow*. CEMW, 8. Columbia UP: New
York, 1965. Pp. 48.

DOBREE, BONAMY. "The novels of C.P. Snow." *LHY*, IV (January
1963), 28-34.
Discusses the first eight volumes of the *Strangers and
Brothers* sequence.

EISELY, LOREN. "The illusion of the two cultures." *ASch*,
XXXIII (1963/64), 387-399.
The Two Cultures.

ENRIGHT, D.J. "Easy lies the head." *New Statesman*,
6 November 1964, 698-699.
S's prose writing is rather orthodox.

FAIRLIE, HENRY. "Cults not cultures." *Spectator*,
1 November 1963, 554.
The Two Cultures. A Second Look.

FIETZ, LOTHAR. "Cambridge und die Diskussion um das Verhält-
nis von Literatur und Naturwissenschaft." *Literatur-Kultur-
Gesellschaft in England und Amerika. Aspekte und Forschungs-
beiträge. Friedrich Schubel zum 60. Geburtstag,* eds. Gerhard Müller-Schwefe & Konrad Tuzinski. Diesterweg: Frankfurt a. M., 1966. Pp. 113-127.
The Two Cultures and following controversy.

FINKELSTEIN, SIDNEY. "The art and science of C.P. Snow."
Mainstream, XIV (September 1961), 31-57.

FISON, PETER. "A reply to Bernard Bergonzi's 'World of Lewis
Eliot'." *TC*, CLXVII (1960), 568-571.
Discusses the series "on its own terms".

FOWLER, ALBERT. "The negative entropy of C.P. Snow."
Approach, 58 (Winter 1966), 7-13.

FULLER, EDMUND. "C.P. Snow: Spokesman of two communities."
Books with men behind them. Random House: New York, 1962.
Pp. 102-134.
"Snow is the best present moderator between the scientific
and literary communities." Discussion of the novels and
the Rede Lecture.

GARDNER, HELEN. "The world of C.P. Snow." *New Statesman,*
29 March 1958, 409-410.
Mainly on *The Conscience of the Rich.*

GERHARDI, WILLIAM *et al.* "Sir Charles Snow, Dr. F.R. Leavis,
and the two cultures." *Spectator*, 16 March 1962, 329-333.
Reactions to the Richmond Lecture.

GOODWIN, DONALD FRANCIS. "The fiction of C.P. Snow." *DA*,
XXVII (1967), 3009A (Iowa).

GRAVES, NORA CALHOUN. "The two culture theory in C.P. Snow's
novels." *DA*, XXVIII (1967), 1434A-1435A (So. Miss.).

GREACEN, ROBERT. "The world of C.P. Snow." *TQ*, IV (Autumn
1961), 266-274.
Fiction and non-fiction.

GREACEN, ROBERT. *The world of C.P. Snow*. Scorpion Press:
Lowestoft, 1962. Pp. 64.

Draws mainly upon the novels; concludes with a bibliography
by Bernard Stone (41-64).

GREEN, MARTIN. "A literary defence of *The Two Cultures*."
CritQ, IV (1962), 155-162; *KR*, XXIV (1962), 731-739.

GREEN, MARTIN. "Lionel Trilling and the 'two cultures'." *EIC*,
XIII (1963), 375-385.

Comment on Trilling's article on the Snow-Leavis controversy.

GULLIVER, ANTONY F. "The political novels of Trollope and
Snow." *DAI*, XXX (1969), 684A (Conn.).

HALIO, JAY R. "C.P. Snow's literary limitations." *NWR*, V
(Winter 1962), 97-102.
Lack of depth.

HALL, WILLIAM F. "The humanism of C.P. Snow." *WSCL*, IV
(1963), 199-208.

Strangers and Brothers look for a viable union between
individualism and social responsibility.

HAMILTON, KENNETH. "C.P. Snow and political man." *QQ*, LXIX
(1962), 416-427.

In rebuttal to Mandel's article, *QQ*, LXIX (1962), 24-37.

HAWKES, PETER. "The day thou gavest." *Spectator*,
7 November 1970, 563-564.

Rev. art. on *Last Things*.

HICKS, GRANVILLE. "Literary horizons." *SatR*,
11 January 1969, 78-79.

Rev. art. on *The Sleep of Reason*.

HUMPHREYS, EMYR. "The 'Protestant' novelist." *Spectator*,
21 November 1952, 681-682.

Discusses themes, characters and plot of the "serious novel
of the middle of this century"; mentions S.

IVASHEVA, V. "Illusion and reality." *InLit*, 6 (1960),
198-203.

The *Strangers and Brothers* sequence is presumably of an
autobiographical nature.

IVASHEVA, V. "Meeting Charles Snow." *SovL*, 8 (1963), 180-182.
Admired for his realism and his portrayals of society.

JAFFA, HERBERT C. "C.P. Snow: Portrait of man as an adult."
Humanist, XXIV (1964), 148-150.
"... sees man as a mature human being."

JOHNSON, PAMELA HANSFORD. "Three novelists and the drawing of
character: C.P. Snow, Joyce Cary and Ivy Compton-Burnett."
E&S, n.s. III (1950), 82-99.

JONES, RICHARD. "The end of the C.P. Snow affair." *Atlantic,*
CCXXVI (September 1970), 112-117.
Rev. art. on *Last Things*.

JURCZAK, CHESTER A. "Humanities or science." *DuqR*, VIII
(Fall 1962), 3-11.
Literary intellectuals and scientists as two polar groups
in *The Two Cultures*.

KARL, FREDERICK R. *C.P. Snow. The politics of conscience.*
With a preface by Harry T. Moore. Southern Illinois UP:
Carbondale, 1963. Pp. IX + 162.
Fiction from *Death under Sail* to *The Affair*; chronologies
of his life and of the events in the *Strangers and Brothers*
sequence.

KARL, FREDERICK R. "C.P. Snow: The unreason of reason." *Contemporary British novelists*, ed. Charles Shapiro. Southern
Illinois UP: Carbondale, Edwardsville, 1965. Pp. 114-124.

KAZIN, ALFRED. "A gifted boy from the Midlands." *Reporter*,
5 February 1959, 37-39. Repr. in *Contemporaries*. Little,
Brown: Boston, 1962. Pp. 171-177.
S's novels report "the struggle of poor boys for careers"
and describe "intellectuals on the make".

KERMODE, FRANK. "Sophisticated quest." *Spectator,*
11 April 1958, 464.
Rev. art. on *The Conscience of the Rich*.

KERMODE, FRANK. "Beckett, Snow, and pure poverty." *Encounter,*
XV (July 1960), 73-77. Repr. in *Puzzles and epiphanies.
Essays and reviews 1958-1961*. Routledge & Kegan Paul:
London, 1962. Pp. 155-163.
S's "power of narrative" as revealed in *The Affair*.

KERMODE, FRANK. "The house of fiction: Interviews with seven English novelists." *PR*, XXX (1963), 61-82.
With S. (74-76).

KETELS, VIOLET B. "Shaw, Snow, and the new men." *Person*, XLVII (1966), 520-531.
S's "new men" are scientists who combine "moral vision and practical judgment".

KREUZER, HELMUT, ed. *Literarische und naturwissenschaftliche Intelligenz. Dialog über die "zwei Kulturen"*. Klett: Stuttgart, 1969. Pp. 273.
Collection of essays by American, English and German writers on the "two cultures" discussion. Selected bibliography.

LEAVIS, F.R. "Two cultures?: The significance of C.P. Snow." *Spectator*, 9 March 1962, 297, 299-300, 302-303.
Answer to the Rede Lecture.

LEAVIS, F.R. *Two cultures? The significance of C.P. Snow. With an essay on Sir Charles Snow's Rede Lecture by Michael Yudkin*. Chatto & Windus: London, 1962. Pp. 45.

LEHAN, RICHARD. "The divided world: *The Masters* examined." *Six contemporary novels. Six introductory essays in modern fiction*, ed. William O.S. Sutherland, Jr. Texas UP: Austin, 1962. Pp. 46-57.

MACDONALD, ALASTAIR. "The failure of success." *DR*, XLIV (1964/65), 494-500.
Rev. art. on *Corridors of Power*.

MACDONALD, ALASTAIR. "Imagery in C.P. Snow." *UR*, XXXII (1965/66), 303-306; XXXIII (1966/67), 33-38.
The imagery of his novels expresses the theme of conflict.

MANDEL, E.W. "C.P. Snow's fantasy of politics." *QQ*, LXIX (1962), 24-37.
On the first eight volumes of the *Strangers and Brothers* sequence. See also K. Hamilton's essay.

MANDEL, E.W. "Anarchy and organization." *QQ*, LXX (1963), 131-141.
Answers K. Hamilton's essay, *QQ* LIX (1962), 416-427.

MARTIN, GRAHAM. "Novelists of three decades: Evelyn Waugh, Graham Greene, C.P. Snow." *The Pelican guide to English literature*, ed. Boris Ford. Vol. VII, *The modern age*.
Contains a short discussion of the *Strangers and Brothers* sequence up to *The Conscience of the Rich*.

MAYNE, RICHARD. "The club armchair." *Encounter*, XXI (November 1963), 76-82.
People in society in the *Strangers and Brothers* sequence.

MILLAR, RONALD. "The play of the book." *TLS*, 19 September 1968, 1053.
Dramatizing *The Affair, The New Men* and *The Masters*.

MILLGATE, MICHAEL. "Strangers and brothers." *Commentary*, XXX (1960), 76-79.
Rev. art. on *The Affair*. S. sees all men in society as essentially similar; he is tolerant, not angry.

MILLGATE, MICHAEL. "Structure and style in the novels of C.P. Snow." *REL*, I (April 1960), 34-41.

MONOD, SYLVERE. "C.P. Snow: *The Sleep of Reason*." *EA*, XXIII (1970), 350-352.
Rev. art.

MUGGERIDGE, MALCOLM. "Appointment with C.P. Snow." *Encounter*, XVIII (February 1962), 90-93.
Excerpt from a TV-interview.

MURRAY, BYRON D. "C.P. Snow: Grounds for reappraisal." *Person*, XLVII (1966), 91-101.
On the Snow-Leavis controversy.

NEWQUIST, ROY. "C.P. Snow." *Counterpoint*. Allen & Unwin: London, 1965. Pp. 553-560.
Interview (1963).

NOON, WILLIAM T., S.J. "Satire: Poison and the professor." *ER*, XI (Fall 1960), 53-56.
Refers to *The Masters* and Amis's *Lucky Jim*.

NOTT, KATHLEEN. "The type to which the whole creation moves?: Further thoughts on the Snow saga." *Encounter*, XVIII (February 1962), 87-88, 94-97.

His view that the "two cultures" should be "unified" suggests that he understands "unification" as *gleich-schaltung*".

NOTT, KATHLEEN. "Whose culture?" *Listener*, 12 April 1962, 631-632; 19 April 1962, 677-678.

Two talks on BBC Third Programme on the Snow-Leavis controversy.

OPPERTSHÄUSER, OTTO. "C.P. Snow." *Englische Literatur der Gegenwart in Einzeldarstellungen,* ed. Horst W. Drescher. Kröner: Stuttgart, 1970. Pp. 47-64.

Discussion of the *Strangers and Brothers* sequence. His position in literary history is still uncertain. Short biography. Bibliography.

PETELIN, G. & JA. SIMKIN. *Čarl'z Persi Snou. Pisatel' i čelovek*. Univ. Press: Rostov-na-Donu, 1963. Pp. 77.

POLANYI, MICHAEL. *"The Two Cultures."* Encounter, XIII (September 1959), 61-64.

PUTT, S. GORLEY. "Technique and culture: Three Cambridge portraits." *E&S*, n.s. XIV (1961), 17-34.
Rede Lecture.

PUTT, S. GORLEY. "The Snow-Leavis rumpus." *AR*, XXIII (1963/64), 299-313.

RABINOVITZ, RUBIN. "C.P. Snow vs. the experimental novel." *CUF*, X (Fall 1967), 37-41.

READ, HERBERT. "Mood of the month, X." *London Mag*, VI (August 1959), 39-43.
The Two Cultures.

ROBERTS, CATHERINE. "Nightingales, hawks, and the two cultures." *AR*, XXV (1965/66), 221-238.

SCHENCK, HILBERT, JR. "Revisiting the 'two cultures'." *CentR*, VIII (1964), 249-261.

SHESTAKOV, DMITRI. "What C.P. Snow means." *SovL*, 1 (1966), 174-179.

He explores the common destiny of his contemporaries, not their individual fates; feels that the important decisions are made in social context.

SHILS, EDWARD. "The charismatic centre." *Spectator*,
  6 November 1964, 608-609.
  Rev. art. on *Corridors of Power*.

SIEGMUND-SCHULTZE, DOROTHEA. "Zur Diskussion des Begriffes
  der Kultur in Großbritannien." *ZAA*, XVIII (1970), 118-130.
  Partly on *The Two Cultures*.

SIMEY, T.S. "Le malaise social dans l'Angleterre d'aujourd-
  'hui." *TR*, 214 (novembre 1965), 40-49.
  Contains references to *The Two Cultures*.

SISK, JOHN P. "Writers and scientists: The two cultures."
  Ramparts, I (September 1962), 17-22.

SMITH, LEROY W. "C.P. Snow as novelist: A delimitation." *SAQ*,
  LXIV (1965), 316-331.
  His novels have no sense of life. Leavis's attack in the
  Spectator (9 March 1962) is justified.

SNOW, C.P. "The 'two-cultures' controversy: Afterthoughts."
  Encounter, XIV (February 1960), 64-68.

SNOW, C.P. "The two cultures: A second look." *TLS*,
  25 October 1963, 839-844.

SNOW, C.P. "C.P. Snow." *Times*, 13 March 1971, 17.
  Personal account of the development of the *Strangers and
  Brothers* sequence.

STANFORD, DEREK. "C.P. Snow: The novelist as fox." *Meanjin*,
  XIX (1960), 236-251.
  Pragmatist and pluralist.

STANFORD, DEREK. "Sir Charles and the two cultures." *Critic*,
  XXI (October-November 1962), 17-21.
  His novels reveal in their popular ethical notions the
  naiveté of the scientist.

STANFORD, DEREK. "A disputed master: C.P. Snow and his
  critics." *Month*, CCXV (1963), 91-94.

STANFORD, RANEY. "Personal politics in the novels of C.P.
  Snow." *Crit*, II:1 (1958), 16-28.
  Traces his links with the tradition of liberal humanism as
  revealed in the *Strangers and Brothers* sequence.

STANFORD, RANEY. "The achievement of C.P. Snow." *WHR*, XVI
   (1962), 43-52.

SYMONS, JULIAN. "Of bureaucratic man." *TLS*, 7 May 1954, 296.
   Repr. in *Critical occasions*. Hamish Hamilton: London, 1966.
   Pp. 68-73.
   Rev. art. on *The New Men*.

THALE, JEROME. "C.P. Snow: The art of worldliness." *KR*, XXII
   (1960), 621-634.
   "Snow's view of the man of power is not so much conservative as worldly. It is based not on ideas or attachment to
   tradition but on experience of the world."

THALE, JEROME. *C.P. Snow*. Writers and Critics. Oliver & Boyd:
   Edinburgh, 1964. Pp. 112.

TRILLING, LIONEL. "The novel alive or dead." *A gathering of
   fugitives*. Secker & Warburg: London, 1957. Pp. 125-132.
   On *The New Men*.

TRILLING, LIONEL. "Science, literature & culture: A comment
   on the Leavis-Snow controversy." *Commentary*, XXXIII (1962),
   461-477. Repr. in *Beyond culture. Essays on literature and
   learning*. Secker & Warburg: London, 1966. Pp. 145-177.

TURCK, SUSANNE. *An interpretation of C.P. Snow's "The Masters"*.
   Diesterwegs neusprachliche Bibliothek, 487. Diesterweg:
   Frankfurt a. M., 1969. Pp. 58.

TURNER, IAN. "Above the Snow line: The sociology of C.P. Snow."
   Overland, 18 (August 1960), 37-43.
   The *Strangers and Brothers* sequence.

VOGEL, ALBERT W. "The academic world of C.P. Snow." *TCL*, IX
   (1963/64), 143-152.
   The *Strangers and Brothers* sequence.

WADDINGTON, C.H. "Humanists and scientists: A last comment on
   C.P. Snow." *Encounter*, XIV (January 1960), 72-73.

WALL, STEPHEN. "The novels of C.P. Snow." *London Mag*, n.s.
   IV (April 1964), 68-74.
   Exposes the "central and crucial weaknesses" of the
   Strangers and Brothers sequence.

WATSON, KENNETH. "C.P. Snow and *The New Men.*" *English*, XV
   (1964/65), 134-139.

WAUGH, AUBERON. "Men of power." *Spectator*, 16 June 1967,
   709-710.
   "Snow is the only novelist in the world ... who reads more
   enjoyably when one is drunk than when one is sober."

WEBSTER, HARVEY CURTIS. "The sacrifices of success." *SatR*,
   12 July 1958, 8-10.
   The success-theme in S's novels.

WEBSTER, HARVEY CURTIS. "C.P. Snow: The scientific humanist."
   *After the trauma. Representative British novelists since
   1920.* Kentucky UP: Lexington, 1970. Pp. 168-190.

WEINTRAUB, STANLEY, ed. *C.P. Snow. A spectrum. Science
   criticism fiction.* Scribner Research Anthology. Scribner's
   Sons: New York, 1963. Pp. XVII + 155.

SPARK, MURIEL (1918)
The Comforters, 1957; *Robinson,* 1958; *Memento Mori,* 1959; *The
Ballad of Peckham Rye,* 1960; *The Bachelors,* 1960; *The Prime
of Miss Jean Brodie,* 1961; *The Girls of Slender Means,* 1963;
The Mandelbaum Gate, 1965; *The Public Image,* 1968; *The
Driver's Seat,* 1970; *Not to Disturb,* 1971.

ANON. "Stag party." *TLS*, 14 October 1960, 657.
   Rev. art. on *The Bachelors.*

ANON. "Mistress of style." *TLS*, 3 November 1961, 785.
   Rev. art. on *The Prime of Miss Jean Brodie.*

ANON. "Hell in the royal borough - ." *TLS*, 20 September 1963,
   701. Repr. in *T.L.S. Essays and reviews from The Times
   Literary Supplement. 1963.* Oxford UP: London, 1964.
   Pp. 100-102.
   Rev. art. on *The Girls of Slender Means.*

ANON. "Talking about Jerusalem." *TLS*, 14 October 1965, 913.
   Repr. in *T.L.S. Essays and reviews from The Times Literary
   Supplement. 1965.* Oxford UP: London, 1966. Pp. 34-36.
   Rev. art. on *The Mandelbaum Gate.*

ANON. "Shallowness everywhere." *TLS*, 13 June 1968, 612. Repr.
in *T.L.S. Essays and reviews from The Times Literary Supplement. 1968.* Oxford UP: London, 1969. Pp. 71-73.
Rev. art. on *The Public Image*.

ANON. "Meal for a masochist." *TLS*, 25 September 1970, 1074.
Rev. art. on *The Driver's Seat*.

ANON. "Grub Street Gothic." *TLS*, 12 November 1971, 1409.
Rev. art. on *Not to Disturb*.

ADLER, RENATA. "Muriel Spark." *On contemporary literature. An anthology of critical essays on the major movements and writers of contemporary literature,* ed. Richard Kostelanetz.
Avon Books: New York, 1964. Pp. 591-596.
Mainly on *The Girls of Slender Means*.

BALDANZA, FRANK. "Muriel Spark and the occult." *WSCL*, VI
(1965), 190-203.

BEDFORD, SYBILLE. "Frontier regions." *Spectator*,
29 October 1965, 555-556.
Rev. art. on *The Mandelbaum Gate*. Refers also to S's previous novels.

BERTHOFF, WARNER. "Fortunes of the novel: Muriel Spark and
Iris Murdoch." *MR*, VIII (1967), 301-332.
Themes, influences and contrasts as shown by the works of
these two writers of the honourable second rank.

BROPHY, BRIGID. *"The Girls of Slender Means* by Muriel Spark."
London Mag, n.s. III (December 1963), 76-80.
Rev. art.

CASSON, ALLAN. "Muriel Spark's *The Girls of Slender Means.*"
Crit, VII:3 (1965), 94-96.

DAVISON, PETER. "The miracles of Muriel Spark." *Atlantic,*
CCXXII (October 1968), 139-142.

DIERICKX, J. "A devil-figure in a contemporary setting: Some
aspects of Muriel Spark's *The Ballad of Peckham Rye.*" *RLV,*
XXXIII (1967), 576-587.

DOBIE, ANN B. *"The Prime of Miss Jean Brodie:* Muriel Spark
bridges the credibility gap." *ArQ,* XXV (1969), 217-228.
With this novel she has moved to a more realistic form.

DOBIE, ANN B. "Muriel Spark's definition of reality." *Crit,*
XII:1 (1970), 20-27.
Examines the relation between the "naturalistic" and the
"supernatural" level of reality in her novels.

ENRIGHT, D.J. "Public doctrine and private judging." *New
Statesman,* 15 October 1965, 563, 566.
Rev. art. on *The Mandelbaum Gate.*

FAY, BERNARD. "Muriel Spark en sa fleur." *NRF,* XXVII (1966),
307-315.
Links her with the English novelists of the 18th-century;
her universe is, however, richer than theirs.

GILLIATT, PENELOPE. "Black laughs." *Spectator,* 21 October 1960,
620-621.
Rev. art. on *The Bachelors.* Refers also to S's previous
novels.

GREENE, GEORGE. "A reading of Muriel Spark." *Thought,* XLIII
(1968), 393-407.

GROSS, JOHN. "Passionate pilgrimage." *NYRB,* 28 October 1965,
12-15.
Rev. art. on *The Mandelbaum Gate.*

GROSSKURTH, PHYLLIS. "The world of Muriel Spark: Spirits or
spooks?" *TamR,* 39 (Spring 1966), 62-67.
She sees the supernatural as the basic reality of existence.

HOLLAND, MARY. "The prime of Muriel Spark." *Observer Colour
Supplement,* 17 October 1965, 8-10.

HOYT, CHARLES ALVA. "Muriel Spark: The surrealist Jane Austen."
Contemporary British novelists, ed. Charles Shapiro.
Southern Illinois UP: Carbondale, Edwardsville, 1965.
Pp. 125-143.

HUGHES, RILEY "Happy malice." *Renascence,* XIV (1961/62), 49-51.
The Bachelors.

HYNES, SAMUEL. "The prime of Muriel Spark." *Commonweal,*
23 February 1962, 562-568.
"Her books are not likely to convert anyone."

JACOBSEN, JOSEPHINE. "A Catholic quartet." *ChS,* XLVII (1964),
139-154.
Discussion of Catholic writers: S., Greene, and the Americans J.F. Powers and Flannery O'Connor.

KERMODE, FRANK. "The house of fiction: Interviews with seven English novelists." *PR*, XXX (1963), 61-82.
With S. (79-82).

KERMODE, FRANK. "The prime of Miss Muriel Spark." *New Statesman*, 27 September 1963, 397-398. Repr. in *Continuities*. Routledge & Kegan Paul: London, 1968. Pp. 202-207.
The Comforters, Memento Mori, The Bachelors, The Prime of Miss Jean Brodie, The Girls of Slender Means.

KERMODE, FRANK. "The novel as Jerusalem: Muriel Spark's *Mandelbaum Gate*." *Atlantic*, CCXVI (October 1965), 92-98. Repr. in *Continuities*. Routledge & Kegan Paul: London, 1968. Pp. 207-216.

LECLAIRE, L.A. "Muriel Spark: *The Go-Away Bird, Robinson, Memento Mori*." *EA*, XIII (1960), 486-487.

LODGE, DAVID. "The uses and abuses of omniscience: Method and meaning in Muriel Spark's *The Prime of Miss Jean Brodie*." *CritQ*, XII (1970), 235-257. Repr. in *The novelist at the crossroads and other essays on fiction and criticism*. Routledge & Kegan Paul: London, 1971. Pp. 119-144.

MALIN, IRVING. "The deceptions of Muriel Spark." *The vision obscured. Perceptions of some twentieth-century Catholic novelists*, ed. Melvin J. Friedman. Fordham UP: New York, 1970. Pp. 95-107.

MALKOFF, KARL. *Muriel Spark*. CEMW, 36. Columbia UP: New York, 1968. Pp. 48.

MALKOFF, KARL. "Demonology and dualism: The supernatural in Isaac Singer and Muriel Spark." *Critical views of Isaac Bashevis Singer*, ed. Irving Malin. New York UP: New York, 1969. Pp. 149-168.

MAYNE, RICHARD. "Fiery particle: On Muriel Spark." *Encounter*, XXV (December 1965), 61-68.
Rev. art. on *The Mandelbaum Gate*. Discusses also her previous novels.

MEIJER, HENK ROMIJN. "Het satirische talent van Muriel Spark." *Tirade*, VI (1962), 157-169.

MÜLLER, NORBERT. "Muriel Spark." *Englische Literatur der Gegenwart in Einzeldarstellungen*, ed. Horst W. Drescher. Kröner: Stuttgart, 1970. Pp. 327-343.

Her writing is decisively influenced by her conversion.
Short biography. Bibliography.

MURPHY, CAROL. "A spark of the supernatural." *Approach*, 60
(Summer 1966), 26-30.
Use of the supernatural in *The Comforters, Memento Mori*
and *The Mandelbaum Gate*.

OHMANN, CAROL B. "Muriel Spark's *Robinson*." *Crit*, VIII:1
(1965), 70-84.

POTTER, NANCY A.J. "Muriel Spark: Transformer of the common-
place." *Renascence*, XVII (1964/65), 115-120.
Good and evil in her novels.

QUINN, JOSEPH A. "A study of the satiric element in the
novels of Muriel Spark." *DAI*, XXX (1970), 3954A
(Purdue).

RAVEN, SIMON. "Heavens below." *Spectator*, 20 September 1963,
354.
Rev. art. on *The Girls of Slender Means*. Refers also to
S's previous novels.

RICKS, CHRISTOPHER. "Extreme instances." *NYRB*, 19 December
1968, 31-32.
Rev. art. on *The Public Image;* general assessment of S's
oeuvre.

SCHNEIDER, HAROLD W. "A writer in her prime: The fiction of
Muriel Spark." *Crit*, V:2 (1962), 28-45.
Discussion of her novels published to date. Her special
gifts: wit, ironic detachment, an eye for detail, ability
to develop character through conversation.

SPARK, MURIEL. "My conversion." *TC*, CLXX (Autumn 1961), 58-63.
Report of an interview conducted by W.J. Weatherby.

SPARK, MURIEL. "How I became a novelist." *B&B*,(November
1961), 9.

STANFORD, DEREK. "The work of Muriel Spark: An essay on her
fictional method." *Month*, CCXIV (1962), 92-99.

STANFORD, DEREK. "The early days of Miss Muriel Spark."
Critic, XX (April-May 1962), 49-53.
Covers her activities while writing her first two novels.

STANFORD, DEREK. *Muriel Spark. A biographical and critical study with a bibliography by Bernard Stone*. Centaur Press: Fontwell, 1963. Pp. 184.

Contains chap. on the novels up to *The Prime of Miss Jean Brodie*.

STUBBS, P.J.A. *A comparative study of the fiction of Iris Murdoch and Muriel Spark*. M. Phil. London (University College), 1968/69.

TUOHY, FRANK. "Rewards and bogies." *Spectator*, 3 November 1961, 634.

Rev. art. on *The Prime of Miss Jean Brodie*.

UPDIKE, JOHN. "Creatures of the air." *NY*, 30 September 1961, 161-167. Repr. in *Assorted prose*. Deutsch: London, 1965. Pp. 204-210.

Rev. art. on *The Bachelors*.

UPDIKE, JOHN. "Between a wedding and a funeral." *Assorted prose*. Deutsch: London, 1965. Pp. 210-214.

Rev. art. on *The Girls of Slender Means*.

VORMWEG, HEINRICH. "Muriel Sparks Welttheaterchen." *Merkur*, XIX (1965), 793-795.

WAUGH, EVELYN. "Something fresh." *Spectator*, 22 February 1957, 256.

Rev. art. on *The Comforters*.

WILDMAN, JOHN HAZARD. "Translated by Muriel Spark." *Nine essays in modern literature,* ed. Donald E. Stanford. Louisiana State University Studies: Humanities Series, 15. Louisiana State UP: Baton Rouge, 1965. Pp. 129-144, 188-190.

She has set herself the task "of bringing good and evil over into concrete objects of consideration and into explicit situations".

STOREY, DAVID (1933)
This Sporting Life, 1960; *Flight into Camden,* 1960; *Radcliffe,* 1963.

ANON. "Kicking against it." *TLS*, 11 March 1960, 157.

Contains rev. of *This Sporting Life*.

ANON. "Journeys here and there." *TLS*, 4 November 1960, 705.
Contains rev. of *Flight into Camden*.

ANON. "- and hell up north." *TLS*, 20 September 1963, 701.
Repr. in *T.L.S. Essays and reviews from The Times Literary
Supplement. 1963*. Oxford UP: London,1964. Pp. 102-103.
Rev. art. on *Radcliffe*.

ANON. "Speaking of writing, II: David Storey." *Times,*
28 November 1963, 15.
Compared with D.H. Lawrence. His novels are thought to be
at the same time realistic and full of poetic symbolism.

BRADBURY, MALCOLM. "*This Sporting Life* by David Storey."
NYTBR, 18 September 1960, 68.
Rev. art.

BRADBURY, MALCOLM. "*Flight into Camden* by David Storey."
NYTBR, 27 August 1961, 4.
Rev. art.

BYGRAVE, MIKE. "David Storey: Novelist or playwright?" *ThQ,*
I (April-June 1971), 31-36.
His later plays have succeeded in overcoming the excessive
symbolism of his novels.

CHURCHILL, THOMAS. "Waterhouse, Storey, and Fowles: Which
way out of the room?" *Crit*, X:3 (1968), 72-87.
On the "claustrophobic dilemma of the 1960's" as shown in
Billy Liar and *Jubb,* in *This Sporting Life,* and in *The
Collector* and *The Magus*.

FURBANK, P.N. "Rags & riches." *Encounter*, XXII (February 1964),
80-82.
Contains rev. of *Radcliffe*.

GLANVILLE, BRIAN. "*This Sporting Life* by David Storey."
London Mag, VII (April 1960), 80-82.
Rev. art.

GROSS, JOHN. "Body and soul." *New Statesman*, 27 September 1963,
410.
Rev. art. on *Radcliffe*.

HALSON, GEOFFREY. "Commentary and notes." David Storey, *This
Sporting Life.* Heritage of Literature Series, 98. Longmans,
Green: London, 1968. Pp. 237-276.

The novel is seen in line with other modern regional and social novels.

KAHRMANN, BERND. "David Storey." *Englische Literatur der Gegenwart in Einzeldarstellungen,* ed. Horst W. Drescher. Kröner: Stuttgart, 1970. Pp. 224-235.
Seen as a regional novelist. Short biography. Bibliography.

MCGUINNESS, FRANK. "The novels of David Storey." *London Mag,* n.s. III (March 1964), 79-83.
This Sporting Life, Flight into Camden, Radcliffe.

MACMANUS, PATRICIA. "*Flight into Camden* by David Storey." *NYHTBR,* 20 August 1961, 12.
Rev. art.

MUDRICK, MARVIN. "News from nowhere." *NYRB,* 9 July 1964, 19-20.
Contains rev. of *Radcliffe.*

NEWTON, J.M. "Two men who matter?" *CQ,* I (1965/66), 284-295.
Rev. art. on *Radcliffe.* Refers also to *This Sporting Life* and *Flight into Camden.*

SPENDER, STEPHEN. "*Radcliffe* by David Storey." *NYHTBR,* 5 April 1964, 6.
Rev. art.

TAYLOR, JOHN RUSSELL. "David Storey: Novelist into dramatist." *P&P,* XVII (June 1970), 22-24.
Mentions his three novels; their links with his four plays.

WATERHOUSE, KEITH. "*This Sporting Life* by David Storey." *SatR,* 17 December 1960, 21.
Rev. art.

TAYLOR, ELIZABETH (1912)
At Mrs. Lippincote's, 1945; *Palladian,* 1946; *A View of the Harbour,* 1947; *A Wreath of Roses,* 1949; *A Game of Hide-and-Seek,* 1951; *The Sleeping Beauty,* 1953; *Angel,* 1957; *In a Summer Season,* 1961; *The Soul of Kindness,* 1964; *The Wedding Group,* 1968; *Mrs. Palfrey at the Claremont,* 1971.

ANON. "A harlequin set." *TLS,* 9 February 1951, 81.
Contains rev. of *A Game of Hide-and-Seek.*

ANON. "The lady of the house." *TLS*, 24 September 1964, 873.
Rev. art. on *The Soul of Kindness*.

ANON. "Home from home." *TLS*, 9 May 1968, 473.
Rev. art. on *The Wedding Group*.

ANON. "Waiting for the end." *TLS*, 27 August 1971, 1017.
Rev. art. on *Mrs. Palfrey at the Claremont*.

AMIS, KINGSLEY. "At Mrs. Taylor's." *Spectator*, 14 June 1957,
784, 786.
Rev. art. on *Angel*; contains general remarks on T's type
of novel.

AUCHINCLOSS, EVE. "Bad characters." *NYRB*, 24 September 1964,
19-20.
Contains rev. of *The Soul of Kindness*.

AUSTEN, RICHARD. "The novels of Elizabeth Taylor." *Commonweal*,
10 June 1955, 258-259.

BROPHY, BRIGID. "*The Wedding Group* by Elizabeth Taylor."
London Mag, n.s. VIII (April 1968), 82-84.
Rev. art.

LIDDELL, ROBERT. "The novels of Elizabeth Taylor." *REL*, I
(April 1960), 54-61.

TOYNBEE, PHILIP (1916)
The Savage Days, 1937; *School in Private*, 1941; *The Barri-
cades*, 1943; *Tea with Mrs. Goodman*, 1947; *The Garden to the
Sea*, 1953; *Pantaloon*, 1961; *Two Brothers*, 1964; *A Learned
City*, 1966; *Views from a Lake*, 1968.

ANON. "Man's fall." *TLS*, 24 July 1953, 473.
Contains rev. of *The Garden to the Sea*.

ANON. "Poetic fiction." *TLS*, 3 November 1961, 791.
Contains rev. of *Pantaloon*.

ANON. "The piece-maker." *TLS*, 6 August 1964, 680.
Rev. art. on *Two Brothers*.

ANON. "The vaults of ambition." *TLS*, 16 February 1967, 125.
Rev. art. on *A Learned City*.

ANON. "Foggy formula." *TLS*, 5 September 1968, 937.

    Rev. art. on *Views from a Lake*. Refers also to *Pantaloon, Two Brothers* and *A Learned City*.

DAVIE, DONALD. "Toynbee's Gerontion." *New Statesman*, 27 October 1961, 615-616.

    Rev. art. on *Pantaloon*. "In particular it draws out what Hugh Kenner has seen in *Gerontion,* the possibility that Eliot's narrator uses the rhetoric of Jacobean blank verse not to reveal but to deceive himself."

EVANS, OLIVER. "Philip Toynbee: *Pantaloon* and David Jones: *In Parenthesis.*" *Crit,* VI:2 (1963), 119-123.

EWART, GAVIN. "Oxford boy makes good/bad/good." *London Mag,* n.s. IV (January 1965), 90-96.

    Short survey of T's work.

SPENDER, STEPHEN. "The miniature and the deluge." *Encounter,* XVII (December 1961), 78-81.

    Contains rev. of *Pantaloon*.

THOMPSON, JOHN. "Poet's novel, novel poem." *NYRB*, 6 May 1965, 23-24.

    Contains rev. of *Two Brothers*.

TREVOR, WILLIAM (1928)

A Standard of Behaviour, 1958; *The Old Boys,* 1964; *The Boarding-House,* 1965; *The Love Department,* 1966; *Mrs. Eckdorf in O'Neill's Hotel,* 1969; *Miss Gomez and the Brethren,* 1971.

ANON. "Hanged by a school-tie." *TLS*, 5 March 1964, 189.

    Rev. art. on *The Old Boys*.

ANON. "Castle Heartrent." *TLS*, 6 May 1965, 345.

    Rev. art. on *The Boarding-House*.

ANON. "Under restraint." *TLS*, 22 September 1966, 873.

    Rev. art. on *The Love Department*. Refers also to *The Old Boys* and *The Boarding House*.

ANON. "Aerial photography." *TLS*, 2 October 1969, 1121.

    Rev. art. on *Mrs. Eckdorf in O'Neill's Hotel;* T's Dublin compared with Spark's Edinburgh.

ANON. "Prayers against loneliness." *TLS,* 15 October 1971, 1247.

    Rev. art. on *Miss Gomez and the Brethren*.

TUOHY, FRANK (1925)

The Animal Game, 1957; *The Warm Nights of January,* 1960; *The Ice Saints,* 1964.

ANON. "Vagaries of the soul." *TLS*, 5 February 1960, 77.
  Contains rev. of *The Warm Nights of January.*

ANON. "Money for a Pole." *TLS*, 9 July 1964, 585.
  Rev. art. on *The Ice Saints.* Refers also to *The Animal Game* and *The Warm Nights of January.*

MCGUINNESS, FRANK. *"The Animal Game; The Warm Nights of January; The Ice Saints."* London Mag, n.s. IV (December 1964), 93-96.
  Rev. art.

WAIN, JOHN (1925)

Hurry on Down, 1953; *Living in the Present,* 1955; *The Contenders,* 1958; *A Travelling Woman,* 1959; *Strike the Father Dead,* 1962; *The Young Visitors,* 1965; *The Smaller Sky,* 1967; *A Winter in the Hills,* 1970.

ANON. "Matters of conscience." *TLS*, 9 October 1953, 641.
  Contains rev. of *Hurry on Down.*

ANON. "Fairly serious." *TLS*, 14 March 1958, 137.
  Rev. art. on *The Contenders.*

ANON. "The man inside." *TLS*, 6 March 1959, 125.
  Rev. art. on *A Travelling Woman.*

ANON. "After the bombardment." *TLS*, 23 March 1962, 197.
  Rev. art. on *Strike the Father Dead.*

ANON. "Rebel with a small cause." *TLS*, 30 April 1970, 471.
  Rev. art. on *A Winter in the Hills.*

BARROWS, JOHN. "John Wain." *JOL*, 13 July 1961, 67-68.
  He will drop the novel for ten years after his forthcoming novel, *Strike the Father Dead,* is published; considers poetry at the centre of literature.

BLUESTONE, GEORGE. "John Wain and John Barth: The angry and the accurate." *MR*, I (1959/60), 582-589.

CHAUCER, DANIEL. "John Wain, *Living in the Present.*" *Shenandoah*, VII (Summer 1956), 60-62.
  Rev. art.

ENGELBORGHS, M. "John Wain en Iris Murdoch." *DWB*, CIII (1958), 50-56.

Hurry on Down, Living in the Present, Under the Net, The Flight from the Enchanter.

HAMILTON, IAN. "Lumbering adulteries." *London Mag,* n.s. X (July/August 1970), 186-190.

Contains rev. of *A Winter in the Hills.*

JONES, JACK. "Inhibition and innocence." *ModA,* III (1958/59), 197-200.

Contains rev. of *The Contenders.*

KERMODE, FRANK. "The house of fiction: Interviews with seven English novelists." *PR*, XXX (1963), 61-82.

With W. (77-79).

MCGUINNESS, FRANK. "*The Smaller Sky* by John Wain." *London Mag,* n.s. VII (October 1967), 95-97.

Rev. art.

MELLOWN, ELGIN W. "Steps toward vision: The development of technique in John Wain's first seven novels." *SAQ*, LXVIII (1969), 330-342.

MONOD, SYLVERE. "John Wain: *A Winter in the Hills.*" *EA,* XXIII (1970), 454-455.

Rev. art.

O'CONNOR, WILLIAM VAN. "John Wain: The will to write." *WSCL,* I (Winter 1960), 35-49. Repr. in *The new university wits and the end of modernism.* With a preface by Harry T. Moore. Southern Illinois UP: Carbondale, 1963. Pp. 30-53, 159-160. The second part of this biographical and literary article deals with his first four novels.

ROTHERMEL, WOLFGANG P. "John Wain." *Englische Literatur der Gegenwart in Einzeldarstellungen,* ed. Horst W. Drescher. Kröner: Stuttgart, 1970. Pp. 133-149.

He is primarily important as an essay writer. His novel *Hurry on Down* was the forerunner of Amis's, Murdoch's and Braine's novels of the mid-50's. Short biography. Bibliography.

WALZER, MICHAEL. "John Wain: The hero in limbo." *Perspective,* X (1958/59), 137-145.

His picaresque heroes move through "inconclusive reality".

YVARD, P. "John Wain: Révolte et neutralité." *EA*, XXIII (1970),
380-394.

Traces his "philosophy of neutrality" from *Hurry on Down* to
The Smaller Sky.

WATERHOUSE, KEITH (1929)

There Is a Happy Land, 1957; *Billy Liar,* 1959; *Jubb,* 1963;
The Bucket Shop, 1968.

ANON. "Teething troubles." *TLS*, 22 March 1957, 173.

Contains rev. of *There Is a Happy Land*.

ANON. "Joking apart." *TLS*, 4 September 1959, 505.

Contains rev. of *Billy Liar*.

ANON. "Heading for a fall." *TLS*, 27 September 1963, 730.

Rev. art. on *Jubb*.

CHURCHILL, THOMAS. "Waterhouse, Storey, and Fowles: Which way
out of the room?" *Crit*, X:3 (1968), 72-87.

On the "claustrophobic dilemma of the 1960's" as shown in
Billy Liar and *Jubb,* in *This Sporting Life,* and in *The Collector* and *The Magus*.

ELLOWAY, DAVID. "Introduction and notes." Keith Waterhouse,
Billy Liar. Alan Sillitoe, *The Loneliness of the Long-
Distance Runner*. Heritage of Literature Series, 85. Long-
mans, Green: London, 1966. Pp. 201-219, 231-253.

MUDRICK, MARVIN. "Then and now." *NYRB*, 19 March 1964, 14,
16-17.

Contains rev. of *Jubb*; sets it against *Billy Liar*.

SCHLEUSSNER, BRUNO. "Keith Waterhouse." *Englische Literatur
der Gegenwart in Einzeldarstellungen,* ed. Horst W. Drescher.
Kröner: Stuttgart, 1970. Pp. 190-206.

He writes 'neo-realistic' fiction. His heroes are tragicomic figures. Short biography. Bibliography.

TAUBMAN, ROBERT. "God is delicate." *New Statesman,*
27 September 1963, 406-407.

Contains rev. of *Jubb* and *There Is a Happy Land*.

WILLIAMS, GORDON M. (1934)
The Last Day of Lincoln Charles, 1965; *The Camp*, 1966; *The Man Who Had Power over Women*, 1967; *From Scenes Like These*, 1968; *The Siege of Trencher's Farm*, 1969; *The Upper Pleasure Garden*, 1970; *They Used to Play on Grass*, 1971 (with Terry Venables).

ANON. "Gordon M. Williams: *The Last Day of Lincoln Charles*." *TLS*, 1 July 1965, 563.
Short rev.

ANON. "In the mob." *TLS*, 28 April 1966, 361.
Rev. art. on *The Camp*. Refers also to *The Last Day of Lincoln Charles*.

ANON. "Boozed." *TLS*, 25 May 1967, 471.
Rev. art. on *The Man Who Had Power over Women*.

ANON. "Growing down." *TLS*, 12 December 1968, 1401.
Rev. art. on *From Scenes Like These*.

ANON. "Rural rumblings." *TLS*, 3 July 1969, 721.
Rev. art. on *The Siege of Trencher's Farm*.

SEYMOUR-SMITH, MARTIN. "Grey days." *Spectator*, 2 June 1967, 649.
Contains rev. of *The Man Who Had Power over Women*.

WILLIAMS, RAYMOND (1921)
Border Country, 1960; *Second Generation*, 1964.

ANON. "On the frontier." *TLS*, 25 November 1960, 753.
Rev. art. on *Border Country*.

ANON. "Shed and spire." *TLS*, 12 November 1964, 1012.
Rev. art. on *Second Generation*.

BERGONZI, BERNARD. "Expatriates." *Spectator*, 18 November 1960, 790-791.
Contains rev. of *Border Country*.

BINDING, WYN. "Some observations on the novels of Raymond Williams." *AWR*, XVI:37 (1967), 74-81.

GOLDSTEIN, LEONARD. "Aspects of Raymond Williams' *Second*
Generation." *Essays in honour of William Gallacher*. Life
and Literature of the Working Class, ed. Anselm Schlösser.
Humboldt-Universität: Berlin, 1966. Pp. 221-233.

WILSON, ANGUS (1913)
Hemlock and After, 1952; *Anglo-Saxon Attitudes,* 1956; *The*
Middle Age of Mrs. Eliot, 1958; *The Old Men at the Zoo,* 1961;
Late Call, 1964; *No Laughing Matter,* 1967.

MCDOWELL, FREDERICK P. "The Angus Wilson collection." *BI*, X
(1969), 9-23.
Manuscripts in the University of Iowa Libraries.

MCDOWELL, FREDERICK P. & E. SHARON GRAVES. *The Angus Wilson*
manuscripts in the University of Iowa Libraries. A catalogue.
Friends of the University of Iowa Library: Iowa City, 1969.
Pp. 16.

ANON. "Corruption rife." *TLS*, 8 August 1952, 516.
Rev. art. on *Hemlock and After.*

ANON. "Mourning becomes Elvira." *TLS*, 18 May 1956, 296.
Rev. art. on *Anglo-Saxon Attitudes;* touches also upon W's
artistic development.

ANON. "Meg Eliot surprised." *TLS*, 21 November 1958, 672.
Rev. art. on *The Middle Age of Mrs. Eliot.* Refers also to
Hemlock and After and *Anglo-Saxon Attitudes.*

ANON. "Beyond the fringe." *TLS*, 29 September 1961, 641.
Rev. art. on *The Old Men at the Zoo.*

ANON. "Not painted - but made up." *TLS*, 12 November 1964,
1013. Repr. in *T.L.S. Essays and reviews from The Times*
Literary Supplement. 1964. Oxford UP: London, 1965.
Pp. 103-105.
Rev. art. on *Late Call.*

ANON. "Playing the game." *TLS*, 5 October 1967, 933. Repr. in
T.L.S. Essays and reviews from The Times Literary Supple-
ment. 1967. Oxford UP: London, 1968. Pp. 201-204.
Rev. art. on *No Laughing Matter.*

AMIS, KINGSLEY. "Dodos less darling." *Spectator*, 1 June 1956, 764-765.

Rev. art. on *Anglo-Saxon Attitudes*.

BERGONZI, BERNARD. "A new Angus Wilson." *NYRB*, 25 February 1965, 21-23.

Rev. art. on *Late Call*; compares it to his previous novels.

BERGONZI, BERNARD. "*No Laughing Matter* by Angus Wilson." *London Mag,* n.s. VII (November 1967), 89-91.

Rev. art.

BILES, JACK I. "An interview in London with Angus Wilson." *SIN*, II (1970), 76-87.

He acknowledges the influence of Richardson, Dickens, Forster, and others. Contemporary fellow-novelists discussed are Golding and Greene.

BURGESS, ANTHONY. "Powers that be." *Encounter*, XXIV (January 1965), 71-76.

Contains rev. of *Late Call*.

COCKSHUT, A.O.J. "Favoured sons: The moral world of Angus Wilson." *EIC*, IX (1959), 50-60.

Hemlock and After, Anglo-Saxon Attitudes.

COX, C.B. "The humanism of Angus Wilson: A study of *Hemlock and After.*" *CritQ*, III (1961), 227-237.

COX, C.B. "Angus Wilson: Studies in depression." *The free spirit. A study of liberal humanism in the novels of George Eliot, Henry James, E.M. Forster, Virginia Woolf, Angus Wilson.* Oxford UP: London, 1963. Pp. 117-153.

DELPECH, JEANINE. "Les masques d'Angus Wilson." *NL,* 10 avril 1969, 3.

DICK, KAY. "Portrait: Angus Wilson's countryside." *Ramparts,* III (November 1964), 5-8.

DRESCHER, HORST W. "Angus Wilson: An interview." *NS,* n.s. XVII (1968), 351-356.

Late Call, its social implications, its concept of evil, and its relation to *Anglo-Saxon Attitudes*.

EDELSTEIN, ARTHUR. "Angus Wilson: The territory behind." *Contemporary British novelists,* ed. Charles Shapiro. Southern Illinois UP: Carbondale, Edwardsville, 1965. Pp. 144-161.

ENGELBORGHS, MAURITS. "Werk van Angus Wilson." *DWB,* CII (1957), 181-189.
Hemlock and After, Anglo-Saxon Attitudes.

ENKEMANN, JÜRGEN. *Die satirische Darstellung gesellschaftlicher Desintegration bei Aldous Huxley, Evelyn Waugh und Angus Wilson. Untersucht am Motiv der Party und an ähnlichen Gruppensituationen.* Diss. T.U. Berlin, 1970. Pp. 279.

GINDIN, JAMES. "Angus Wilson." *Harvest of a quiet eye. The novel of compassion.* Indiana UP: Bloomington, 1971. Pp. 277-304.
He never judges his "estranged central characters from any single or assured point of view, never establishes an imperative that would have made life more rewarding or satisfactory for the central character." Concentrates on the form of the "open novel".

GRANSDEN, K.W. *Angus Wilson.* WTW, 208. Longmans, Green: London, 1969. Pp. 31.

HALIO, JAY L. "Response *vs.* responsibility: Angus Wilson's *The Old Men at the Zoo." Crit,* V:1 (1962), 77-82.

HALIO, JAY L. "The novels of Angus Wilson." *MFS,* VIII (1962/63), 171-181.
Hemlock and After, Anglo-Saxon Attitudes and *The Middle Age of Mrs. Eliot* are written in the tradition of the novel of manners.

HALIO, JAY L. *Angus Wilson.* Writers and Critics. Oliver & Boyd: Edinburgh, 1964. Pp. 120.

HASAN, R. *A linguistic study of contrasting features in the style of two contemporary English prose writers, William Golding and Angus Wilson.* Diss. Edinburgh, 1963/64.

HOPE, FRANCIS. "Grace and favour." *New Statesman,* 27 November 1964, 834, 836.
Rev. art. on *Late Call.*

JOHNSON, B.S. "Getting on." *Spectator,* 13 November 1964, 644.
Rev. art. on *Late Call.*

195

KATONA, ANNA. "Angus Wilson's fiction and its relation to the English tradition." *ALitASH*, X (1968), 111-127.

His work combines a kind of social fiction with the novel of sensibility and thus stands in the tradition of the 19th century (George Eliot).

KERMODE, FRANK. "Mr. Wilson's people." *Spectator,* 21 November 1958, 705-706. Repr. in *Puzzles and epiphanies. Essays and reviews 1958-1961.* Routledge & Kegan Paul: London, 1962. Pp. 193-197.

Rev. art. on *The Middle Age of Mrs. Eliot.*

KERMODE, FRANK. "The house of fiction: Interviews with seven English novelists." *PR*, XXX (1963), 61-82.

With W. (68-70).

LINDBERG, MARGARET. "Angus Wilson: *The Old Men at the Zoo* as allegory." *IEY*, 14 (Fall 1969), 44-48.

MCGUINNESS, FRANK. "*Late Call* by Angus Wilson." *London Mag,* n.s. IV (January 1965), 100-102.

Rev. art.

MILLGATE, MICHAEL. "Angus Wilson." *Writers at work. The Paris Review interviews,* ed. Malcolm Cowley. Viking: New York, 1958. Pp. 251-266.

On his writing habits and his novel technique. *Anglo-Saxon Attitudes* is talked about in detail.

MORTIMER, JOHN. "A fatal giraffe." *Spectator*, 29 September 1961, 431.

Rev. art. on *The Old Men at the Zoo.*

POSTON, LAWRENCE. "A conversation with Angus Wilson." *BA*, XL (1966), 29-31.

On the Dickens tradition, Zola, Henry James, the novels from *Hemlock and After* to *Late Call.*

PRITCHETT, V.S. "Bad-hearted Britain." *New Statesman,* 29 September 1961, 429-430.

The British professional classes in *The Old Men at the Zoo.*

PRITCHETT, V.S. "Ventriloquists." *NYRB*, 18 January 1968, 10, 12, 14.

Contains extensive rev. of *No Laughing Matter.*

RAVEN, SIMON. "Angus agonistes." *Spectator*, 6 October 1967, 396-397.

Rev. art. on *No Laughing Matter*.

SCHEER-SCHÄZLER, BRIGITTE. "Angus Wilson." *Englische Literatur der Gegenwart in Einzeldarstellungen*, ed. Horst W. Drescher. Kröner: Stuttgart, 1970. Pp. 104-132.

Though he is regarded as the protagonist of Victorian tradition, his main aim is to show the ambiguities of life and to plead for their tolerance. Short biography. Bibliography.

SCHLÜTER, KURT. *Kuriose Welt im modernen englischen Roman. Dargestellt an ausgewählten Werken von Evelyn Waugh und Angus Wilson.* Schmidt: Berlin, 1969. Pp. 247.

Hemlock and After, Anglo-Saxon Attitudes, The Middle Age of Mrs. Eliot, The Old Men at the Zoo (126-233); bibliography (244-245).

SCHLÜTER, KURT. "Angus Wilson." *Englische Dichter der Moderne. Ihr Leben und Werk. Unter Mitarbeit zahlreicher Fachgelehrter,* eds. Rudolf Sühnel & Dieter Riesner. Schmidt: Berlin, 1971. Pp. 536-545.

Biographical and literary essay. Selected bibliography.

SCHLÜTER, KURT. "Angus Wilson: *The Middle Age of Mrs. Eliot.*" *Der moderne englische Roman. Interpretationen,* ed. Horst Oppel. Schmidt: Berlin, 1971 (rev. ed.). Pp. 361-377.

SCOTT-KILVERT, IAN. "Angus Wilson." *REL*, I (April 1960), 42-53.

Short stories and early novels. Argues that he has pursued "more closely than any of his contemporaries or successors, the conception of the novel as a comic or satirical criticism of manners expressed in naturalistic terms."

SERVOTTE, HERMAN. "Experiment en traditie: Angus Wilson *No Laughing Matter.*" *DWB,* CXIII (1968), 324-335.

Rev. art.

SERVOTTE, HERMAN. "A note on the formal characteristics of Angus Wilson's *No Laughing Matter.*" *ES,* L (1969), 58-64.

Stresses the "literariness" of this novel.

SHAW, VALERIE A. "*The Middle Age of Mrs. Eliot* and *Late Call:* Angus Wilson's traditionalism." *CritQ,* XII (1970), 9-27.

SMITH, WILLIAM JAMES. "Angus Wilson's England: The novelist as social historian." *Commonweal*, 26 March 1965, 18-21.

Late Call and *Anglo-Saxon Attitudes;* mentions *Hemlock and After, The Middle Age of Mrs. Eliot* and *The Old Men at the Zoo.*

SPIEL, HILDE. *Welt im Widerschein. Essays.* Beck: München, 1960. Pp. 298.

Contains passages on W. (75-81).

SUDRANN, JEAN. "The lion and the unicorn: Angus Wilson's triumphant tragedy." *SIN*, III (1971), 390-400.

No Laughing Matter.

SYMONS, JULIAN. "Politics and the novel." *TC*, CLXX (Winter 1961/62), 147-154.

Contains discussions of *The Old Men at the Zoo* (151-153).

TAYLOR, GRIFFIN. "'What doth it profit a man ...?': Three British views of the null and the void." *SR*, LXVI (1958), 132-146.

Anglo-Saxon Attitudes, Murdoch's *The Sandcastle,* Macaulay's *The Towers of Trebizond.*

VALLETTE, JACQUES. "Lettres Anglo-Saxonnes: Angus Wilson un peu par lui-même." *MdF*, 1142 (1958), 313-316.

Style, use of irony and humour.

WAIN, JOHN. "Books: Comment on widowhood." *NY*, 11 April 1959, 164-166.

W's critical commentary on English society in the era of the Welfare State is sometimes overexplicit.

WILSON, ANGUS. "The novelist and the narrator." *English studies today.* Second Series, ed. G.A. Bonnard. Francke: Bern, 1961. Pp. 43-50.

A "plea for the unfashionable literary criticism which concerns itself with the biography of the author." Draws heavily on his own novels.

WILSON, ANGUS. *The wild garden. Or, speaking of writing.* Secker & Warburg: London, 1963. Pp. 150.

The book came out of the three Ewing Lectures. W. talks about the relation of his life to the themes of his writing.

WOGATZKY, KARIN. *Angus Wilson: "Hemlock and After".* A study in ambiguity. Schweizer Anglistische Arbeiten, 62. Francke: Bern, 1971. Pp. VIII + 129.

ZIMMERMAN, MURIEL. "The fiction of Angus Wilson." *DA*,
   XXVIII (1968), 4195A-4196A (Temple).

WILSON, COLIN (1931)
Ritual in the Dark, 1960; *Adrift in Soho*, 1961; *The World of
Violence*, 1963; *Man Without a Shadow*, 1963; *Necessary Doubt*,
1964; *The Glass Cage*, 1966; *The Mind Parasites*, 1967; *The
Philosopher's Stone*, 1969; *The Killer*, 1970; *The God of the
Labyrinth*, 1970; *The Black Room*, 1971.

ANON. "Dionysiac delights." *TLS*, 4 March 1960, 141.
   Rev. art. on *Ritual in the Dark*.

ANON. "Outward bound." *TLS*, 8 September 1961, 593.
   Contains rev. of *Adrift in Soho*.

ANON. "A Sphinx at the yard." *TLS*, 27 February 1964, 161.
   Rev. art. on *Necessary Doubt*.

ANON. "Shazam!" *TLS*, 10 July 1969, 745.
   Short rev. of *The Philosopher's Stone*.

BRYDEN, RONALD. "Childe Colin." *Spectator*, 4 March 1960,
   329.
   Contains rev. of *Ritual in the Dark*.

BRYDEN, RONALD. "Adrift in England." *Spectator*,
   8 September 1961, 329-330.
   Contains rev. of *Adrift in Soho*.

CAMPION, SIDNEY R. *The world of Colin Wilson. A biographical
   study*. Muller: London, 1962. Pp. XVII + 254.
   Contains chap. on *Ritual in the Dark* and passages on
   Adrift in Soho.

COOPER, WILLIAM. "Existentialist nerve twitch." *Nation*,
   25 August 1956, 162-164.

CURRAN, STUART. "'Detecting' the existential Blake." *BlakeS*,
   II (Fall 1969), 67-76.
   Refers to *The Glass Cage* and its protagonist, a Blake
   scholar.

DILLARD, R.H. "Towards an existential realism: The novels of
   Colin Wilson." *HC*, IV (October 1967), 1-12.

GREENWELL, TOM. "The two Colin Wilsons." *B&B*, (June 1960), 9.
  Social provocateur and serious literary figure.

HIBBS, CHRISTOPHER. "The curious case of Colin Wilson." *B&B*,
  (January 1971), 16-17.
  Short critical assessment of his publications. No case can
  be made for his being a "good writer".

LUNN, SIR ARNOLD. "The infallibility of Colin Wilson." *Month*,
  CCXII (1961), 278-286.
  Mainly concerned with his "philosophy".

SPIEL, HILDE. *Welt im Widerschein. Essays.* Beck: München,
  1960. Pp. 298.
  Contains passages on W. (81-86).

TODD, OLIVIER. "Colin Wilson, ou le lumpen-intellectuel." *TM*,
  XIV (1958/59), 748-754.
  Mainly on his "philosophy" (*The Outsider* and *Religion and
  the Rebel*).

WIDMER, KINGSLEY. *The literary rebel.* With a preface by
  Harry T. Moore. Southern Illinois UP: Carbondale, 1965.
  Pp. VII + 261.
  Sees current 'rebels' in line with a tradition of rebellion.
  Mainly on the American situation. W's writings are dis-
  cussed briefly.

I N D E X